MARINE WILDLIFE

OF THE GROS MORNE NATIONAL PARK REGION

1 Stamp's Lane, St. John's, NL, Canada, A1E 3C9
WWW.BREAKWATERBOOKS.COM

LIBRARY AND ARCHIVES CANADA CATALOGUING IN PUBLICATION
Wroblewski, J. S. (Joseph S.)
Marine wildlife of the Gros Morne National Park region / Joe Wroblewski.
Includes bibliographical references and index.
ISBN 978-1-55081-410-1
1. Marine animals--Newfoundland and Labrador--Gros Morne National Park.
2. Marine resources conservation--Newfoundland and Labrador--Gros Morne National Park. 3. Gros Morne National Park (N.L.). I. Title.
QH92.2.W76 2013 591.77'31 C2013-901010-6

Publication of this book was financially supported in part by the Community-University Research for Recovery Alliance (CURRA) project. The CURRA was funded by the Social Sciences and Humanities Research Council (SSHRC) of Canada and Memorial University, with additional financial and in-kind support from numerous community partners and groups.

We acknowledge the support of the Canada Council for the Arts, which last year invested $154 million to bring the arts to Canadians throughout the country. We acknowledge the Government of Canada through the Canada Book Fund and the Government of Newfoundland and Labrador through the Department of Tourism, Culture and Recreation for our publishing activities.

PRINTED AND BOUND IN CANADA.

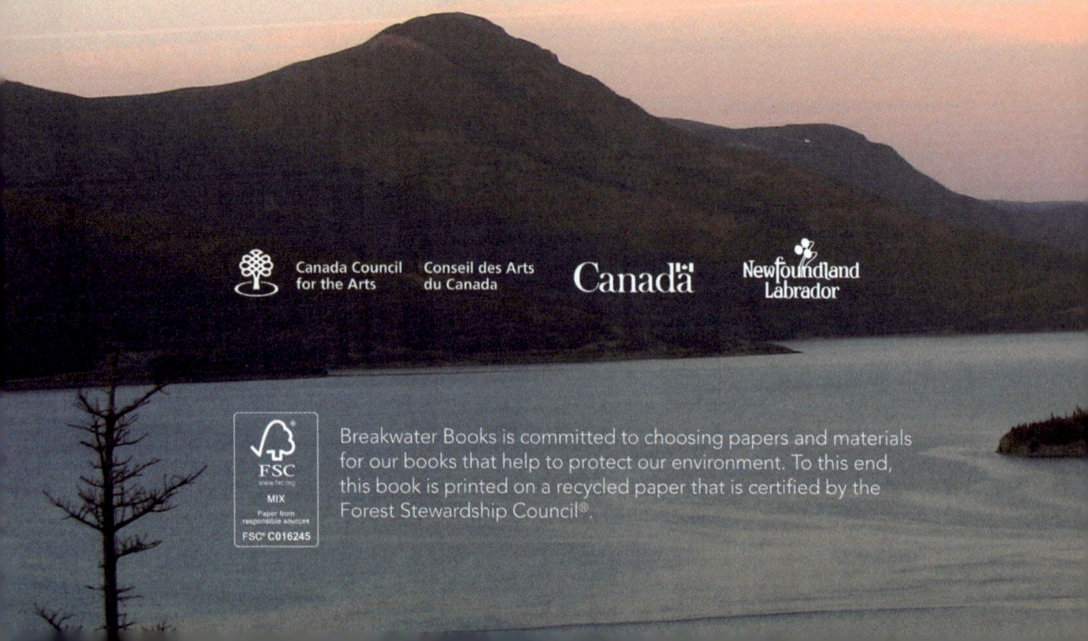

Canada Council for the Arts | Conseil des Arts du Canada
Canada
Newfoundland Labrador

FSC www.fsc.org MIX Paper from responsible sources FSC® C016245

Breakwater Books is committed to choosing papers and materials for our books that help to protect our environment. To this end, this book is printed on a recycled paper that is certified by the Forest Stewardship Council®.

JOE WROBLEWSKI

ILLUSTRATIONS BY LEAH K. WROBLEWSKI

MARINE WILDLIFE

OF THE GROS MORNE NATIONAL PARK REGION

BREAKWATER

View of the Outer Basin of Bonne Bay from Photographer's Lookout near Norris Point. The pointed peak of Pic à Tenerife Mountain rises over the tree-covered hills in the background to the left. The Tablelands (mountains nearly barren of plant life) appear in the far background to the right.

FOREWORD

BY DR. BARBARA NEIS

THE COMMUNITY-UNIVERSITY Research for Recovery Alliance (CURRA) was a six-year research and community engagement program funded by the Social Sciences and Humanities Research Council (SSHRC), Memorial University, and with financial and in-kind support from numerous other agencies (www.curra.ca). Our objective was to combine the knowledge and skills of Memorial University researchers, in multiple disciplines, with the resources, insights, and local knowledge of community groups on Newfoundland's west coast in order to look for ways to rebuild the collapsed fisheries and threatened communities in the region. This beautiful and informative book, *Marine Wildlife of the Gros Morne National Park Region*, is an outstanding product of that collaboration.

Bonne Bay is a complex fjord environment that is home to an unusually rich and diverse variety of marine wildlife. This wildlife plays a crucial role in the local ecology, as well as in the lives of people who live in the region and those who visit. Bonne Bay is the jewel at the centre of the Park and hugely important to the Gros Morne Region as a whole.

Since much of the life and activity that exists in Bonne Bay resides below the surface, that life and the changes in it are not easily visible to most of us. Fishing people and others have, for many decades, lived from and on the Bay, but their knowledge has not been fully documented or made accessible to others. The Bonne Bay Marine Station is an exquisite resource where, for forty years, researchers have conducted their research, trained students, and interacted with local people and visitors. But, until now, much of what they had learned from their work was dispersed and difficult to access. *Marine Wildlife of the Gros Morne National Park Region* changes this.

The book seeks to make visible to people in the region, researchers, and the almost 200,000 visitors who come to the Gros Morne area each year, the marine ecology of Bonne Bay, including many of the species that inhabit its waters. It invites us to explore this region in a new way, to embark on a journey that will help us begin to understand the 'sea around us.' It reminds us that our coasts, the Bay, and the ocean as a whole are fragile and changing, but rarely for the better.

Marine Wildlife of the Gros Morne National Park Region is an essential step in the development of effective governance for Bonne Bay in the future and for fuelling constructive discussions about how this beautiful, complex subarctic/temperate fjord ecosystem could be more effectively integrated into planning and development strategies for the region. It invites us—all of us—to become stewards of the Bay and of the ocean of which it is a part, and gives us some of the tools we need to undertake this enormous and vital task.

I hope this book is the first of many resources on the marine ecology, fisheries, and communities in the region available for use by educators, students, and community groups as they seek to steward and benefit from the region's ecological, cultural, and social richness into the future.

CONTENTS

76

158

IN MEMORIAM

Dr. Donald H. Steele

Professor of Biology and lifelong steward of the environment

ACKNOWLEDGEMENTS

A GOAL OF the CURRA project was to assist fishing communities in the rebuilding of collapsed fish stocks and the recovery of fisheries in the northern Gulf of St. Lawrence and elsewhere. Towards that goal, this book provides information on the diversity of marine wildlife, especially fishes, in the Gros Morne National Park region. Living marine resources are important to the local economy. Nearshore waters are a nursery ground for many commercial fish species harvested in the Gulf of St. Lawrence.

The information on the fish fauna of Bonne Bay presented here is based upon data collected by Memorial University students and their instructors (Drs. Joe Wroblewski, David Methven, and Craig Purchase) during the field course "Estuarine Fish Ecology" taught annually at the Bonne Bay Marine Station in Norris Point. Special thanks are extended to the teaching assistants for the field course: Erin Carruthers, Liuming Hu, Arnault Le Bris, and Shanshan Liu. The author wishes to acknowledge Dr. Robert Hooper, Director of the Bonne Bay Marine Station, and Fiona Cuthbert and Allison Eaton, Managers of the Marine Station, for assistance during the field courses. Thanks are also extended to Marine Station employees William Coffey and Dennis Rumbolt for their assistance in boating operations.

Drs. Tom Knight and Darroch Whitaker, of the Western Newfoundland and Labrador Field Unit of Parks Canada, provided information on the freshwater fishes inhabiting Gros Morne National Park. Several colleagues contributed photographs of marine wildlife for the book, and they are greatfully acknowledged in the Photography Credits. Charles Conway of the Geography Department at Memorial University created the regional maps in the book.

The author would like to thank these colleagues for reviewing sections of the book manuscript: Michael Burzynski, Dr. Evan Edinger, Alain Fréchet, Dr. Patrick Gagnon, Dr. Richard Haedrich, Dr. Gene Herzberg, Dr. Jack Lawson, Wayne Ledwell, Dr. William Montevecchi, Dr. David Methven, Dr. Craig Purchase, Dr. David Schneider, Dr. Becky Sjare, Dr. Garry Stenson, and Dr. Darroch Whitaker.

Finally, the author wishes to acknowledge James Langer, the managing editor, and Rhonda Molloy, the graphic designer, for their outstanding work in producing this book.

Ten Mile Pond viewed from the top of Gros Morne mountain.
(PHOTOGRAPH BY ARNAULT LE BRIS)

PREFACE

THIS BOOK IS about the marine wildlife that inhabits the estuarine and marine waters bordering Gros Morne National Park in western Newfoundland. Although several books have been written about the Park and its unusual geology, there has been little published about the marine life in coastal waters adjacent to the Park. Bonne Bay, a fjord-estuary near the southern border of the Park, remains in a largely unspoiled, natural state. Bonne Bay has become a focus for stewardship efforts by coastal communities because the marine ecosystem supports small boat commercial fisheries, recreational sport fishing, pleasure boating, and ecotourism. Public knowledge about the environment is the foundation of the stewardship of nature. The land in Gros Morne National Park is protected by federal legislation designed for managing human activity in a National Park. However, the waters of Bonne Bay currently have no special protection other than the federal regulations for managing Canada's coastal waters. It is hoped that the information presented in this book will encourage continued community-based stewardship of the terrestrial and freshwater environments of Gros Morne National Park and the adjacent estuaries and marine waters of the Gulf of St. Lawrence.

Joe Wroblewski
St. John's, NL
2013

Map of the boundaries of Gros Morne National Park. The official boundary between the Park and marine coastal waters is the mean low-tide mark. Note that Bonne Bay and St. Paul's Inlet are outside the Park boundary.

GROS MORNE NATIONAL PARK, GULF OF ST. LAWRENCE, AND BONNE BAY

1

GROS MORNE NATIONAL PARK – A WORLD HERITAGE SITE

Located on the west coast of the island of Newfoundland, Gros Morne National Park is a site of world-wide significance as the unusual rocks in the area tell the story of the earth's turbulent geological history.[1] Since the park holds some of the world's best examples of the processes of plate tectonics and glaciation, it has been designated a World Heritage Site by the United Nations Educational, Scientific and Cultural Organization (UNESCO).

Efforts to preserve this unique landscape began in 1973 when 1,800 km^2 of the Long Range Mountains of the Great Northern Peninsula of western Newfoundland were established as the Gros Morne National Park Reserve, but the full significance of the land's unusual geology was not realized at that time. The initial purpose of establishing the Park Reserve was to protect the natural beauty of the landscape.[2] The reserve was named after the mountain peak Gros Morne, or "large mountain standing alone," and tourists and local people visited the area to enjoy the seacoast, forests, and mountains.

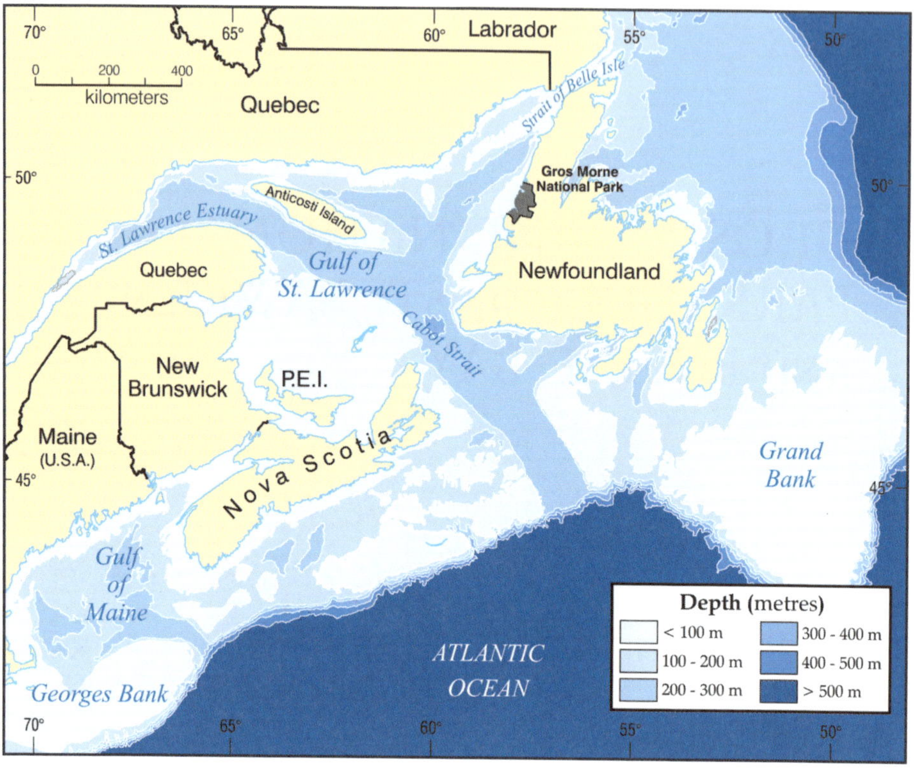

Map showing location of Gros Morne National Park in western Newfoundland in relation to the Gulf of St. Lawrence. The Gulf is a semi-enclosed sea with two openings to the Atlantic Ocean: the Strait of Belle Isle in the northeast Gulf and the Cabot Strait in the southern Gulf.

View of the Outer Basin of Bonne Bay from the top of The Tablelands. Gros Morne mountain appears in the centre background. (PHOTOGRAPH BY ARNAULT LE BRIS)

Coastal community of Norris Point (foreground) with Gros Morne mountain in the background. (PHOTOGRAPH BY ARNAULT LE BRIS)

Western Brook Pond in Gros Morne National Park is in the foreground. The Gulf of St. Lawrence appears along the horizon in the far background. (PHOTOGRAPH BY ARNAULT LE BRIS)

View of the fjord lake in the Western Brook Pond region looking southeast from Snug Harbour. (PHOTOGRAPH BY ARNAULT LE BRIS)

Trilobite fossil in a rock cliff of Bonne Bay. The fossil is evidence that the region was once an ancient sea.[3] NOTE: Canadian quarter coin is placed for scale.

Scientists began to discover the significance of the geological features of the area and promoted the recognition of the Gros Morne Park Reserve as a World Heritage Site. Designation by UNESCO came in 1987. The local rock features tell the story of the earth's complex geological history in a manner not seen elsewhere, and geologists have learned much about the movements of the earth's crust by studying rocks in the park area. In 2005, the Park Reserve became a National Park under the Canada National Parks Act.[4]

A very unusual geological feature within Gros Morne National Park is the area where the earth's mantle has been pushed to the surface by movements within the earth. The area called "The Tablelands" was once part of the earth's mantle, several kilometres deep

A valley in the Tablelands within Gros Morne National Park. The reddish colouration of the land is caused by iron mineral. Bonne Bay can be seen in the far right background. (PHOTOGRAPH BY ARNAULT LE BRIS)

View of Western Brook in the coastal plains of Gros Morne National Park with the Long Range Mountains in the background. The mouth of the Western Brook Pond fjord is in center background. (PHOTOGRAPH BY ARNAULT LE BRIS)

in the planet's interior.[5] The earth's mantle is rich in magnesium and iron and so are the rocks of The Tablelands. This high concentration of iron gives the landscape a reddish colouration. Very little vegetation develops here as the soil lacks many of the minerals that plants require for growth and the high concentrations of magnesium and iron are toxic to many forms of plant life.

Fossils in park rocks indicate that this part of Newfoundland was once beneath a tropical ocean during Cambrian and Ordovician times.[6] Much more recently, in the geological history of the earth, the land was covered by glaciers during the "Ice Age," and the movements of a series of glaciers carved the fjords of Western Brook Pond and Bonne Bay. Rising of the land, after the tremendous weight of melting glaciers was removed, has isolated Western Brook Pond from the sea. The fjord of Bonne Bay is still connected to the sea, although a shallow sill near Norris Point almost blocks the water of the inner fjord from mixing with the Gulf of St. Lawrence.

Moving ice during the most recent glaciation (10,000 to 85,000 years ago)[7] had a profound effect on the present-day freshwater fish fauna of Newfoundland, including the fishes present in Gros Morne National Park. The glaciation caused the extinction of the pre-existing freshwater fishes on the island, and when the glaciers receded, the freshwater habitat that became available was recolonized by salinity tolerant (estuarine) fishes from mainland North America that were able to cross the Gulf of St. Lawrence. No truly freshwater fishes (e.g. northern pike and yellow perch) could cross the ocean barrier.[8] Thus the present day freshwater fish fauna in Newfoundland is composed of only a few species. Those species present in freshwater on the island are salinity tolerant (e.g. the banded killifish, mummichog, Arctic char, Atlantic salmon, and brook trout). Freshwater sports fisheries for Atlantic salmon and brook trout are now important components of the economy of Newfoundland and Labrador.[9]

A brook trout in Western Brook in Gros Morne National Park.
(PHOTOGRAPH BY ARNAULT LE BRIS)

The Atlantic salmon is the most valuable fish in the recreational freshwater fishery in Newfoundland and Labrador.

The sandbar at the mouth of Western Brook. Atlantic salmon enter Western Brook from the sea through this narrow estuary.

GULF OF ST. LAWRENCE

Gros Morne National Park borders approximately 280 km of coastline along the Gulf of St. Lawrence. The Gulf is a semi-enclosed sea with only two connections to the Atlantic Ocean: the Cabot Strait and the Strait of Belle Isle. Water from the Labrador Sea flows into the Gulf through the Strait of Belle Isle, which is only 20 km across at its narrowest point. Most of the freshwater input to the Gulf comes from the watershed of the St. Lawrence Estuary. In winter, sea ice usually forms in the northern Gulf by mid-January and melts by late April.

The deepest point in the Gulf of St. Lawrence occurs at 535 m in the Laurentian Channel of the southern Gulf, but generally the waters in the northern Gulf are 200 to 300 m deep.[10]

Commercial fisheries conducted in the Gulf land approximately 200,000 tonnes of finfish and shellfish each year, worth several-hundred-million dollars annually.[11] The Gulf groundfish fishery

harvests Atlantic cod, white hake, witch flounder, winter flounder, American plaice, Atlantic halibut, Greenland halibut (also known as "turbot"), lumpfish, and yellowtail flounder. Pelagic fishes caught in the Gulf include redfish, Atlantic herring, Atlantic mackerel, capelin, haddock, pollock, and Atlantic bluefin tuna. Fish harvested from the estuaries of the Gulf include the alewife, rainbow smelt, American eel, and Atlantic tomcod. Crustaceans harvested from the Gulf's marine waters include northern shrimp, American lobster, snow crab, and Atlantic rock crab while the molluscs harvested include the shortfin squid, sea scallop, blue mussel, Atlantic surf clam, and soft-shelled clam.[12]

The Gulf of St. Lawrence is a highly productive marine ecosystem. Seaweed broken from the sea bottom by storm waves has washed up on the beach near Western Brook.

A longliner and two smaller inshore fishing boats at the wharf in Rocky Harbour.
(PHOTOGRAPH BY ARNAULT LE BRIS)

BONNE BAY – A FJORD-ESTUARY NEAR THE SOUTHERN BORDER OF GROS MORNE NATIONAL PARK

Bonne Bay is nearly surrounded by Gros Morne National Park. Outer Bonne Bay is an embayment of the coastline of western Newfoundland and connects directly with the Gulf of St Lawrence. The inner bay has three arms: South Arm, East Arm, and Deer Arm. The three main rivers that flow into Bonne Bay are Deer Brook, Southeast Brook, and the Lomond River. These are the main sources of freshwater that drain from the boreal forested watershed into the bay. Along the shoreline, there are a number of rocky beaches at the base of steep cliffs.

Geologically, Bonne Bay is a fjord formed over a period of about 1.6 million years as a series of glaciers flowed to the sea. Fjords typically have steep sides and a submarine sill that separates the inner fjord from coastal waters.[13] A sill forms where soil and rock is dropped by a retreating glacier.[14] Near Norris Point, the sill, at its shallowest, is 14 m in depth while the greatest depth in East Arm is approximately 230 m.[15]

The arms of Bonne Bay were deepened by successive glaciations during the most recent Ice Age. View of Gadds Harbour (left of centre) looking south from the hills behind Norris Point. (PHOTOGRAPH BY ARNAULT LE BRIS)

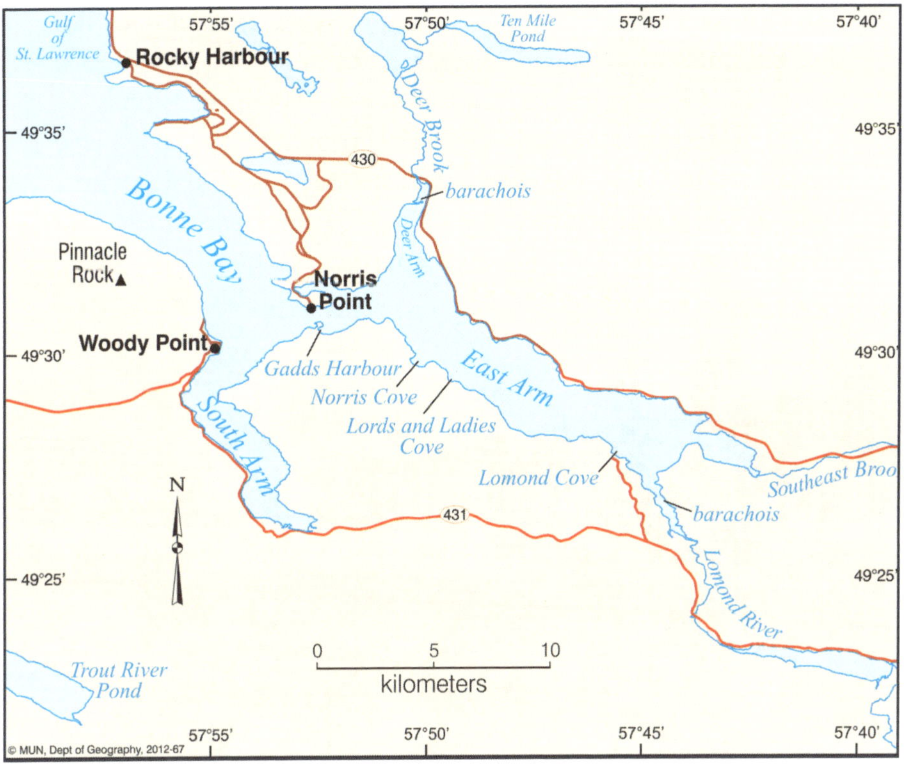

Map of Bonne Bay showing location of Gadds Harbour, Norris Cove, Lords and Ladies Cove, Lomond Cove, the barachois in the Deer Brook delta, and the barachois in the Lomond River delta.

Gros Morne's terrestrial ecosystem is protected by federal legislation designed to manage human activity in all National Parks. However, the marine ecosystem of Bonne Bay currently has no special protection other than the federal regulations set to manage coastal waters,[16] so the future and health of this unique area depends on public stewardship of the marine environment and conservation of the bay's marine resources.

TOP PHOTO: The Lomond River delta looking up-river.

LEFT PHOTO: These pillars at Lomond Cove are remnants of an ice house built to keep food fresh for men who worked in the woods to supply a saw mill near the mouth of the Lomond River.[17]

Longliners landing mackerel at the wharf in Norris Point. Seiners harvest mackerel and capelin in the Outer Basin of Bonne Bay. (PHOTOGRAPH BY ARNAULT LE BRIS)

Commercial fishing boats at the wharf in Norris Point. Shown to the left in the photo is the main building of the Bonne Bay Marine Station.[18] (PHOTOGRAPH BY CRAIG PURCHASE)

A lobster fishing boat carrying modern wire lobster traps to the wharf in Norris Point at the end of the lobster fishing season.[19]

View of The Tablelands (background) from the shoreline of Bonne Bay. Seaweeds growing along the shoreline are uncovered at low tide.
(PHOTOGRAPH BY CRAIG PURCHASE)

MARINE ECOSYSTEM OF BONNE BAY

2

Marine algae and animal life can easily be seen just by walking along the shoreline of Bonne Bay. Seaweeds and mussels lie attached to rocks in the intertidal zone. Sea stars and crabs inhabit tide pools. Sticklebacks swim in schools a little further from the shoreline. One might see a marine mammal, such as a minke whale, surfacing in the distance while seabirds fly over the waters of the bay in search of food.

The sea has an ecosystem, just as the land has a cycle of life. The position of an organism in the marine food chain is called its trophic level.[1] In the marine ecosystem, the base of the food chain is the algal life. Photosynthetic algae are the first trophic level. Microscopic algae that drift in the sea are called "phytoplankton." Seaweeds and marine grasses growing where sunlight reaches the sea bottom also contribute to photosynthetic production.

Algae are eaten by herbivorous animals, the second trophic level, and tiny herbivores that drift with the currents are called zooplankton.[2] The next link in the marine food chain is composed of fish that eat zooplankton (for example Atlantic herring). Plankton (both living and recently dead) are then consumed by benthic animals (for example clams, mussels, scallops, and shrimp), which are in turn eaten by a variety of fish and seabirds. Fishes which eat other fishes are called "piscivorous" fishes (for example Atlantic cod). Marine mammals and seabirds consume the zooplankton and fish. Then bacteria recycle dead vegetable and animal matter back into nutrients for algae, completing the cycle of life.

ALGAE AND ESTUARINE PLANTS

Primary producers in the marine ecosystem of Bonne Bay include single-celled algae, multi-cellular algae (commonly known as seaweeds), flowering sea grasses, and salt marsh plants. Microscopic phytoplankton create most of the photosynthetic production in the seawater. Seaweeds, sea grasses, and salt marsh plants that grow along the shores of Bonne Bay also contribute to the primary production of organic matter, the food for herbivores.[3] Some seaweeds and estuarine plants are destroyed each winter by landfast ice scour of the shoreline. Seaweeds, sea grasses, and salt marsh plants are perennial vegetation (i.e. living for more than one growing season). All species of algae and estuarine plants contribute to the functioning of the fjord-estuary ecosystem.

PHYTOPLANKTON

In nearshore coastal waters of higher latitudes, including Bonne Bay, the spring bloom of phytoplankton is initiated by snow-melt runoff from the land, which forms a lens of fresh water on the surface. This freshwater lens dampens the wind-driven mixing of the upper water column, so phytoplankton can remain near the sea surface and absorb sufficient sunlight to grow. Sunlight energy and inorganic nutrients dissolved in the water column are converted into phytoplankton biomass through the process of photosynthesis.[4] Phytoplankton cells will grow and divide until the nutrients are depleted. Seawater can appear green due to an abundance of microscopic phytoplankton, and zooplankton feeding on phytoplankton will excrete waste products that then become more nutrients for the phytoplankton. At the end of the growth season in the fall, phytoplankton no longer have sufficient sunlight to grow, and phytoplankton cells remain dormant during the winter until they can divide and grow again in the spring.

SEAWEEDS

There are three taxonomic categories of seaweed, grouped according to their dominant type of photosynthetic pigment: red algae (phylum Rhodophyta), brown algae (phylum Phaeophyta) and green algae (phylum Chlorophyta).[5] Seaweeds have a different structure than terrestrial plants as seaweeds do not have roots, stems, and leaves like true vascular plants. The main body of a seaweed is called the thallus, and it has various shapes and forms depending on the species. The thallus can be leaflike, branching, filamentous, or encrusting.[6] In kelp species, the thallus is flattened and is called a blade. The stem-like region of the kelp is called a stipe, and the stipe attaches to the sea bottom by a structure called the holdfast. The life cycle of kelp species differs from land plants that produce flowers and seeds. Kelp blades produce spores which settle on the sea bottom and grow into microscopic filaments. These filaments have a sexual reproductive stage, which subsequently produces new kelp blades.[7]

A number of subarctic and cold-temperate seaweed species can be found in Bonne Bay.[8] The brown algae species present include the rockweed, knotted wrack, sea colander, hollow-stemmed kelp, and smooth cord weed. Green algae species present include the sea lettuce and hollow green weed. Red algae species found in Bonne Bay include Irish moss, twig weed, frayed weed, tubed weed, Dumont's red weed, wire weed, and several crustose red algal species (*Lithothamnium glaciale*, *L. lemoineae*, *Phymatolithon laevigatum* and *P. lenormandi*).

LEFT PHOTO: The cobble beach at Norris Cove with wave-torn seaweed left behind by a falling tide.
RIGHT PHOTO: Clumps of rockweed and knotted wrack growing on rocks in the intertidal zone.

ROCKWEED "Bladder Wrack"

Fucus vesiculosus

Rockweed is a brown algae commonly found in the rocky intertidal zone of the Gulf of St. Lawrence, including Bonne Bay. Air bladders in the bumpy branches will pop if squeezed or stepped upon.

Phylum Phaeophyta, the taxonomic category for brown algae.

DESCRIPTION The blades of the rockweed are flat with a midrib and a Y-shaped fork at the end. The rockweed has paired, pea-size air bladders within the blade, which float the submerged blades up toward the surface where more sunlight is available for photosynthesis. The colouration of rockweed is usually olive, but can vary from golden yellow to deep green. The blades may grow to almost a metre in length in ideal environmental conditions.[9]

HABITAT The rockweed is found in the littoral zone of the Arctic south to North Carolina and can often be observed in the intertidal zone attached to rocks. It is a perennial seaweed.

RESOURCE USE The rockweed is food for herbivores, such as snails. Decaying rockweed is food for detritus eaters.

KNOTTED WRACK

Ascophyllum nodosum

The knotted wrack is a brown algae common in the rocky intertidal zone of Bonne Bay.

Phylum Phaeophyta, the taxonomic category for brown algae.

DESCRIPTION The knotted wrack has long, narrow fronds with short branchlets. The "knots" are air bladders and are not paired as in the rockweed. The colouration of the knotted wrack is olive, but may be golden or yellow brown. The fronds can grow to 60 centimetres or more in length.[10]

HABITAT The knotted wrack is found in the littoral zone of the Arctic south to Long Island Sound and can often be observed in the intertidal zone attached to rocks. It is a perennial seaweed.

RESOURCE USE The knotted wrack is food for herbivores and detritivores. It can be used as packing material for lobsters stored for market in crates. Beds of knotted wrack exposed at low tide are particularly slippery when stepped on.

SEA COLANDER
Agarum clathratum

The sea colander is a brown alga that grows attached to the sea bottom in subtidal waters. This specimen was dislodged by storm waves and washed ashore at Norris Cove. The blade, stipe, and holdfast or "anchor" are shown in the photograph left to right.

DESCRIPTION The blade of the sea colander has a midrib and is characteristically riddled with holes. The colouration is dark brown, and the blade of this seaweed can grow to a length of 2 to 3 metres.[11]

Phylum Phaeophyta, the taxonomic category for brown algae.

HABITAT The sea colander can be found in subtidal waters of the Arctic Ocean south to Cape Cod. It is a perennial seaweed.

RESOURCE USE The sea colander is food for herbivores and produces a chemical to repel sea urchins. Large kelp species like the sea colander provide many marine animals (such as crabs, lobsters, and fishes) shelter from predators.[12]

CABBAGE KELP "Hollow-stemmed kelp"
Saccharina longicruris

The cabbage kelp is a brown alga present in subtidal waters of Bonne Bay. In the photograph, the kelp's holdfast is attached to a rock encrusted by coralline red algae.

DESCRIPTION The blade of the cabbage kelp is long with ruffled edges and without a midrib. The colouration is brown. The blade of this seaweed can grow to a length of 5 metres, but lengths of more than 10 metres have been reported for cabbage kelp growing in deep water.[13]

HABITAT The cabbage kelp is found in subtidal waters on both sides of the Atlantic Ocean. In the northwest Atlantic, the cabbage kelp ranges from the Arctic Ocean to Cape Cod, Massachusetts. It is a perennial seaweed.

Phylum Phaeophyta, the taxonomic category for brown algae.

RESOURCE USE Cabbage kelp beds provide food and shelter for many marine organisms.[14] Kelps of the genus *Laminaria* can be dried, crushed, and used as a natural food supplement rich in vitamins and minerals. Kelp has traditionally been used as a garden fertilizer in Newfoundland and Labrador.

SMOOTH CORD WEED

Chorda filum

The smooth cord weed is a brown algae that grows in the lower intertidal zone and subtidal waters of the Gulf, including Bonne Bay. Note the holdfast is attached to a cobble stone. This specimen was dislodged by storm waves and washed ashore.

Phylum Phaeophyta, the taxonomic category for brown algae.

DESCRIPTION The cord-like blades of the thallus are whip-like, without branches. The core is hollow and buoyant in seawater, helping the blades float toward the surface where sunlight is available for photosynthesis. The colouration of the smooth cord weed is brown, and the blades can grow to a length of 4 metres or more, while the blade thickness remains about 6 millimetres.[15]

HABITAT The smooth cord weed is found in the littoral zone of the Arctic south to Long Island Sound. The holdfast attaches to shells or stones. It is an annual seaweed, maturing in summer.[16]

RESOURCE USE The smooth cord weed is food for herbivores and, when growing in subtidal waters, provides many marine animals, including juvenile fishes, shelter from predators

FLOWERING SEAGRASSES

Most vegetation on land consists of plants which reproduce by generating seeds. There are only a few plant species living in the sea that produce flowers, seeds, and fruit. One of these seed plant species, the eelgrass, is present in river deltas in Bonne Bay and St. Paul's Inlet. A second seed plant species, widgeon grass or ditch grass, can be found in many coastal regions throughout the world, and has been collected near the mouth of the Lomond River and from St. Paul's Inlet.

These flowering seagrasses have the same structural form as many land plants: stems, roots, and leaves.[17] Eelgrass and widgeon grass have root systems that grow into the marine sediment. Seagrass plants can live totally submerged without exposure to air at low tide. Like lawn grass, seagrass grows horizontal stems and vertical leaves.

EELGRASS "Goosegrass"

Zostera marina

Top photo: An eelgrass bed in the delta of Deer Brook exposed at low tide.
Bottom photo: The long leaves of eelgrass move with the current like a swimming eel, hence the common name.

DESCRIPTION Eelgrass is a flowering seagrass with leaves, stems, and roots. Stems growing horizontally in the bottom sediments are called rhizomes or runners from which grow vertical stems.[18] The long leaves of the eelgrass arise from these vertical stems. It is a perennial plant, living longer than two years.[19] Tiny flowers and fruit are produced on the stem during the summer.

HABITAT The eelgrass is found in shallow water with a mud-sand bottom along the west coast of the North Atlantic, from the Arctic to South Carolina. It can also be found along the Pacific Coast.[20]

RESOURCE USE The eelgrass plays an important ecological role in the estuaries of the Gulf of St. Lawrence, including Bonne Bay. Eelgrass beds stabilize mud bottoms and provide shelter for many small marine animals, including commercially important fish larvae, such as Atlantic cod.[21] The Brant, a small goose resembling a Canada Goose with a dark neck, feeds on eelgrass. This is likely the origin of the nickname "goosegrass."[22]

Phylum Anthophyta, the taxonomic category of seed plants that include the freshwater lily and salt marsh plants.

SALT MARSH PLANTS

Salt marsh plants have the same structural form as many land plants (stems, roots, and leaves), produce flowers and seeds,[23] and grow in intertidal zones with mud sediment. Unlike seagrasses, salt marsh plants must have periodic exposure to air at low tide to grow and reproduce.[24] Salt marsh plants are found along river deltas and the shores of bays in temperate regions of the world's oceans. Their distribution in high latitudes is restricted by ice scouring of the shoreline and in low latitudes is limited by the high temperature of seawater.[25]

Smooth cordgrass is usually the dominant plant of the lower marsh in temperate costal regions of the world.[26] An abundant plant in the low marsh of St. Paul's Inlet is the seaside arrowgrass. Various species of grasses and rushes grow in the upper salt marsh which is underwater only during spring tides and storm surges. The salt marsh habitat transitions to terrestrial habitat with increasing elevation of the land.

TOP PHOTO: Salt marsh plants grow in mud sediment of the upper barachois at Deer Brook delta. The barachois is only about a metre deep at high tide.

Zonation in vegetation with increasing land elevation in the salt marsh can be seen in the left photo.

SMOOTH CORDGRASS

Spartina alterniflora

Smooth cordgrass is a salt marsh plant that grows in intertidal areas with mud sediment. It can be found along the shores of the Deer Brook delta and Lomond River delta in Bonne Bay.

DESCRIPTION Smooth cordgrass grows in clumps of vertical stems connected by horizontal roots called rhizomes. Long, flat blades grow from the stems, and small flowers may be produced during the summer. Smooth cordgrass can grow as high as 3 metres, but plants in nutrient poor sediments are smaller.[27]

HABITAT This plant forms salt marshes in many temperate coastal regions of the world. It grows in the portion of the intertidal zone that is covered by water much of the time.

RESOURCE USE The smooth cordgrass plays an ecological role similar to eelgrass by stabilizing mud sediment and providing shelter for many small marine animals, including the juvenile life stage of many sport and commercially important fishes.[28]

Phylum Anthophyta, the taxonomic category of seed plants that include the freshwater lily and salt marsh plants. It is classified with the Family Poaceae, the true grasses.

Sand dune plants are considered part of the terrestrial ecosystem of Gros Morne National Park. The regulatory boundary of the Park extends to the mean low tide mark.

INVERTEBRATE ANIMALS

Unlike marine algae and estuarine plants, marine animals cannot produce their own nutrition. Animals eat other organisms for sustenance.[29] Animals that lack a backbone are called "invertebrates." Major taxonomic groups of marine invertebrates include the phyla Porifera, for sponges; Cnidaria, for animals with stinging cells (e.g. hydrozoans, jellyfish, corals, and sea anemones); Echinodermata, for "spiny skinned" animals (e.g. sea stars, sea urchins, sand dollars, and sea cucumbers); Annelida, for marine segmented worms (e.g. polychaetes); Mollusca, for animals with

STRAWBERRY CORAL "Sea strawberry"
Gersemia rubiformis

The strawberry coral is a benthic invertebrate animal that lives in the Gulf of St. Lawrence and in the East Arm of Bonne Bay. The photograph shows a redfish seeking the shelter of the coral. (PHOTOGRAPH COURTESY OF EVAN EDINGER)

Phylum Cnidaria, order Octorallia (eight tentacled polyps) which includes the soft corals, gorgonians, sea feathers, and sea pens.[32]

DESCRIPTION The body form of the strawberry coral is the polyp, typified by the sea anemone.[30] The strawberry coral is formed of colonies branching from a stem-like base which is attached to the sea bottom.[31] The branches are not rigid, as in reef corals, and can sway with the ocean current. Soft corals are long lived and slow growing. When disturbed, the strawberry coral contracts its body into a small pink-white ball. This is the animal's appearance when found entangled in fishing gear.

HABITAT The strawberry coral is found in the Arctic Ocean, the northwest Atlantic Ocean, and the northern Gulf of St. Lawrence,[33] including Bonne Bay.[34] It lives on hard bottom substrate at depths from 10 to 1000 metres,[35] and feeds on zooplankton caught by the stinging cells. Soft corals have few predators. However, they can be caught as bycatch in bottom trawls and gillnets used in the groundfish fishery.

RESOURCE USE Soft corals such as the strawberry coral have an important role in the marine ecosystem of the Gulf of St. Lawrence. Several species of fish and invertebrates use soft corals for shelter.[36]

a soft body usually covered by a shell of calcium carbonate (e.g. snails, mussels, scallops, and clams, but also shell-less octopods and squids); and Arthropoda, with a subphylum Crustacea, for animals with a hard exterior skeleton of chitin and mandibles for feeding (e.g. copepods, krill, amphipods, shrimp, crabs, and lobsters).[37] There are also taxonomic groupings of less common marine invertebrates, which are not discussed here.[38]

ASTERIID SEA STAR "Starfish"

Asterias rubens

Asteriid sea stars are familiar to tide pool explorers. Top photo shows the rough skin on the dorsal surface (upper side) of the sea star. Lower photo shows the ventral surface with contractile tube feet in grooves along each arm and the mouth in the center.[39]

DESCRIPTION The body form of asteriid sea stars, like all echinoderms, has a five-part, radial pattern.[40] Asteriid sea stars have five arms with rough skin, tiny pincers on the dorsal surface (upper side) and four rows of tube feet in the groove under each arm.[41] Other species of sea stars have two rows of tube feet in the groove along the underside of the arms. The colouration of Asteriid sea stars can be olive, brown, yellow, orange, red, or purple,[42] and these sea stars can grow to a diameter of about 50 centimetres.

HABITAT The sea star species *Asterias rubens* is found in most seas of the world, including the Gulf of St. Lawrence.[43] It inhabits rocky and sandy sea bottoms from the intertidal zone down to the edge of the continental shelf. Sea stars prey upon clams, scallops, mussels, and other sea stars. Demersal fishes, such as the Atlantic cod, will eat sea stars.

RESOURCE USE Sea stars are fun for children to observe in tide pools. Predation by sea stars in oyster beds, clams beds, and mussel aquaculture strings can affect the profitability of shellfish fisheries and aquaculture operations.

Asteriid sea stars (that is species of the genera *Asterias* and *Leptasterias*) are members of the phylum Echinodermata, the taxonomic category for spiny-skinned, exclusively marine invertebrates.

BIVALVE MOLLUSCS

Bivalve molluscs are invertebrate animals that have two joined shells called "valves." Scallops, mussels, and clams are bivalve molluscs. They filter seawater to obtain their food, mainly plankton. Some mollusc species, such as the soft-shelled clam, live in mud sediment. Other species, such as the Iceland scallop, can attach itself to a hard bottom substrate with a bundle of tough threads called a "byssus." Scallops which are unattached by byssal threads can escape sea star predators by closing the valves rapidly, akin to jet propulsion.[44]

SEA SCALLOP

"Giant scallop; Deep-sea scallop"

Placopecten magellanicus

The sea scallop is a benthic invertebrate animal that lives in subtidal waters of the Gulf and in the East Arm of Bonne Bay.
(PHOTOGRAPH BY ROBERT BRIGGS)

Phylum Mollusca, class Bivalvia, order Ostreoida, family Pectinidae, the taxonomic category for marine scallops.[45]

DESCRIPTION The sea scallop has a ribbed shell and can grow to a maximum shell height (i.e. the longest distance from the shell hinge to shell margin) of about 20 centimetres.

HABITAT The sea scallop is found in the northwest Atlantic Ocean, ranging from the Labrador continental shelf to Cape Cod, Massachusetts. It lives on hard bottom substrate in subtidal waters down to a depth of approximately 180 metres. The sea scallop inhabits the Gulf of St. Lawrence,[46] including the subtidal waters of Bonne Bay.[47]

RESOURCE USE Sea scallops are harvested commercially by dredging on the Grand Banks and on the continental shelf off the south coast of Newfoundland. The fishery for sea scallops is worth about $2 million annually.[48]

BLUE MUSSEL

Mytilus edulis

The blue mussel is a benthic invertebrate animal that lives in the intertidal zone and upper subtidal zone. (PHOTOGRAPH BY DAVID INNES)

DESCRIPTION The blue mussel has a smooth shell, and the colouration is glossy bluish or bluish black.[49] Blue mussels attach themselves to solid substrate with tough threads and can grow to a maximum shell height of about 10 centimetres.

HABITAT The blue mussel has a circumpolar distribution.[50] In the western Atlantic Ocean, it ranges from the Canadian Arctic Ocean south to the coast of South Carolina. Often found attached to rocks in the intertidal zone and subtidal waters close to the shoreline, it is common throughout the Gulf of St. Lawrence,[51] including Bonne Bay.[52]

RESOURCE USE The blue mussel is tasty seafood. It can be steamed and eaten if harvested from non-polluted waters or purchased as an aquaculture product. Sales of blue mussels produced by aquaculture in insular Newfoundland are worth about $8 million annually.[54]

Phylum Mollusca, class Bivalvia, order Mytiloida, family Mytilidae, the taxonomic category for marine mussels.[53]

CRUSTACEANS

Arthropods (phylum Arthropoda) are invertebrate animals with a hard exterior skeleton (exoskeleton) and segmented body with jointed appendages. Familiar terrestrial insects are arthropods.[55] Marine arthropods that have a pair of appendages on the head used for feeding are called "mandibulates," and include crustaceans (subphylum Crustacea) such as copepods, amphipods, and mysids.

Decapod crustaceans have five pairs of leg-like jointed appendages, some of which may be clawed.[56] These crustaceans living in the Gulf include shrimps, crabs, and lobster.[57] The meat from decapod crustaceans is tasty seafood. A commercially-important decapod crustacean, the northern shrimp inhabits the Gulf of St. Lawrence and the continental shelf of Newfoundland and Labrador. The northern shrimp fishery is worth about $150 million annually to the provincial economy. The northern shrimp feeds on marine

TOP PHOTO: An amphipod collected from the intertidal zone of Bonne Bay. LEFT PHOTO: Mysids collected from a swarm along the shoreline of Bonne Bay.[58]

worms and detritus along the ocean bottom during the day and moves up into the water column to feed upon copepods and krill at night. Northern shrimp are preyed upon by commercially important fish species such as Greenland halibut and Atlantic cod.

Commercially important crab species living in the Gulf of St. Lawrence are the snow crab, Atlantic rock crab, and toad crab.[59] The snow crab fishery in Newfoundland and Labrador is worth about $200 million annually.[60] The Atlantic rock crab and toad crab are underutilized species.

SNOW CRAB

Chionoecetes opilio

The snow crab is a decapod crustacean that lives in the Gulf of St. Lawrence, including the Outer Basin of Bonne Bay. The shape of the tail flap on the abdomen is rounded in females (bottom photo) and more triangular in males (not shown).

DESCRIPTION The body shape of the snowcrab is oval. The claws of the snow crab are smaller than the claws of lobster. The male snow crab at maturity is larger than the female.

HABITAT The snow crab inhabits continental shelf waters of the northwestern Atlantic Ocean and from west Greenland, along the Labrador and Newfoundland coastlines, the Gulf of St. Lawrence, and south into the Gulf of Maine. The snow crab lives on muddy or sand-mud bottom substrates and feeds on marine worms, sea urchins, brittle stars, and bivalve molluscs.

RESOURCE USE The snow crab is the most valuable shellfish species harvested in Newfoundland and Labrador.[61] The mesh size of crab pots is regulated so the female escapes from the pot while the male is retained. Only the males are harvested, as a fishery conservation measure. There is a stock of snow crab in Outer Bonne Bay, which supports a local fishery.[62]

Phylum Arthropoda, class Malacostraca, order Decapoda, and family Oregoniidae.[63]

ATLANTIC ROCK CRAB "Peekytoe Crab"

Cancer irroratus

The underside of an Atlantic rock crab, a decapod crustacean. The triangular shape of the tail flap on the abdomen indicates this individual is a male. The female rock crab has a wider and more rounded tail flap.

DESCRIPTION The body shape of the Atlantic rock crab is broadly oval, and the colouration is yellowish with reddish or purple brown. The underside is whitish yellow. The rock crab can grow to a maximum carapace length of about 13 centimetres.

Phylum Arthropoda, class Malacostraca, order Decapoda, and family Cancridae.[64]

HABITAT The Atlantic rock crab are found in waters of the western North Atlantic Ocean, ranging from Labrador to the coast of South Carolina.[65] It inhabits the sea bottom from the intertidal zone down to a depth of about 750 metres.

RESOURCE USE In New England, rock crabs that are caught as by-catch in lobster pots are marketed as whole crabs or as disjointed claws. The rock crab is an underutilized species in the Gulf of St. Lawrence.[66]

TOAD CRAB "Spider Crab"

Hyas araneus

The toad crab is a decapod crustacean that lives in shallow subtidal waters of the Gulf, including Bonne Bay.

DESCRIPTION The body shape of the toad crab is triangular. The rostrum is nearly triangular, and the colouration is reddish to olive. The toad crab can grow to a maximum carapace length of about 10 centimetres.[67]

Phylum Arthropoda, class Malacostraca, order Decapoda and family Oregoniidae, the taxonomic category that includes true crabs.[68]

HABITAT Toad crab are found in the Arctic Ocean south to the coastline of Rhode Island. It inhabits mud sea bottoms in subtidal waters down to a depth of about 10 metres.

RESOURCE USE The toad crab is an underutilized species in the Gulf of St. Lawrence.[69]

Perhaps the most famous decapod crustacean living in the Gulf of St. Lawrence is the American lobster. The economic value of the lobster fishery in Atlantic Canada is about $550 million. The lobster fishery in Newfoundland and Labrador is worth about $25 million annually.[70] Lobster are harvested using traps in Bonne Bay by inshore fishermen working in small boats.

AMERICAN LOBSTER

Homarus americanus

The American lobster is a decapod crustacean that lives in subtidal waters of the Gulf, including Bonne Bay.

DESCRIPTION The American lobster has five pairs of appendages. The first three pairs have claws, with huge pincers on the first pair. The colouration is greenish brown; however, many variations include red, blue, and bilateral split colouration. American lobsters can grow to 90 centimetres in length.

HABITAT The American lobster is found only in the northwest Atlantic Ocean, ranging from the Strait of Belle Isle south to Cape Hatteras, North Carolina.[71] The lobster lives at depths ranging from shallow subtidal waters to the edge of the continental shelf. Adult lobsters prey upon marine worms, snails, sea urchins, starfish, scallops, clams, and shrimp.

RESOURCE USE The American lobster is considered a seafood delicacy.[72] Harvesting lobster contributes a significant portion to the annual income of many inshore fishermen in Atlantic Canada.[73] The American lobster supports an inshore fishery in the East Arm of Bonne Bay.[74]

Phylum Arthropoda, class Malacostraca, order Decapoda, and family Nephropidae, the taxonomic category that also includes the European lobster.[75] A close relative of the lobster is the crayfish, which is found in many freshwater habitats in North America.

VERTEBRATE ANIMALS

The major taxonomic group for animals with a skeletal rod is the phylum Chordata. Animals that have a skeletal rod of bone or cartilage that helps support the body are called "vertebrates." Fishes, amphibians, reptiles, birds, and mammals are vertebrates.[76]

FISHES

Fish are cold-blooded, vertebrate animals.[77] All fish possess a backbone made of either cartilage or bone. The body temperature of the cold-blooded fish is the same as its water surroundings. Fish possess gills for respiration, absorbing oxygen dissolved in the water. Most fish have a body covered by scales although scales are minor or absent in some fishes (e.g. the juvenile American eel of less than 10 centimetres, has no scales). The body is covered by a protective mucus layer. Many fish species have a lateral line with sensory cells on the skin. Fish use fins and a tail to swim through their aquatic habitat, although some fish have modified fins (e.g. the pelvic fins of the Atlantic snailfish form a sucker for attachment to rocks) or lack fins (e.g. the pelvic fins are absent in the American eel).[78]

Whales, dolphins, porpoises, and seals are not fish, but rather air-breathing, warm-blooded mammals.[79] Warm-blooded animals obtain their body heat from metabolism of their food. Marine mammals give live birth and nurse their young. While some fish bear live young (e.g. the Acadian redfish), no fish nurse their young like mammals.

All fish species fall within one of two major taxonomic groupings: those with jaws and those without jaws.[80] The Atlantic hagfish is a jawless fish that lives in the deep waters of the Gulf of St. Lawrence, and possibly the depths of Bonne Bay. However, the fishes living in the nearshore waters of Bonne Bay all possess jaws. The taxonomic group of fishes with jaws can be further divided into three taxonomic classes: fishes with a cartilaginous skeleton (class Chondrichthyes); fishes with a bone skeleton along with fleshy, lobed fins (class Sarcopterygii); and fishes with a bone skeleton along with rayed fins (class Actinopterygii). There are no lobed-fin fishes in North American waters, so we are only concerned here with cartilaginous fishes (skates and sharks) and bony fishes with rayed fins.[81]

CARTILAGINOUS FISHES: SKATES

Skates are pancake-shaped fishes with a cartilaginous skeleton.[82] The flattened body is an adaptation to its bottom-dwelling or "demersal" way of life. The mouth is located on the ventral (underneath) surface of the body. Skates have breathing holes or "spiracles" on the top of the head and breathe by pulling water into the spiracles and across the gills located on the ventral surface. Large pectoral fins are attached to the sides of the head, giving the appearance of "wings." The skate swims with an undulating motion of the tips of the pectoral fins and can bury itself by stirring up sand or mud by flapping its fins.[83]

Views of the dorsal (left sketch) and ventral (right sketch) views of a winter skate to show the names of a typical skate's body parts.

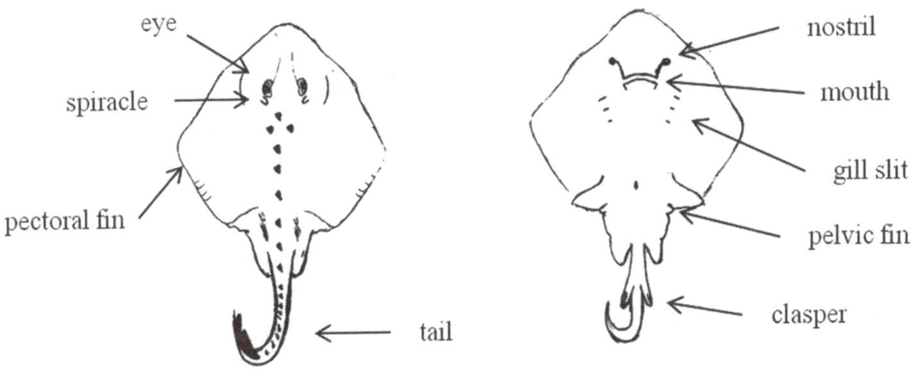

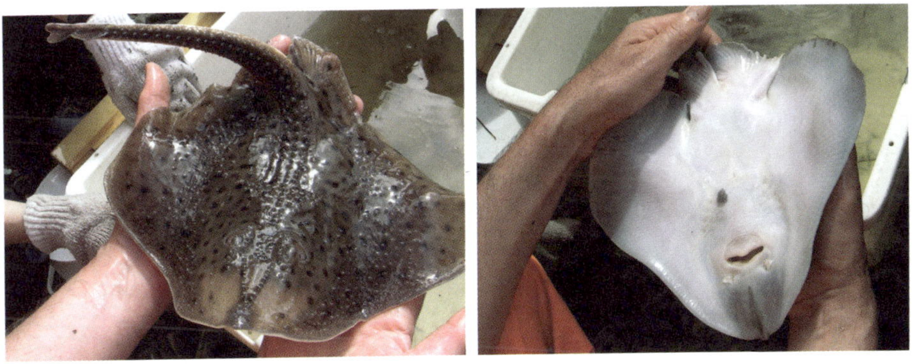

The winter skate is a pancake-shaped fish with a skeleton of cartilage. The pectoral fins adjoined to the head resemble the wings of an airplane.

As the male skate becomes sexually mature, it develops a mating organ with "claspers" where the pelvic fins join the tail. The eggs in the female skate are internally fertilized by the male. The fertilized egg develops a tough exterior case with stiff pointed "horns" at the corners. The egg capsule, known as "mermaid's purse," is released by the female skate on the sea bottom. The embryo lives off the yolk of the egg and leaves the egg capsule as a free-swimming juvenile skate.

CARTILAGINOUS FISHES: SHARKS

Sharks are torpedo-shaped fishes with a cartilaginous skeleton.[84] The body is shaped for swimming in the water column, a "pelagic" way of life. A shark swims by moving its tail from side to side. Carnivorous sharks have a large head and a large mouth with sharp teeth. Only a few species of shark are planktivorous.

The spiny dogfish is a torpedo-shaped fish with a cartilaginous skeleton. (PHOTOGRAPH BY RYAN MARTIN)

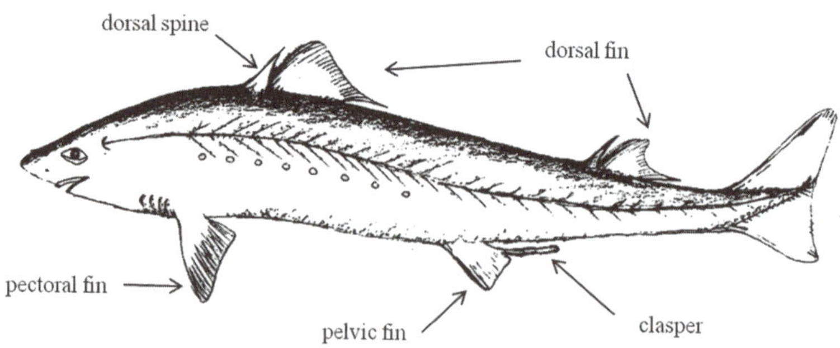

Sketch of a spiny dogfish to show the names of the body parts of a typical shark. The pectoral fins and pelvic fins are paired (one on each side of the body).

The "pups" are free-swimming juveniles when born by the female dogfish. (PHOTOGRAPH BY RYAN MARTIN)

Like skates, mating in sharks is by internal fertilization. The pelvic fins of the adult male shark are modified into "claspers" for delivery of sperm to the female. The female shark produces only a few large eggs, and in some shark species, the individual fertilized egg is released as an egg case into the sea. In other shark species, the fertilized egg is retained within the body of the female. The gestation period may extend for nearly two years, unusually long for a vertebrate animal. The "pups" are free-swimming juvenile sharks when born by the female.

BONY FISHES

Fishes with a bone skeleton and fins attached to the body by soft supportive rays are called "ray-finned fishes." Paired pectoral and pelvic fins are used for steering, while the dorsal and anal fins help the fish maintain stability while swimming.[85] There are many body shapes of ray-finned fishes as each fish species adapts to its specialized habitat.

SPINDLE-SHAPED PELAGIC FISHES

Fishes that are fast swimmers, such as the Atlantic salmon, have a spindle-like body shape that is wide in the middle and tapered at both ends.[86]

The Atlantic salmon is an example of a bony fish with rayed fins and a spindle-shaped body form. Note the adipose fin behind the single dorsal fin. The adipose fin is a distinguishing characteristic of salmonid (trout-like) fishes. (PHOTOGRAPH BY DAVID METHVEN)

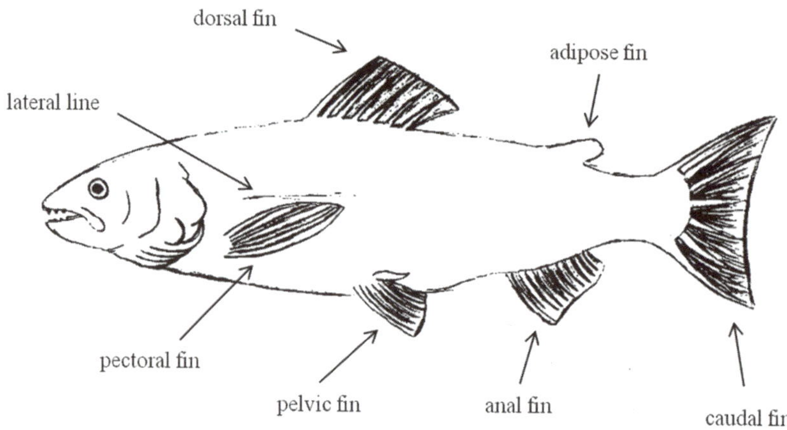

Sketch of an Atlantic salmon to show the names of body parts of a typical bony fish with rayed fins and a spindle-shaped body form. The pectoral fins and pelvic fins are paired while the dorsal, caudal, and anal fins are not paired. Salmonid species have an adipose fin on the back just before the caudal fin.

FLAT-SHAPED DEMERSAL FISHES (FLOUNDERS)

"Flatfish" is the name given to fish species that lie on their side when resting on the sea bottom.[87] Some flounder species lie on their right side while other species lie on their left side. Both eyes are on the topside of the head, so the fish can see with both its eyes as it lies on the sea bottom. The underside is pale while the topside is pigmented so the flounder blends with the bottom habitat. Flatfish swim with their eyed side upward and the eyeless side downward toward the ocean floor.

There are usually four stages in the life cycle of a marine bony fish: the egg stage, the larval stage, the juvenile stage, and the reproductive adult stage. Life begins with the fertilization of the egg cell produced in the ovary of the female fish. Some fish species (e.g. the Atlantic cod) spawn by releasing eggs and sperm into the water, whereupon the fertilized egg drifts with the currents. Other fish species (e.g. the Atlantic herring) lay demersal eggs which adhere to the sea bottom. Some fish species (e.g. the striped wolffish) exhibit "parental-care" behaviour, protecting the mass of fertilized eggs on the sea bottom from predation until the eggs hatch.

The winter flounder is an example of a bony fish with rayed fins and a flat-shaped body form. This species is a "right-eyed flounder" in that both eyes are on the right side of the head.

The young fish hatches from the egg usually in the larval form. The planktonic larval stage lasts until the fish undergoes "metamorphosis," when the features of the juvenile stage (e.g. rayed fins and perhaps spines) first appear in the developing body. Upon metamorphosis, the juvenile stage of some fish species will settle to the sea bottom (e.g. Atlantic cod). The morphed juvenile stage of other species will remain pelagic, swimming constantly in the water column (e.g. Atlantic herring).

The juvenile stage lasts until the fish becomes sexually mature and spawns. Some species reproduce only once in a lifetime (e.g. American eel) while others spawn each year after maturation (e.g. Atlantic cod). Fish reach their maximum length and age near

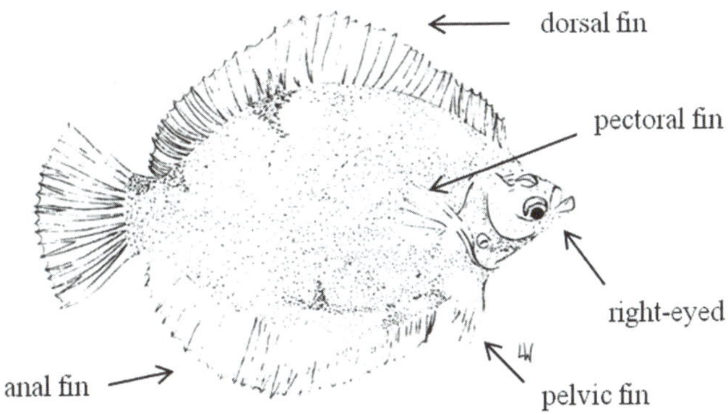

Sketch of a winter flounder to show the names of the body parts of a typical flat-shaped, "right-eyed" flounder. The pectoral fins and pelvic fins are paired while the dorsal, caudal, and anal fins are not paired.

the end of life. The age of a bony fish can usually be determined by counting the annual growth rings in body scales or in the otoliths, the two ear-stones that form the balance mechanism in the fish's skull.

A flounder begins life as most marine bony fishes. That is, the egg hatches releasing the planktonic larval stage which then metamorphoses into the juvenile stage. But as the juvenile flounder develops, one eye migrates to the side of the body that becomes the pigmented topside. Flounders are classified as left-eyed or right-eyed flatfish, depending on which side of the body has both eyes. An example of a right-eyed flatfish that inhabits Bonne Bay is the winter flounder, and a left-eyed flatfish inhabiting Bonne Bay is the windowpane flounder.

The fish species known to be present in Bonne Bay are described in the next chapter.

REPTILES

Reptiles are air-breathing, cold-blooded vertebrate animals.[88] Reptiles have scales, plates, or bony shields covering the body, and claws on the feet. A young reptile hatching from the egg looks like the parent except for its smaller size. The taxonomic category for reptiles includes marine species of crocodiles, turtles, lizards, and snakes. Most marine reptiles inhabit tropical seas, and only the leatherback sea turtle and the loggerhead sea turtle migrate north into the cold waters of the northwest Atlantic Ocean.[89]

While swimming nearshore, the leatherback sea turtle may become entangled in fishing gear, especially gillnets, and could then drown since sea turtles must reach the surface to breathe.[90]

The leatherback is protected under Canadian Federal Legislation, the Species At Risk Act (SARA), as a species in danger of becoming extinct.[91] The number of leatherback turtles in the Atlantic and Pacific Oceans has declined greatly in the past two decades, and thus it is a species of conservation concern.[92]

The loggerhead turtle is known to feed in waters off eastern

Newfoundland during the summer and fall,[93] but the loggerhead population in the northwestern Atlantic is declining due to loss of nesting habitat in the Caribbean and mortality as bycatch in pelagic longline fisheries on Georges Bank and the Grand Banks. Like the leatherback, the loggerhead sea turtle is a species of conservation concern.[94] However, the loggerhead is not yet protected under the SARA.

LEATHERBACK SEA TURTLE

"Lute turtle" *Dermochelys coriacea*

The leatherback sea turtle is a warm-temperate ocean species that commonly visits the Gulf of St. Lawrence and coastal waters of eastern Newfoundland and Labrador to feed. This air-breathing marine reptile can become entangled in fishing gear and drown. The turtle in the photo was rescued and released by the Whale Release and Strandings Group of Newfoundland and Labrador. (PHOTOGRAPH BY WAYNE LEDWELL)

DESCRIPTION The leatherback sea turtle has a shield of leathery skin covering its body rather than the hard plate possessed by most turtle species. There are prominent ridges along the back, and its fore-flippers are long and used for swimming great distances. Unlike most reptiles, the leatherback turtle has no claws. The largest sea turtle, the leatherback can grow to approximately 2 metres in length and 500 kilograms or more in weight.[95]

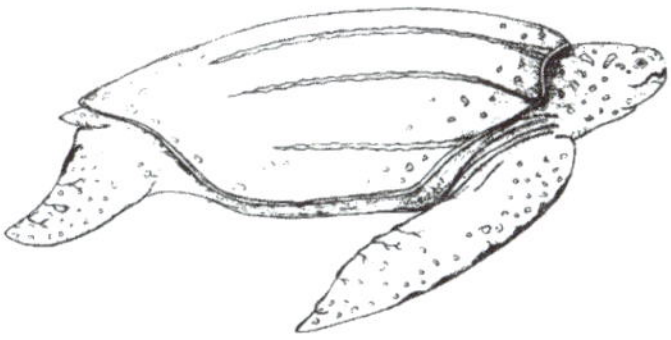

HABITAT The leatherback turtle has been observed in the Gulf of St. Lawrence and Bonne Bay.[96] This turtle mates at sea, and the female homes to nesting sites in the Caribbean and lays her eggs in sand above the surf line.

Phylum Chordata, family Dermochelyidae.[97]

The leatherback feeds near the sea surface, consuming mostly jellyfish. It can appear in nearshore coastal waters of the Gulf of St. Lawrence during the summer months when jellyfish blooms occur. Unfortunately, the leatherback may mistake floating plastic grocery bags for jellyfish, and the ingested plastic may block the digestive tract, causing the turtle to starve to death.

RESOURCE USE The leatherback sea turtle is a favourite species of marine-life watchers.

MAMMALS

CETACEANS (WHALES, DOLPHINS, AND PORPOISES)

Mammals are air-breathing, warm-blooded vertebrate animals which give live birth and nurse their young.[98] Whales, dolphins, and porpoises are categorized by biologists as "cetaceans," which have a blowhole in the animal's head. There are two main taxonomic categories of whales: baleen whales and toothed whales. Baleen whales filter feed on plankton and small fish screened from mouthfuls of seawater by the baleen plates. Toothed whales prey on squid and fish.

Baleen whales observed in the Gulf of St. Lawrence include the humpback, the minke, the fin whale, and occasionally the northern right whale. The blue whale is rarely present.[99]

HUMPBACK WHALE "Hump"

Megaptera novaeangliae

The humpback is a baleen whale that can be seen in summer feeding on capelin in the Gulf of St. Lawrence and occasionally in the Outer Basin of Bonne Bay. (PHOTOGRAPH BY JESSICA FLIGHT)

DESCRIPTION The body of the humpback whale is streamlined and nearly hairless. It has a broad head with wart-like knobs. The dorsal fin is located at about two-thirds of the length of the back and appears to be on a hump when the whale is diving, hence its common name. Long flippers are located at about one third of the body length. The colouration of the humpback is black on the back with white undersides. The flippers are white. The average length of an adult is about 13 metres.

HABITAT The humpback whale is found in all oceans in both hemispheres. The humpback breeds and gives birth in the tropics and migrates to feeding grounds in high latitudes. A mature female produces a calf every two years, and the gestation period is ten to twelve months. The calf suckles milk from the mother for about a year.[100] In the northwest Atlantic Ocean, humpbacks overwinter in the West Indies and migrate north to Newfoundland and Labrador to feed during the summer and fall. Sightings in the Gulf of St. Lawrence, where they feed on capelin, krill, sand lance, and squid, are common.

RESOURCE USE Whaling stations were established in southern Labrador by the Basques people from the Bay of Biscay in Europe during the 16th century.[101] Commercial whaling in the waters of Newfoundland and Labrador was conducted by the English, Norwegians, and Americans during the late 1800s and early 1900s.[102]

The current abundance of the humpback whale in the Canadian Arctic Ocean and the western North Atlantic is estimated to be several thousand individuals, and therefore not at risk of extinction.[103] However, the humpback whale is still a species of conservation concern because of frequent entanglements in fishing gear.[104]

The fin whale is a large whale, second in size only to the blue whale.[105] Like the blue whale, the fin whale is sometimes killed or injured by ship strikes. The current number of fin whales in the Atlantic Ocean is so low that this species is protected under the SARA legislation when in Canadian coastal waters.[106]

The International Whaling Commission (IWC) was established in 1946 to manage the whaling industry globally. In 1972, Canada banned commercial whaling.[107] A moratorium on commercial hunting of large whales declared by the IWC came into effect in 1986.[108] The global abundance of humpback whales, blue whales, fin whales, sperm whales, sei whales, and minke whales had declined dramatically before the establishment of the IWC moratorium. Right whales in the Southern Hemisphere were already severely depleted by commercial whaling by the mid-1800s.[109] Japan, Norway, and Russia did not agree with the IWC moratorium and continue today to hunt certain species, particularly the minke whale.[110] Canada withdrew from the IWC in 1981 as it has no commercial whaling industry.

Aboriginal peoples of the Canadian Arctic are allowed to take bowhead whales, narwhals, and beluga whales in subsistence food harvests.[111] These harvests by aboriginal groups are regulated by Fisheries and Oceans Canada (DFO).

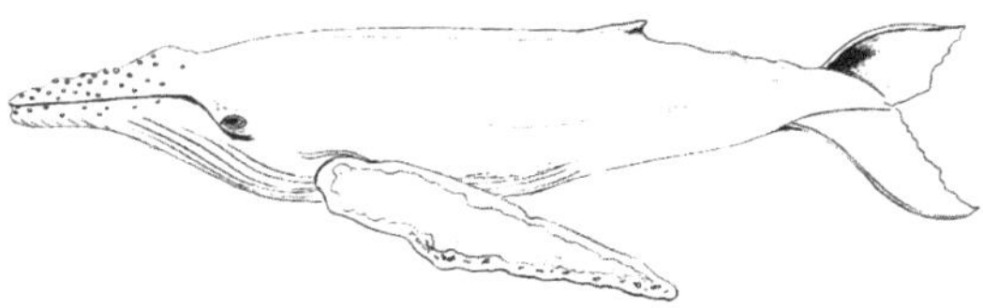

Phylum Chordata, class Mammalia, order Cetacea, sub-order Mysticeti (baleen whales), and the family Balaenopteridae, the taxonomic category for baleen whales having throat groves, rigid baleen plates, and a broad, flat rostrum.[112]

Currently, the number of North Atlantic right whales is estimated to be less than 350 individuals. Again, threats to the survival of the species are accidental collisions with vessels and entanglements in fishing gear.[113] The right whale is considered in danger of extinction by biologists, but the species is not yet provided with legal protection under SARA.[114]

MINKE WHALE "Herring hog"

Balaenoptera acutorostrata

The minke is a small baleen whale that can often be seen in the East Arm of Bonne Bay during the summer. (PHOTOGRAPH BY CRAIG PURCHASE)

Phylum Chordata, class Mammalia, order Cetacea, suborder Mysticeti (baleen whales), and the family Balaenopteridae.[115]

DESCRIPTION The minke whale has a narrow, triangular shaped head with a central ridge. The dorsal fin is located at about two-thirds of the length of the back and is pointed and hooked backward. The flippers are short in comparison to the humpback. The colouration is blue-grey with light chevron bands from behind the flippers up the side. The underside is light grey to white. The minke is the smallest of the baleen whales with a maximum length of about 9 metres.

HABITAT The minke whale is found worldwide in tropical, temperate, and polar seas. In the North Atlantic Ocean, minkes follow the same general migration pattern as humpback whales, leaving tropical waters in spring and reaching feeding grounds off Newfoundland and Labrador by early summer. They return to lower latitudes in the late fall, although some remain in northern waters during the winter months. There are reports of minke whales becoming trapped in sea ice. This whale can often be seen in the Gulf of St. Lawrence,[116] including Bonne Bay, feeding on krill, squid, and small fish). Females can produce a calf every year, more frequently than all other baleen whales.[117] The gestation period is about 11 months, and the calf suckles milk from the mother for about six months. Its natural predator is the killer whale. Minke whales appear to be naturally abundant in the Gulf, and the species is not thought to be of conservation concern. However minkes can become entrapped in fishing gear.[118]

RESOURCE USE Norway and Japan continue to hunt minke whales despite the moratorium established by the IWC in 1986.[119]

The blue whale is the largest whale, and reportedly the largest animal on Earth today.[120] The number of blue whales in the Northwest Atlantic Ocean is fewer than 250 individuals and the species is considered at risk of extinction.[121] Blue whales swimming at the sea surface are sometimes struck by ships or become entangled in fishing gear, and when in Canadian waters, the animals are protected under the SARA legislation.

HARBOUR PORPOISE "Puffin Pig"

Phocoena phocoena

The harbour porpoise is a small "toothed whale" which occasionally visits the East Arm of Bonne Bay. Note the blowhole at the top of the head.

DESCRIPTION The body of the harbour porpoise is stout, the head is round, and there is no beak. The nickname "puffin pig" stems from the resemblance of the snout to that of a pig, and the sound of the porpoise breathing at the surface resembles a snort.[122] The colouration is dark grey with black on the back and lighter grey on the sides. The underside is whitish with white under the chin and on the belly. The harbour porpoise is the smallest toothed whale with a maximum length of about 2 metres.[123]

HABITAT The harbour porpoise is found in temperate and subarctic coastal waters of the North Atlantic, North Pacific, and Black Sea. In the northwest Atlantic Ocean, it ranges from Greenland and Labrador south to the eastern seaboard of the US. As its common name implies, it is often observed in harbours. This porpoise is non-migratory and can become trapped in sea ice in bays, fjords, and estuaries during the winter months. Females can produce a calf every two years.[124] The gestation period is about 11 months, and the calf suckles milk for about eight months. The harbour porpoise feeds on squid, krill and fish, especially capelin, herring and mackerel. Predators of the harbour porpoise are sharks and killer whales.

Phylum Chordata, class Mammalia, order Cetacea, suborder Odontoceti (toothed whales), and the family Phocoenidae.[125]

RESOURCE USE As the harbour porpoise can frequently be seen in fjords, bays, and estuaries, it is familiar to whale watchers. It is currently not subject to commercial or aboriginal subsistence hunting in Canada.

Large baleen whales, such as the fin and humpback, have not been observed in the East Arm of Bonne Bay. These large animals apparently avoid the shallow sill at the entrance to the inner bay, between Gadds Harbour and Norris Point. But humpbacks and fin whales have been seen in South Arm and the Outer Basin of Bonne Bay, feeding on capelin and other "bait" fish during the summer. The smaller minke whale will often enter East Arm, usually between June and October.

Toothed whales observed in the Gulf of St. Lawrence include the beluga whale, the long-finned pilot or "pothead" whale, the northern bottlenose whale, and the killer whale. Sperm whales are occasionally sighted in the Gulf.[126]

The beluga whale is a year-round resident of the St. Lawrence Estuary, and individuals from this population may appear off the coast of western Newfoundland. This population of beluga is considered "threatened" by ship traffic and pollution of the St. Lawrence Estuary. It is protected under the SARA.[127]

Killer whales can sometimes be observed in coastal waters off Newfoundland and Labrador, including the northern Gulf of St. Lawrence, where they feed on seals and fish (e.g. Atlantic salmon). The killer whale population in the northwest Atlantic Ocean and eastern Arctic Ocean is small, and there are threats to their continued existence from hunting by Greenlanders. The population is therefore of conservation concern.[128]

Dolphins and porpoises are taxonomically classified as toothed whales.[129] Species commonly found in the Gulf of St. Lawrence are the Atlantic white-sided dolphin, the white-beaked dolphin, and the harbour porpoise.[130]

The harbour porpoise can often be seen in the Gulf of St. Lawrence, including Bonne Bay. In the Gulf, they appear to be naturally abundant, but the species is thought to be of conservation concern because of the high incidence of entanglement in fishing gear, especially gillnets.[131] This animal is not yet protected under SARA.[132]

PINNIPEDS (SEALS)

Seals, sea lions, and walrus are categorized by biologists as "pinnipeds" or "flipper-footed" marine mammals.[133] The fore and hind limbs are flipper-like. There are three taxonomic families of pinnipeds: Phocidae or true seals (e.g. seals that have no external ears); Otariidae or eared seals (e.g. fur seals and sea lions which have external ear flaps); and Odobenidae (walrus). True seals inhabit the Gulf, but sea lions are not found in the Atlantic. The Atlantic walrus inhabits the Arctic region and may stray south to Newfoundland waters, but sightings are rare in the Gulf of St. Lawrence.

Seals are prominent members of the marine mammal fauna in the Gulf of St. Lawrence. The harbour seal and grey seal are year-round residents of the Gulf and the estuary of the St. Lawrence River. The

HARBOUR SEAL

"Spotted Seal; Dodder (adult); Ranger (immature)"
Phoca vitulina

An adult (left) and young harbour seal (right) lying on the rocks at St. Paul's Inlet.
(PHOTOGRAPH BY JESSICA FLIGHT)

DESCRIPTION The body shape of the harbour seal is stout. The head is small in relation to the body. The muzzle is short and dog-like, and the colouration is light grey with dark spots. The average length of an adult is about 160 centimetres.

HABITAT Widely distributed in the central and eastern Arctic Ocean, this seal ranges from Greenland south to the eastern seaboard of the US. It is commonly observed in nearshore waters of the Gulf of St. Lawrence. The harbour seal is non-migratory and has a relatively sedentary behavior. It often hauls itself out of the water onto rocky ledges and breakwaters to rest and bask in the sun. Mating occurs during the summer, and pups are born the following spring. The harbour seal feeds on fish (flatfish, Atlantic cod, herring, and sculpins) and crustaceans (crabs). Its predators are sharks and killer whales.

RESOURCE USE The harbour seal is familiar to marine life watchers.

Phylum Chordata, class mammalian, order Carnivora, suborder Pinnipedia, and the family Phocidae.[134]

harp seal and the hooded seal are highly migratory. Harps and hoods spend their summers feeding in Arctic waters and migrate south to give birth on the sea ice off southern Labrador in the Gulf of St. Lawrence.[135] The ringed seal and bearded seal have a circumpolar distribution and occasionally appear in the Gulf during the winter.[136]

HARP SEAL "Whitecoat (newborn pup); Raggedy Jacket (2-4 weeks old); Beater (yearling); Bedlamer (immature harp more than one year old)"
Pagophilus groenlandica

Female harp seal and pup on sea ice in the Gulf. Note the harp-shaped black band on the back and sides. (PHOTOGRAPH BY DARROCH WHITAKER)

Phylum Chordata, class Mammalia, order Carnivora, suborder Pinnipedia, and the family Phocidae.[138]

DESCRIPTION The head of the harp seal is small in relation to its body size, and the nose is pointed. The colouration is white with dark patches. Adults have a horseshoe-shaped band or "harp" on the back and sides, hence its common name. Males have a black harp pattern while the pattern in females is paler. The average length of an adult harp seal is about 170 centimetres.[137]

HABITAT There are three breeding populations of harp seal: The White Sea population, the Jan Mayer Island population in the Arctic Ocean, and the population in the northwest Atlantic Ocean. The harp seal population in the northwest Atlantic breeds in the early spring on sea ice in the Gulf of St. Lawrence, off southeastern Labrador, and on the northeast coast of Newfoundland. Pups are born on the ice, nursed by the female for 10 to 12 days, and have a coat of white fur. As the young seal grows, the fur develops irregular black spots. After mating, adult harp seals migrate back to the northern feeding grounds.[139] The diet of the harp seal is mainly fish (e.g. Arctic cod, capelin, and Atlantic cod) and invertebrates (shrimp and krill).[140]

RESOURCE USE Harp seals have been hunted for centuries by coastal peoples.[141] Products for human use from sealing include meat for food, seal oil capsules rich in omega-3 fatty acids for pharmaceuticals, leather for clothes, and handicrafts. Canadian Inuit have constitutionally protected rights to harvest seals for food and ceremonial purposes. Other coastal peoples harvest seals for food security and personal use of seal products.[142]

BIRDS

Seabirds are considered marine wildlife as they are part of the marine food chain.[143] Birds are air-breathing, warm-blooded, vertebrate animals with feathers covering the body. Most bird species can fly. Birds reproduce by laying and incubating eggs,[144] and most provide parental care to their young. Of the approximately 8,500 species of birds, only about 250 species are adapted to a marine habitat.[145] Many marine birds exhibit seasonal feeding and breeding migration behavior. Seabirds cannot breed at sea and must nest on land. The availability of food and nesting sites determines the presence of seabird breeding colonies along a coastline.

The avian wildlife of the Gulf of St. Lawrence includes seabirds, shorebirds, sea ducks, and birds of prey.[146] Some seabird species are adapted to feeding near the coast (e.g. gulls, terns, cormorants, and guillemot), while other seabirds feed offshore (e.g. petrels, kittiwakes, gannets, murres, razorbills, and puffins). Shorebirds (e.g. sandpipers, phalaropes, and plovers) feed in the intertidal zone. Sea ducks (e.g. eiders, scoters, and harlequin ducks) can dive underwater to feed on benthic crustaceans and bivalve molluscs. Birds of prey are carnivores, and some species (e.g. the bald eagle and osprey) will take marine and estuarine fishes as well as terrestrial prey.[147]

A bald eagle perched on a tree rooted on a cliff at Gadds Harbour. Eagles and osprey prey upon flatfish in the shallow waters of Bonne Bay. (PHOTOGRAPH BY ARNAULT LE BRIS)

The piping plover and the red knot are shorebirds present in the Gulf region that are species of conservation concern. Sea ducks present in the Gulf that are species of conservation concern are the harlequin duck and the Barrow's goldeneye.[148] The harlequin duck is also known as "Lords and Ladies" because of its regal colour plumage. A cove in the East Arm of Bonne Bay has the name Lords and Ladies Cove (see map Chap. 1). Harlequin ducks are regularly seen along the rocky shores of Bonne Bay from late fall until early spring.

The piping plover is considered "endangered" of extirpation and is therefore protected by both provincial (NL ESA) and federal (SARA) legislation.[149] After an absence of thirty-four years, piping plovers returned to Gros Morne National Park in 2009

PIPING PLOVER
Charadrius melodus

A piping plover running in the surf zone on the beach at the mouth of the Western Brook.
(PHOTOGRAPH BY DARROCH WHITAKER)

DESCRIPTION The piping plover has a short, plump body shape. The legs are long, the bill is short, and the colouration is tan on the back and white on the belly. The legs are yellow, and the bill is yellow with a black tip.[150]

Phylum Chordata, class Aves, order Charadriiformes, and the family Charadriidae, which includes , sandpipers, phalaropes, herons, and inland species such as snipes and woodcocks.[151]

HABITAT The piping plover ranges from southern Canada to the northeastern and central US. There are few breeding individuals of this bird species in Canada. It will build a nest in an open area of a sand or pebble beach along the shoreline of an inland prairie lake or marine estuary. Breeding success has fallen due to human disturbance of nesting habitats.

RESOURCE USE The piping plover is a favorite of shorebird watchers.

Dr. Darroch Whitaker of Parks Canada and a student monitor a piping plover nest (LEFT PHOTO) on the sandbar at the mouth of Western Brook (RIGHT PHOTO).

and now nest at Shallow Bay and Western Brook Beach.[152]

Coastal feeding seabirds commonly seen in the Gulf of St. Lawrence and the Bonne Bay region are the great black-backed gull, the herring gull, the ring-billed gull, and the black-headed gull.[153] The Iceland gull and the glaucous gull regularly occur along the coast in winter.[154]

The ivory gull nests in the Arctic in summer and overwinters along the southern edge of the pack ice in the North Atlantic Ocean. In some years, it may follow pack ice into the Gulf. The ivory gull population breeding in Canada has declined to the extent that the species is listed as "endangered" by both the provincial and federal governments, and is protected by NL ESA and SARA legislation.[155]

Terns are similar to gulls in body structure except that terns have a sharp-pointed bill and a forked tail rather than the hooked bill and square tail of gulls.[156] While gulls scavenge whatever food is available, terns dive in surface waters to catch small fish. Terns commonly seen over Gulf coastal waters are the Caspian tern, the common tern, and the Arctic tern.

The Atlantic puffin is a favorite of seabird watchers. There is a colony of nesting puffins in the Magdalen Island archipelago in the southwestern Gulf of St. Lawrence.[159]

Offshore feeding seabirds commonly seen over the open waters of the Gulf are the northern gannet, the great cormorant, the double-crested cormorant, the black-legged kittiwake, the Atlantic puffin, the black guillemot, the common murre, the thick-billed murre, and the razorbill.[157] Offshore feeding seabirds eat mostly small pelagic fish, such as capelin and sand lance.[158]

A Leach's storm petrel flying over open water at night can be attracted to man-made light, and storm petrels sometimes become injured by flying into the lighted windows of offshore oil platforms and ships at sea.

Birds are an important factor in the ecotourism industry of Bonne Bay and Gros Morne National Park as many people enjoy contact with nature through bird watching.

Herring gulls along the shore of Bonne Bay. The Tablelands can be seen in the background. (PHOTOGRAPH BY ARNAULT LE BRIS)

ESTUARINE ENVIRONMENT OF BONNE BAY

An estuary is defined as a coastal embayment where the seawater is significantly diluted with freshwater draining from the land.[160] There are four types of estuaries: drowned river valleys, fjords with freshwater input, sandbar-built estuaries, and estuaries formed by land subsidence or geological faulting of the earth.

Bonne Bay is a fjord with freshwater input from the Lomond River and Southeast Brook flowing into the East Arm and Deer Brook flowing into Deer Arm. These three riverine sources contribute most of the freshwater that mixes with the seawater

Low tide at the Deer Brook delta where Deer Brook flows into Bonne Bay.

in the fjord. The volume of freshwater flowing into Bonne Bay is significant all year round, especially in the spring during snow melt on the land. This freshwater input causes Bonne Bay to have an estuarine circulation.

A characteristic of estuarine circulation is a brackish surface layer flowing toward the ocean above a salty bottom layer flowing toward the head of the estuary. Physical oceanographic measurements made at the sill near Norris Point show clear evidence of this two layer flow.[161] Surface flow over the sill is toward the Gulf. There is a compensating inflow of seawater from the Gulf below this surface layer of brackish water. The salinity of surface waters in Bonne Bay shows a gradient from freshwater near the head of the bay to saltwater at the mouth of the bay.

A slick at the sea surface occurs at the boundary between water masses of different salinities and temperatures. Slicks in Bonne Bay are a visual indicator of the estuarine circulation of Bonne Bay. The mixing of river water with the saline water from the Gulf creates a convergence zone where fish and marine mammals often feed.
(PHOTOGRAPH BY ARNAULT LE BRIS)

Local winds and the tides also effect the estuarine circulation of Bonne Bay.[162] The mean tidal range is 1.4 metres.[163] There are two high tides and two low tides each lunar day (24 hours and 50 minutes), a semidiurnal tide pattern.[164] The wind direction is usually along the axis of the fjord because the steep cliffs steer the wind. A strong wind rushing down off the plateau of the Long Range Mountains to the coastal lowlands is called a "katabatic" wind (from the Greek word "katabatikos," meaning "going downhill").[165] Katabatic winds blowing over the surface waters of Bonne Bay occur only under certain weather conditions, but these winds can quickly result in a rough sea state dangerous for recreational boaters and kayakers.

Deer Brook is a freshwater habitat of fishes that live in both fresh and salt water. Atlantic salmon, brook trout, rainbow smelt, threespine stickleback, Atlantic tomcod, alewife, American eel, and ninespine stickleback can be found in Deer Brook and also in the waters of Bonne Bay.

FISH FAUNA OF BONNE BAY

3

BIODIVERSITY OF FISHES

There are more than 25,000 species of fish on Earth.[1] This large number of different life forms (biodiversity) of fishes is related to the variety of aquatic habitats available on the planet.[2] Species adapt to these different habitats, specializing in ways of feeding, reproducing, and avoiding predation. There are about 15,500 species of marine fishes.[3]

Estuarine environments at northern latitudes have a relatively low biodiversity of fishes.[4] An estuary is a harsh environment where the water temperature, salinity, and oxygen content can change quickly.[5] Only a few fish species have evolved a physiology tolerant to both warm and cold waters, low and high salinity, and oxygen depletion events. However, estuaries are highly productive at the base of the food chain and so can support a relatively large biomass of fishes.[6]

The fish species known to be present in Bonne Bay[7] are described in the following pages. There are undoubtedly other fish species inhabiting the bay which have not been observed and recorded. The deep waters of Bonne Bay have yet to be explored. The deepest waters of Bonne Bay are in East Arm where the bottom depth is more than 200 m, and a scientific survey of these deep waters would provide additional information on the fish fauna. Many of the fish species living in the deep channels of the Gulf of St. Lawrence (e.g. Atlantic hagfish, Atlantic halibut, and Greenland halibut)[8] might also be found in the depths of Bonne Bay.

VARIETY OF FISH HABITATS

Bonne Bay has a variety of fish habitats, each of which supports a different assemblage of fish species.[9] These habitats differ in seaweed coverage, bottom substrate type, water depth, seawater temperature range, and salinity range. Some locations along the shoreline have dense marine vegetation while other locations have only sparse seaweeds. The bottom substrate changes with increasing depth from a hard rocky bottom of sand, pebbles, cobble, and boulders to a soft mud bottom of sand and silt.

A few of the fish species living year-round in Bonne Bay exhibit a specific habitat association. The northern pipefish, for example, inhabits the eelgrass beds at Deer Brook delta and Lomond River delta. Some fish species are found in more than one habitat type. For instance, the winter flounder and threespine stickleback are almost ubiquitous. The habitat most suitable for a fish species may change with the fish's life cycle stage as is the case with Atlantic cod. Juvenile cod inhabit shallow waters near the shoreline,[10] but adult cod are found in deeper waters of the bay. Shallow water vegetated with seaweed provides a nursery ground for many fish species in Bonne Bay while the deeper waters further from the shoreline are the feeding ground of many adult fishes.

The fishes commonly found in the estuarine and marine waters of Bonne Bay can be categorized according to their habitat use, specifically where they feed and spawn. These fishes can be grouped rather simply. There are fishes living in both freshwater and the sea (Part I); fishes living near the shoreline in intertidal waters, in barachois, and in eelgrass beds (Part II); and fishes living off the shoreline in subtidal coastal waters (Part III).

PART I FISHES LIVING IN BOTH THE FRESHWATER OF THE PARK AND THE SEA

ANADROMOUS FISHES

Anadromous fishes are species that are born in freshwater, migrate from freshwater to the sea to feed and grow, and then return to freshwater to spawn.[11] Anadromous fishes that can be found during the summer months in Bonne Bay include the Atlantic salmon, sea-run brook trout, rainbow smelt, threespine stickleback, Atlantic tomcod, and alewife. The Arctic char, sea lamprey, and Atlantic sturgeon are also anadromous fishes of Atlantic Canada, but these species have not been recorded as present in the marine or estuarine waters of Bonne Bay.

The Atlantic salmon is perhaps the most famous anadromous species. The Lomond River, Deer Brook, Western Brook, and Trout River in Gros Morne National Park have salmon populations. After growing for several years in freshwater, young salmon will descend their natal river and pass through the estuary to feed in the Atlantic Ocean off west Greenland. Salmon will spend a year or more at sea, growing to sexual maturity. During their return migration to freshwater to spawn, they transit coastal waters such as Bonne Bay on the journey back to natal rivers and streams.

The return migration from the ocean to freshwater rivers occurs during the summer. Salmon spawn on gravel beds in fast-flowing, shallow areas of a river. The female will create a depression in the gravel bed with her tail. There is no parental care of the spawned eggs. Adult salmon that survive spawning will return to the ocean where they can feed and recover. After one or two years at sea, the adult salmon could breed again. Large Atlantic salmon are repeat spawners, reproducing perhaps several times before dying. The eggs in the gravel bed hatch, and the young, called "alevins," emerge. The alevin develops into the fry and then the parr stage. Parr salmon live in the freshwater environment for one to four years, whereupon they develop into the smolt stage and migrate to the sea.Juvenile salmon remain in the sea for up to four years before they grow to sexual maturity and return to freshwater.

Many Atlantic salmon populations throughout the range of the species have decreased in abundance due to overfishing, pollution of rivers, and blockage from spawning habitat with the construction of dams on rivers. Several Atlantic salmon populations in Atlantic Canada are considered "in danger of extinction" or "threatened" by the Committee on the Status of Endangered Wildlife in Canada (COSEWIC).[12] Today there is a nearly world-wide ban on commercial salmon fishing for insular Newfoundland. The historical fishery for Atlantic salmon in Newfoundland and Labrador used trap nets and gillnets set along the coastline to catch pre-spawning salmon as they moved from the ocean toward their natal rivers, but the Federal Government of Canada declared a moratorium on commercial fishing for Atlantic salmon in 1992. The pink flesh of Atlantic salmon is fatty but nutritious and tasty. Aquaculture operations have filled the market demand since the ban on commercial fishing for wild Atlantic salmon.[13]

Salmon populations in Newfoundland have recovered somewhat from their lowest numbers, but conservation is still a concern. Regulations for recreational fly fishing for salmon in freshwater are strictly enforced. Fishing for salmon in the rivers of Gros Morne National Park requires a Parks Canada-issued license. Atlantic salmon populations in the rivers of northern Quebec and Labrador[14] are among the few remaining abundant wild populations in the world.

ATLANTIC SALMON

"Sea salmon; Silver salmon; Black Salmon"
Salmo salar

(Top photo) This Atlantic salmon was transiting Bonne Bay while migrating back to either the Lomond River or Deer Brook when captured. Note the hooked lower jaw or "kype" of this male specimen. This fish has been deposited into the collection of preserved species at The Rooms, Provincial Museum in St. John's. (Bottom photo) Young salmon, called "parr," can be found in the Lomond River and Deer Brook. Note the red dots between the "parr marks" (bluish bars).
(PHOTOGRAPH BY CRAIG PURCHASE)

DESCRIPTION The body shape of the Atlantic salmon is spindle-like. Adults are stouter than juveniles. There is an adipose fin behind the single dorsal fin, just above the single anal fin. The tailfin is slightly forked. The salmon has no spines, and colouration varies with life cycle stage. Young Atlantic salmon after one year of age are called "postyearling parr" and have dusky bars on the side called "parr marks." Red dots appear between these parr marks.[15] Immature Atlantic salmon about three years old and 15 centimetres in length are called "smolts." Smolts turn silvery as they migrate to the sea.[16]

Phylum Chordata, class Actinopterygii, order Salmoniformes, and family Salmonidae, the taxomonic category of freshwater fishes, known as "salmonids."[17]

While at sea, the salmon's dorsal surface is black, the sides are silvery, and the belly is white. There are black flecks scattered along the sides. During the spawning period in freshwater, the salmon loses its silvery colour and becomes reddish brown. Breeding males have reddish-orange spots, and the lower jaw becomes hooked, forming a "kype." After spawning, the surviving parents are known as "slinks." Slinks will darken in colour on their journey back to the ocean to feed and grow further. Salmon can grow to 1.5 metres in length and weigh 38 kilograms.

HABITAT The Atlantic salmon is native to coastal watersheds along both the northeast and northwest North Atlantic Ocean, including the watersheds of Iceland and southern Greenland.[18] Atlantic salmon can be found in coastal waters, fast-flowing streams and rivers, and some lakes. In North America, the Atlantic salmon ranges from Ungava Bay, along the coasts of Newfoundland and Labrador, the Gulf of St. Lawrence, and south to the Connecticut River. Many rivers in the Atlantic Provinces support populations of Atlantic salmon. There are landlocked populations in Newfoundland where they are called ovananiche.

Salmon fry and parr living in streams and rivers feed upon small benthic invertebrates and aquatic insects such as black flies and mayflies. While at sea, salmon feed upon krill, shrimp, squid, and fish such as capelin, herring, and sand lance. Salmon rarely feed while migrating through freshwater to their natal spawning grounds. The major predators of Atlantic salmon in estuaries are seals.[19]

RESOURCE USE The Atlantic salmon is perhaps the most prized freshwater game fish in the world. Recreational anglers are only allowed to fly fish in rivers for pre-spawning Atlantic salmon. The fighting ability of a salmon hooked on a fly rod is renowned. There is a subsistence food fishery for Atlantic salmon conducted by aboriginal groups in Labrador.

"Sea-run" brook trout or "sea trout" are found in marine waters, but these fish were born in freshwater. These freshwater trout have migrated to the sea to feed and grow. After several weeks in estuarine and marine waters, sea-run brook trout will return to freshwater to spawn, so by definition these fish are anadromous. Some individuals of the brook trout populations in the Lomond River and Deer Brook will leave the freshwater and enter Bonne Bay to feed during the summer. These sea trout then return to the Lomond River or Deer Brook and spawn in the fall. Brook trout spawn in streams and rivers over gravel bottoms. The fertilized eggs buried in gravel develop over the winter and hatch in the spring.

Not all individuals in an anadromous brook trout population will migrate to the sea. Those that do descend to the sea will feed there for only a few weeks. A scientific field experiment conducted by students at the Bonne Bay Marine Laboratory found that brook trout tagged in Deer Brook entered East Arm and remained there feeding for only about a month (mid-June to mid-July) before returning to Deer Brook. A few of the tagged brook trout crossed the sill at Norris Point and moved into the Outer Basin of Bonne Bay for a few days. These sea-run trout eventually returned to Deer Brook.[20]

Anadromous rainbow smelt are similar to Atlantic salmon in that they feed and grow in marine waters for several years and then ascend rivers and streams to spawn. The homing of rainbow smelt to natal waters is not as precise as the homing behavior of salmon. Rainbow smelt grow to sexual maturity at sea and gather into schools in river estuaries during the fall and winter. In the spring, rainbow smelt begin their spawning migration into freshwater. Smelt spawn in fast-flowing streams over rock, sand, and gravel substrate. Some smelt will spawn in the brackish water of estuaries. The eggs are sticky and adhere to hard substrate. Deer Brook delta in Bonne Bay is a nursery ground for rainbow smelt, as juveniles have been collected there.[21]

BROOK TROUT

"Mud trout; brook char"
Salvelinus fontinalis

(Top photo) A sea-run brook trout caught in Deer Arm. Note the white leading edge of the pelvic fins. (Bottom photo) The juvenile brook trout has parr marks similar to the juvenile Atlantic salmon. Brook trout parr can be distinguished from salmon parr by the bluish halos around the red dots between the parr marks. Salmon parr do not have bluish halos around the red dots.
(PHOTOGRAPH BY ARNAULT LE BRIS)

Phylum Chordata, class Actinopterygii, order Salmoniformes, and family Salmonidae, the taxomonic category of freshwater fishes, known as "salmonids."[22]

DESCRIPTION The body shape of the brook trout is spindle-like. An adipose fin lies between the dorsal fin and the tail. The tailfin is slightly forked, and there is a single anal fin. The brook trout has no spines, and the colouration varies with life cycle stage. In adults, the back is dark brown or black, the sides are green to brown with pale spots, and there are red spots surrounded by bluish halos. The belly is white. The pectoral, pelvic, and anal fins are white along the leading edge. Sea-run brook trout become silvery, but the white leading edges of the fins and the red spots on the sides remain. The silvery colouration is lost when the sea trout returns to freshwater. Large breeding males may develop a hooked lower jaw or "kype." Brook trout in breeding colouration have bright orange and red pigmentation, especially on the belly of the male. Brook trout can grow to 45 centimetres in length and weigh 6 kilograms.[23]

HABITAT The brook trout is native to cold-temperate watersheds in eastern North America, but has been introduced to freshwaters elsewhere in North America and Europe for recreational angling. Brook trout can be found in streams, ponds, and lakes throughout the Atlantic Provinces and the Great Lakes region. Some individuals of freshwater populations in coastal watersheds will descend rivers to feed in estuaries and nearshore marine waters. Sea-run brook trout can be found in coastal waters from Baffin Island south to Cape Cod, Massachusetts.

While at sea, brook trout will feed on zooplankton and small fish such as sand lance. In the freshwater environment, brook trout feed on aquatic insects, snails, clams, and small fish. Brook trout are food for terrestrial birds of prey and freshwater and marine piscivorous fishes.[24]

RESOURCE USE The brook trout is a favorite sports fish of recreational anglers fishing rivers, streams, and ponds. Fishing for brook trout in the freshwaters of Gros Morne National Park requires a Parks Canada-issued license. Sea-run brook trout are fished recreationally in nearshore marine waters. There is a subsistence food fishery for sea-run brook trout conducted by aboriginal groups in Labrador. Brook trout are raised in freshwater aquaculture operations and marketed fresh. The flesh of sea-run brook trout is orange red and tasty when fried or baked.

RAINBOW SMELT

"American smelt; Frostfish; Icefish"
Osmerus mordax

Anadromous mature smelt pass through Bonne Bay to reach freshwater streams to spawn. These rainbow smelt caught in Deer Arm were likely migrating to Deer Brook.

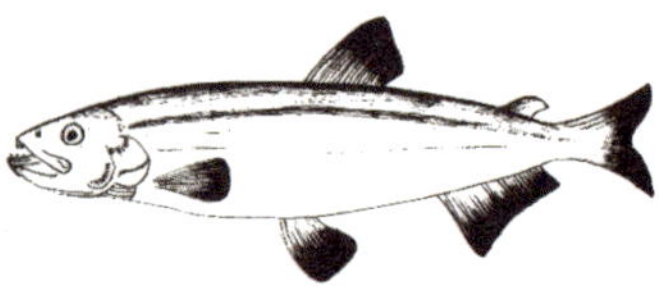

DESCRIPTION The body of the rainbow smelt is slender. The lower jaw projects slightly beyond the upper jaw, and there are teeth on the tip of the tongue. There are no spines. A small adipose fin is located behind the dorsal fin and above the anal fin. The tailfin is forked. Scales on the body are large.[25] The colouration of the rainbow smelt is dark olive green on the back with silvery sides which reflect pink, blue, and purple iridescence, hence the common name. The silvery belly has tiny dusky dots. Rainbow smelt can grow to a maximum length of 35 centimetres.[26]

Phylum Chordata, class Actinipterygii, order Osmeriformes, and family Osmeridae, a taxonomic category of marine, freshwater, and anadromous fishes inhabiting coastal and inland waters of the northern hemisphere.[27]

HABITAT The rainbow smelt is found along both the east coast and west coast of North America and in many inland freshwater systems. On the east coast of North America, the rainbow smelt ranges from Hamilton Inlet of Labrador south to the Gulf of Maine. Smelt from the southern Gulf of St. Lawrence migrate through the St. Lawrence River system as far inland as Lake Superior. There are both landlocked and anadromous populations of rainbow smelt.

Rainbow smelt feeding in the marine environment eat marine worms, amphipods, krill, and small fishes. Landlocked freshwater populations feed on various aquatic insects, zooplankton, and small fish. Landlocked smelt are preyed upon by piscivorous freshwater fishes such as lake trout, and brook trout. In coastal waters, smelt are prey for Atlantic salmon, Atlantic cod, seals, and piscivorous birds.[28]

RESOURCE USE In Eastern Canada and New England, a winter recreational fishery for rainbow smelt in lakes is undertaken by fishing through the ice with hook and line, hence the nicknames "frostfish" and "icefish." Smelt are also commercially harvested in estuaries of the Gulf of St. Lawrence using nets and traps during the fall and winter.[29] Smelt are marketed fresh as dressed fish. Rainbow smelt are lean and taste sweet when pan fried.

The threespine stickleback matures in the first year of life. Freshwater populations of threespine stickleback spawn in the shallow water of rivers or tributaries throughout the Atlantic Provinces, the St. Lawrence River, the Ottawa River, and the Lake Ontario Basin. Marine populations exhibit an anadromous

THREESPINE STICKLEBACK "Pinfish"

Gasterosteus aculeatus

The anadromous threespine stickleback can often been seen swimming near the shoreline of Bonne Bay, especially in barachois environments. (PHOTOGRAPH BY CRAIG PURCHASE)

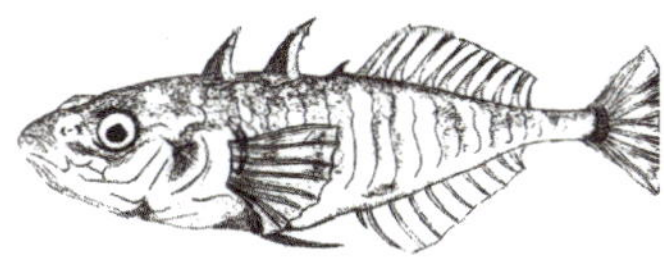

DESCRIPTION The body shape of the threespine stickleback is spindle-like. The mouth is small. Three sharp spines precede the dorsal fin, hence the common name. The anal fin has one spine. The pelvic fins each have a spine. All these sharp spines on the body give rise to the nickname "pinfish." There is a lateral keel formed by bony plates on the body just before the tail, which can be felt if held between one's thumb and forefinger. The three dorsal spines and the keel near the tail distinguish the threespine stickleback from other stickleback species.[30] The colouration is dark olive on the back, and the sides are silvery, sometimes with dark mottling. The belly is silvery. During breeding season, males exhibit red colouration on the belly. The maximum recorded length is 10 centimetres.[31]

Phylum Chordata, class Actinopterygii, order Gasterosteiformes, and family Gasterosteidae, the taxonomic category of small fish with dorsal and pelvic fin spines, called "sticklebacks."[32]

HABITAT The threespine stickleback is found in both freshwater and marine waters of the temperate northern hemisphere.[33] In the northwest Atlantic Ocean, it is found in James Bay and along the coastline from Newfoundland and Labrador south to New York. Threespine sticklebacks have been observed at the surface of the open ocean, far from a coastline.

The threespine stickleback eats small invertebrates, such as copepods, when feeding at sea and aquatic insects, such as chironomids, mosquito larvae, and pupae, when feeding in freshwater. The threespine stickleback is preyed upon by many piscivorous fishes and piscivorous birds.[34]

RESOURCE USE Schooling threespine stickleback are fun for children to try to catch when exploring tidal creeks and barachois environments, but otherwise are not utilized by people.

migration behavior, and these sticklebacks will migrate into freshwater to spawn during the warm summer months. Anadromous migrations can ascend rivers and tributaries far inland. Individuals that survive spawning in freshwater will return to the marine environment in the fall.

Marine populations can also spawn in the brackish waters of tidal creeks. Individuals in breeding colouration were collected in the barachois at Deer Brook delta and in the barachois at Lomond

River delta in Bonne Bay.[35] The male builds a nest using bits of aquatic vegetation and sand grains. The female deposits her eggs in the nest which are then fertilized by the male, and the male guards the nest until the eggs hatch.

The anadromous Atlantic tomcod inhabits estuaries, especially the mouth of rivers and streams, eelgrass beds, and salt marshes. In the fall, tomcod leave estuarine waters and migrate up rivers and streams into tidally-influenced, brackish waters. During the winter, tomcod spawn over sandy gravel bottoms, often under ice. The adhesive eggs stick to seaweed, gravel, cobble, and boulders on the bottom.

Marine populations of alewife undergo an anadromous migration, ascending tributary rivers along the coast of the Atlantic

ATLANTIC TOMCOD "Tommycod; Snig"
Microgadus tomcod

The anadromous Atlantic tomcod inhabits brackish coastal waters. Atlantic tomcod have been captured near Gadds Harbour in Bonne Bay. (PHOTOGRAPH BY RYAN MELANSON)

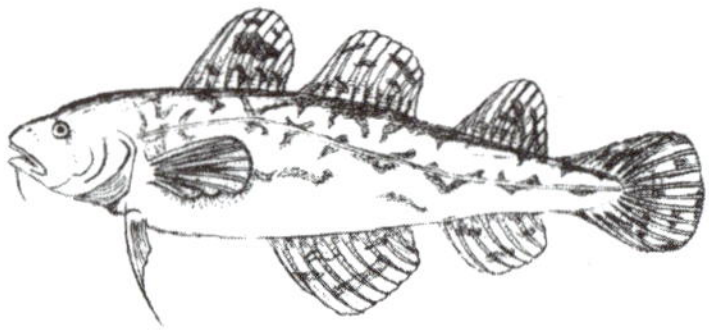

DESCRIPTION The body shape of Atlantic tomcod is "cod-like." The eye is small relative to the eye of Atlantic cod.[36] The snout is rounded, and there is a slender barbel on the underside of the lower jaw. There are three dorsal fins and two anal fins. The caudal fin is rounded. The pelvic fins each have a long filament.[37] The barbel and the pelvic fin filaments are dragged along the bottom to help detect prey. The colouration is olive green with yellowish tinges, paling on the sides to a greyish or yellow white belly. The sides and fins are mottled with dark blotches and marbled markings while the lateral line is pale. The tomcod has a maximum length of about 40 centimetres.[38]

HABITAT The Atlantic tomcod is found only in near-shore waters of the western North Atlantic, ranging from the Hamilton Inlet-Lake Melville region of coastal Labrador, south to Cape Hatteras in North Carolina. Atlantic tomcod are most abundant in estuaries around Newfoundland provinces, especially the St. Lawrence River system. Alewife have been caught in fish-counting fence traps set in Western Brook and in Deer Brook, indicating that alewifes from the Gulf of St. Lawrence ascend into freshwater systems of Gros Morne National Park.[39]

The alewife in coastal waters form large schools when migrating. In spring, the alewife will enter freshwater tributary systems to spawn in rivers and streams, lakes and ponds. Some alewife display homing behavior and return to their natal spawning grounds. The alewife returns to the sea shortly after spawning. The young born in freshwater during the spring descend to the sea during the summer and fall. Juvenile alewife feed and grow to maturity in the ocean and then return to freshwater to spawn.

and Nova Scotia and in the St. Lawrence River. Tomcod can live in freshwater, and there are landlocked populations in lakes of Newfoundland, Quebec, and Nova Scotia.[40]

Atlantic tomcod feed upon benthic crustaceans, especially amphipods. They also prey upon marine worms, small molluscs, and small fishes (especially sticklebacks). Juvenile tomcod are preyed upon by piscivorous estuarine fishes, especially sculpins.

RESOURCE USE There are recreational fisheries for Atlantic tomcod in the Maritime Provinces, particularly in the Miramichi estuary of New Brunswick.[41] During winter, tomcod are caught by hook and line through the ice, and in summer, tomcod are caught by people fishing off wharves. The white fillet of tomcod is tasty.

Phylum Chordata, class Actinopterygii, order Gadiformes, and family Gadidae, the taxonomic category for cod-like fishes. Most fishes in this family are marine, but some species, including the Atlantic tomcod, inhabit estuaries and are anadromous.[42]

ALEWIFE "Gaspereau"

Alosa pseudoharengus

The alewife is an anadromous species living in the Gulf of St. Lawrence. Upstream migrating alewife have been captured in Western Brook, Deer Brook, and Trout River.[43]

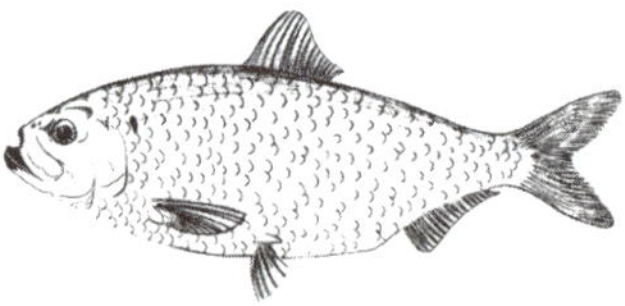

DESCRIPTION The alewife is deep bodied and the head is relatively small.[44] The belly has a keel of saw-toothed "scutes." The alewife does not have spines. There is a single dorsal fin and a single anal fin. The tail fin is forked. The colouration is dark greyish green on the back and silvery on the sides and belly. There is a dusky black spot on either side of the body just behind the gill cover at eye level. The alewife can grow to 40 centimetres in length.[45]

Phylum Chordata, class Actinopterygii, order Clupeiformes, and family Clupeidae, the taxonomic category of freshwater and marine pelagic fishes, called "herrings."[46]

HABITAT Found only in coastal waters and tributary freshwaters of the Northwest Atlantic Ocean, the alewife ranges from the west coast of Newfoundland south to the coast of North Carolina, including waters of the Gulf of St. Lawrence, the Bay of Fundy, and the Gulf of Maine. Landlocked populations are found in the Great Lakes region and many freshwater systems of eastern North America.

The alewife at sea is a plankton feeder, consuming zooplankton such as copepods, krill, fish eggs, and larvae. Alewife are prey for many piscivorous marine fishes such as spiny dogfish, Atlantic cod, pollock, and silver hake.[47]

RESOURCE USE Schools of alewife are caught in weir traps[48] at the mouth of rivers in the Gulf of St. Lawrence.[49] Alewife is an excellent food fish, but bony. It is marketed as fresh or frozen fillets or as smoked, pickled, or salted fillets. The alewife is also used to bait lobster traps and crab pots.

CATADROMOUS FISHES

Catadromous fishes are species that are born in the ocean, migrate to freshwater to feed and grow, and then return to the ocean to spawn.[50] Two catadromous fish species are found in Bonne Bay: the American eel and the ninespine stickleback.

The spawning migration of the American eel to the sea begins during the fall and early winter. Immature "yellow eels" in rivers migrate downstream into estuaries. Some of these individuals may move back upstream in the spring. Mature "silver eels" will continue to move through the estuaries and coastal waters and swim to the deep waters of the southwestern North Atlantic where they home to their natal spawning ground. The American eel apparently dies after spawning, although the spawning event has never been observed.

The fertilized egg develops into a willow-leaf-shaped larva which drifts with the currents of the North Atlantic. Ocean currents eventually carry the developing eel to the coast of North America. The young eels, called "elvers," then swim into estuaries and the freshwater rivers and streams of eastern and southern North America. Some elvers migrate though Bonne Bay to reach Deer Brook and the Lomond River.

Most elvers migrate upstream into the uppermost inland reaches of river systems. Some elvers remain in freshwater systems along the coastline. Upstream migrating elvers have been captured in Deer Brook. The juvenile American eel feeds and grows in freshwater systems for five to ten years or longer. Attaining sexual maturity, the eel returns to the breeding ground in the North Atlantic. Silver eels transit the estuaries of the Gulf of St. Lawrence on their way to the sea and have been reported as observed in Bonne Bay.[51]

The abundance of the American eel in Newfoundland and Labrador freshwater systems has declined to the point that the provincial government has designated the freshwater eel as "vulnerable" to extirpation under the Endangered Species Act.[52]

The ninespine stickleback shares with the American eel the distinction of being one of the only two catadromous species in the fish fauna of Bonne Bay.[53] Freshwater populations of ninespine stickleback living near the coastline of the Gulf of St. Lawrence migrate downstream in the spring to shallow marine waters and estuaries to spawn. The ninespine stickleback has been collected in freshwater streams in Gros Morne National Park,[54] and these fish may migrate into brackish waters in Bonne Bay to spawn.

AMERICAN EEL "Whip; Freshwater eel"
Anguilla rostrata

The American eel is a catadromous fish that lives in rivers and streams and migrates to the sea to spawn. American eel have been collected in Deer Brook, Lomond River, Western Brook, and Trout River.[55]

DESCRIPTION The body shape of the American eel is serpentine. The head is pointed, and the jaws have needle-like teeth. The single dorsal fin is continuous with the rounded tailfin and anal fin. The eel has no spines, and the pelvic fins are absent.[56] The skin secretes mucus as a protective coating, and the colouration varies with life cycle stage. Immature eels are black or olive brown on the back and yellowish white on the belly, and these are called "yellow eels." Mature eels beginning their catadromous migration to the sea turn silvery on the sides and belly and are called "silver eels." The juvenile American eel lives in freshwater rivers and streams for several decades until it attains sexual maturity and moves downstream to the sea to spawn and die in the deep waters of the southwestern North Atlantic Ocean. Female eels can grow up to 1.5 metres in length while males have a smaller maximum size.[57]

Phylum Chordata, class Actinopterygii, order Anguilliformes, and family Anguillidae, the taxonomic category of catadromous fishes known as freshwater eels.[58]

HABITAT The American eel inhabits the estuaries and freshwater tributaries of the east coast of North America, the Gulf of Mexico, and the Caribbean. It ranges from the Hamilton Inlet-Lake Melville estuary of Labrador and south to Panama and the West Indies.

Larval eels developing at sea are planktivores. In the freshwater environment, yellow eels will eat aquatic insects, benthic invertebrates such as crayfish, snails, and worms, and small fish such as young salmon and brook trout. While in the estuarine environment, yellow eels will eat marine worms, crustaceans, and bivalve molluscs.

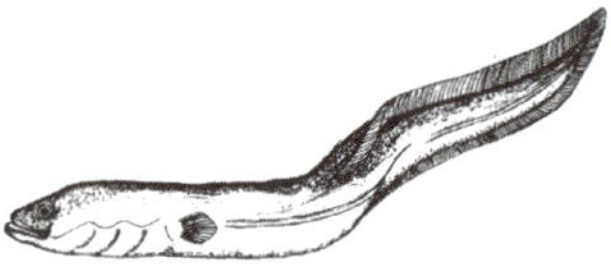

Larval eels, elvers, and small yellow eels are preyed upon by piscivorous fishes and piscivorous birds. Migrating silver eels may fall prey to large predaceous fishes and birds of prey such as eagles and osprey.[59]

RESOURCE USE The commercial fishery for downstream migrating silver eels in the St. Lawrence River system began during the mid-1800s. Eels were caught in the shallow water of rivers and streams using hoop nets, baited pots, and baited trot lines.[60] The eels were pickled and exported to Europe for human consumption. Today eels are marketed as fresh or frozen dressed fish. The flesh of American eel is fatty and, thus, is often sold processed as smoked, jellied, or marinated. There is only a minor fishery for the American eel in the Gulf of St. Lawrence estuary.[61]

The ninespine stickleback has been collected in St. Paul's inlet.[62] The male builds a nest in tidal pools using filamentous algae or eelgrass and guards the fertilized eggs. The individuals that survive spawning will migrate back to freshwater in the fall.

NINESPINE STICKLEBACK

"Pinfish; Tiny burnstickle"

Pungitius pungitius

The ninespine stickleback has been collected in freshwater streams of Gros Morne National Park[63] and may make a catadromous migration into brackish waters of Bonne Bay to spawn.

DESCRIPTION The ninespine stickleback is the most slender of the stickleback species found in Bonne Bay. Its head is relatively large, and the mouth is small. The dorsal fin is preceded by usually nine (but possibly 7 to 12) short spines,[64] hence its common name. The anal fin has one spine. The tailfin is rounded or slightly forked. The slender caudal peduncle (where the tail joins the body) has a keel formed by bony plates, similar to the keel of the threespine stickleback. The colouration of the ninespine stickleback is olive brown or grey on the back with the upper sides of the body having faint barred marks. The belly is silvery. The ninespine stickleback has a maximum size of about 7 centimetres.[65]

Phylum Chordata, class Actinopterygii, order Gasterosteiformes, and family Gasterosteidae, the taxonomic category of small fish with dorsal and pelvic fin spines, called "sticklebacks."[67]

HABITAT The ninespine stickleback has a circumpolar distribution in the Northern Hemisphere.[66] It inhabits freshwater, estuarine, and marine environments. There are freshwater populations of ninespine stickleback in Canadian inland waters from Alberta, Manitoba, and Saskatchewan eastward to the Great Lakes and the upper St. Lawrence Valley. Freshwater populations near the coast are usually catadromous, moving from lakes or ponds into shallow marine waters or estuaries to spawn.

There are marine populations of ninespine stickleback living in nearshore coastal waters ranging from Hudson Bay eastward to the Newfoundland and Labrador coast, the Gulf of St. Lawrence, and south to New Jersey. Members of these coastal populations may be anadromous, migrating from marine waters into freshwater to spawn.

The ninespine stickleback feeds on copepods in marine waters and aquatic insects in freshwater. Its predators include piscivorous fishes and piscivorous birds feeding in shallow waters.[68]

RESOURCE USE Ninespine stickleback are fun for children to try to catch when exploring tidal pools, eelgrass beds, and barachois environments, but otherwise are not utilized by people.

PART II

FISHES LIVING NEAR THE SHORELINE OF BONNE BAY

There are several fish species found in Bonne Bay that live near the shoreline. These fishes are adapted to life in shallow water affected by the incoming and outgoing tides. Three distinct fish habitats occur along the shoreline of Bonne Bay: the rocky intertidal zone, the shallow lagoon known as a "barachois,"[1] and the eelgrass bed environment.

FISHES IN THE ROCKY INTERTIDAL ZONE

The intertidal zone is commonly called "the landwash."[2] Fishes living in the intertidal zone of Bonne Bay, such as the rock gunnel and Atlantic snailfish, are relatively small in size.

The rock gunnel can often be found in the rocky intertidal zone where it remains under rocks and seaweeds at low tide. Gunnels will move from the intertidal zone into subtidal waters to spawn during the winter. The female deposits her eggs in a cluster on the sea bottom, often in crevices between rocks, and the eggs are guarded by the female or male gunnel until they hatch. The rock gunnel is likely a year-round resident species of Bonne Bay, as both juvenile and adult life stages have been collected.[3]

◀ Low tide at Lords and Ladies Cove (TOP PHOTO) and Lomond Cove (BOTTOM PHOTO) in the East Arm. The rocky intertidal zone is the habitat of the rock gunnel and the Atlantic snailfish.

The Atlantic snailfish lives in the rocky intertidal zone and the shallow subtidal zone and can often be found attached by its suction disk to the lower sides of rocks. The snailfish matures at one year of age. Spawning occurs during the late winter and spring. The female lays her eggs in a clump on the bottom in the intertidal zone, and the male will guard the eggs until hatching.

ROCK GUNNEL "Butterfish; Tansy"

Pholis gunnellus

The rock gunnel inhabits the rocky intertidal zone of Bonne Bay and is nicknamed "butterfish" because gunnel are as slippery as butter and difficult to pick up.

DESCRIPTION The body shape of the rock gunnel is elongate. The head is relatively small with a blunt snout. There is one dorsal fin that extends from the head to the tail, and the single anal fin also joins the tail. The caudal fin is rounded. Although the dorsal and anal fins have tiny spines, the skin of rock gunnels feels very smooth, hence the nickname "butterfish." The colouration varies with its background environment, but is usually olive to reddish brown. The belly is pale white to yellowish white, and there is a dark band across the eye and a row of black spots along the dorsal fin.[4] The rock gunnel has a maximum length of about 30 centimetres.[5]

HABITAT The rock gunnel is found on both sides of the North Atlantic Ocean.[6] In the northwest Atlantic, it ranges from the coasts of Labrador and Newfoundland, the Gulf of St. Lawrence, and south to Delaware Bay. The rock gunnel feeds on marine worms, amphipods, and other small benthic crustaceans. Predators of the rock gunnel are piscivorous fishes and piscivorous birds feeding in the intertidal zone.[7]

RESOURCE USE Rock gunnels are fun for children to try to find and catch when exploring the intertidal zone, but otherwise are not utilized by people.

Phylum Chordata, class Actinopterygii, order Perciformes, and family Pholidae, the taxonomic category of small marine fishes living in the littoral zone in the North Atlantic and North Pacific Oceans, known as gunnels.[8]

ATLANTIC SNAILFISH "Seasnail"

Liparis atlanticus

The Atlantic snailfish can be found by turning over cobble and boulders in the intertidal zone of Bonne Bay. (Bottom photo) The pelvic fins form a suction disk for clinging to rocks.

DESCRIPTION The body shape of the Atlantic snailfish is moderately elongate. There is one dorsal fin with a notch and a single anal fin.[9] The caudal fin is truncate or square while pectoral fins are fanlike, and the pelvic fins are modified in shape to form a suction disk. The colouration is dark olive with darker sides on the body, and the belly is greyish white. The Atlantic snailfish has a maximum length of about 15 centimetres.[10]

HABITAT The Atlantic snailfish is found only in the northwest Atlantic Ocean. It ranges from Ungava Bay, along the Labrador and Newfoundland coasts, the Gulf of St. Lawrence, and southward to the coast of New York. The snailfish feeds on marine worms, amphipods, and other small crustaceans. Predators of the Atlantic snailfish are piscivorous fishes hunting in the intertidal and subtidal zone, especially winter skate and sea ravens.[11]

RESOURCE USE
The Atlantic snailfish is fun for children to find under rocks when exploring the intertidal zone, but otherwise is not utilized by people.

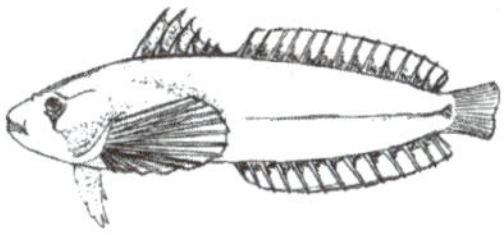

Phylum Chordata, class Actinopterygii, order Scorpaeniformes, and family Liparidae, the taxonomic category of small marine fishes found in all oceans from the Arctic to the Antarctic known as snailfish.[12]

FISHES IN A BARACHOIS

"Barachois' is the word used by some people of Atlantic Canada for a shallow lagoon of nearly freshwater separated by a sandbar or strip of land from more saline waters.[13] The barachois near the mouth of Deer Brook receives freshwater from the river. Brackish water from the Deer Brook delta enters the barachois at high tide. The barachois has a bottom substrate composed of sand and mud. The barachois is at most 1.5 metres deep. The sandbar that separates the barachois from the river delta was formed over time by sediment carried by the river. There is a similar barachois near the mouth of the Lomond River in the East Arm.

Fishes living in the barachois of the Deer Arm delta and in the barachois of the Lomond River delta include the blackspotted stickleback and the fourspine stickleback. These two species may complete their lifecycles entirely within the barachois and adjacent river delta environments. The blackspotted stickleback and fourspine stickleback usually do not enter the fully freshwater environment of tributary rivers. The threespine stickleback is also commonly found in the barachois environment, but the threespine stickleback will enter freshwater. The threespine stickleback performs an anadromous migration from the estuary into tributary rivers and streams to build a nest and spawn.

LEFT PHOTO: The sandbar that separates the barachois (to the right of the bar) from the Deer Brook delta. The barachois is the habitat of the blackspotted stickleback, fourspine stickleback, and threespine stickleback. RIGHT PHOTO: The barachois of the Lomond River delta.

The blackspotted stickleback is the most marine of all stickleback species found in Bonne Bay and is physiologically adapted to the salinity of seawater. Spending most of its one-year lifespan in nearshore coastal waters, the blackspotted stickleback lives near the surface among floating vegetation. In the spring, this stickleback will move to shallow waters near the shoreline, especially tide

BLACKSPOTTED STICKLEBACK

"Twospined stickleback"

Gasterosteus wheatlandi

The blackspotted stickleback lives in barachois environments of Bonne Bay.

DESCRIPTION The body shape of the blackspotted stickleback is stouter than the threespine stickleback. There are two large spines and one small spine preceding the dorsal fin. The caudal fin is truncate or square. There is no keel on the caudal peduncle as is present in the threespine stickleback and ninespine stickleback species.[14] The colouration is yellowish green on the back. The sides are silvery with black spots, and the belly is silvery. The blackspotted stickleback has a maximum length of about 7 centimetres.[15]

HABITAT The blackspotted stickleback is found only in the northwest Atlantic Ocean and has a restricted range. It occurs in coastal waters from northern Newfoundland to New York, including the Gulf of St. Lawrence and the Gulf of Maine. The blackspotted stickleback feeds on copepods while living in marine surface waters. While living in shallow water near the shoreline, it will feed on small marine worms and copepods. Blackspotted sticklebacks are preyed upon by piscivorous fishes and piscivorous birds.[16]

Phylum Chordata, class Actinopterygii, order Gasterosteiformes, and family Gasterosteidae, the taxonomic category of small fish, called "sticklebacks," with dorsal and pelvic fin spines."[17]

RESOURCE USE The blackspotted stickleback is fun for children to try to catch when exploring barachois environments, but otherwise are not utilized by people.

pools and barachois environments where it spawns. The male will build a nest of filamentous seaweed, and the female will deposit her eggs in the nest. After fertilizing the eggs, the male will maintain the nest while the eggs incubate. The blackspotted stickleback dies soon after breeding.[18]

The fourspine stickleback is found in estuaries and coastal waters of the Gulf of St. Lawrence. It has been collected in both the barachois of the Deer Brook delta and the barachois of the Lomond River delta.[19] Estuarine populations of fourspine stickleback rarely enter freshwater tributaries, but there are unusual freshwater populations of fourspine stickleback in Gros Morne

National Park.[20] The fourspine stickleback matures at one year of age. Spawning takes place during the early summer in a barachois environment or river delta. The male will build a nest of filamentous seaweed, and the female will deposit her eggs in the nest. After fertilizing the eggs, the male maintains the nest while the eggs incubate. Some females will survive and breed the following year.

FOURSPINE STICKLEBACK "Pinfish"

Apeltes quadracus

The fourspine stickleback is present in the barachois environments of Bonne Bay.

Phylum Chordata, class Actinopterygii, order Gasterosteiformes, and family Gasterosteidae, the taxonomic category of small fish with dorsal and pelvic fin spines, called "sticklebacks."[23] The fourspine stickleback can be found in marine, brackish water and freshwater.

DESCRIPTION The body of the fourspine stickleback is moderately elongate. There are four (possibly 5) spines preceding the dorsal fin,[21] while the anal fin has one spine and each pelvic fin has a single spine. The caudal fin is truncate with rounded corners. The caudal peduncle is slender, and there is no keel as present in the threespine stickleback and ninespine stickleback species. The colouration is olive green to brownish on the back and upper sides, while the lower sides and belly are silvery. This stickleback has a maximum length of about 5 centimetres.[22]

HABITAT The fourspine stickleback is found only in the northwest Atlantic. It inhabits estuaries and coastal waters of eastern North America from northern Newfoundland to Virginia. The fourspine stickleback feeds on amphipods and copepods. Predators of the fourspine stickleback are piscivourous fishes and piscivorous birds.[24]

RESOURCE USE The fourspine stickleback is fun for children to try to catch when exploring barachois environments, but otherwise are not utilized by people.

FISHES IN AN EELGRASS BED

Many fishes living near the shoreline of Bonne Bay can also be found in eelgrass beds (e.g. the stickleback species),[25] but one species is particularly associated with eelgrass beds: the northern pipefish. By noting its body shape, one can discern that the northern pipefish is adapted to the eelgrass environment. Its body is long and slender and blends into the eelgrass, hiding the pipefish from predators.

TOP PHOTO: The Lomond River delta at low tide, looking upriver. In areas that are almost always submerged, there is a shift from pebble and cobble to finer sediments such as silt and sand. This provides an ideal habitat for eelgrass, which occurs in large beds throughout this area.

LEFT PHOTO: An eelgrass bed in the Lomond River delta. The eelgrass bed is the habitat of the northern pipefish.

Northern pipefish in Bonne Bay are living at the northern latitudinal limit of the range of the species. Northern pipefish mature at one or two years of age. The reproductive behaviour of pipefish is unusual. The female deposits her eggs in the brood pouch located under the tail of the male pipefish. The eggs are fertilized at this time, and the male carries the fertilized eggs in his brood pouch until they hatch in about ten days.[26]

NORTHERN PIPEFISH "Pipefish"

Syngnathus fuscus

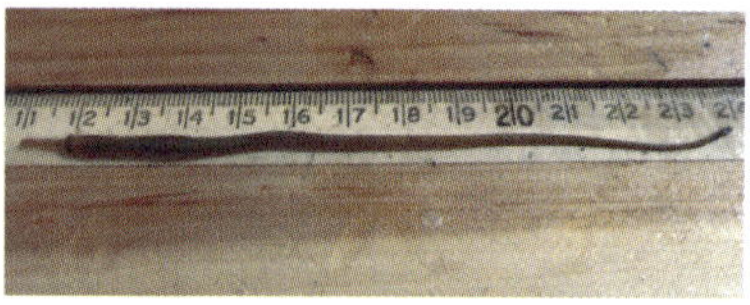

Top photo: This northern pipefish was held briefly in an aquarium to take a close-up photograph of the trumpet shaped mouth. (PHOTOGRAPH BY CRAIG PURCHASE) Bottom photo: The northern pipefish lives in eelgrass beds of the Deer Brook delta and the Lomond River delta in Bonne Bay.

DESCRIPTION The body of the northern pipefish is elongate and armored with bony plates. The mouth is small and trumpet shaped. The northern pipefish has one dorsal fin, but lacks pelvic fins. The anal fin is tiny in females and absent in males. The caudal fin is rounded. The colouration can change to match its surroundings, but is usually brownish with dark mottling. The belly is golden yellow. The northern pipefish has a maximum length of about 30 centimetres.[27]

HABITAT The northern pipefish is found only in the western Atlantic Ocean. The northern pipefish inhabits beds of seaweed and eelgrass in coastal bays, salt marshes, and estuarine waters, ranging from the southern Gulf of St. Lawrence and south to Florida and the northern Gulf of Mexico. The northern pipefish feeds on small prey items such as copepods, amphipods, fish eggs, and fish larvae. The northern pipefish is preyed upon by piscivorous fishes.[29]

Phylum Chordata, class Actinopterygii, order Syngnathiformes, and family Syngnathidae, the taxomomic category for small marine fishes commonly known as pipefishes and seahorses.[28]

RESOURCE USE The northern pipefish is not utilized by people.

PART III

FISHES LIVING IN SUBTIDAL WATERS OF BONNE BAY

Many of the fishes found in Bonne Bay live off the shoreline in subtidal waters, i.e. waters deeper than the intertidal zone.[1] Some of these fishes can also be found in the Gulf of St. Lawrence.[2] Subtidal zone fishes include demersal species living near the sea bottom and pelagic species living in the water column.

DEMERSAL FISHES IN SUBTIDAL WATERS OF THE BAY

Demersal fishes living in subtidal waters include the winter skate, thorny skate, radiated shanny, daubed shanny, Arctic shanny, alligatorfish, sea raven, longhorn sculpin, shorthorn sculpin, grubby, Atlantic cod, Greenland cod, winter flounder, and windowpane flounder.[3]

Subtidal waters of Deer Arm. Gros Morne Mountain appears in the background.

The winter skate inhabits subtidal waters down to a depth of approximately 100 metres and has been collected from sand and gravel sea bottoms in Bonne Bay.[4] With the decline in the abundance of winter skate in the southern Gulf of St. Lawrence, COSEWIC has designated winter skate as "endangered," but the winter skate is not listed under SARA.[5] As the winter skate is a species of conservation concern, it should be returned to the sea alive if caught unintentionally.

WINTER SKATE "Big skate; Eyed skate"

Leucoraja ocellata

Views of the dorsal (left photo) and ventral (bottom photo) surfaces of a winter skate collected from the seabed in subtidal waters of Bonne Bay.[6] Note the arrow-shape pattern of dorsal thorns along the centre of the back.

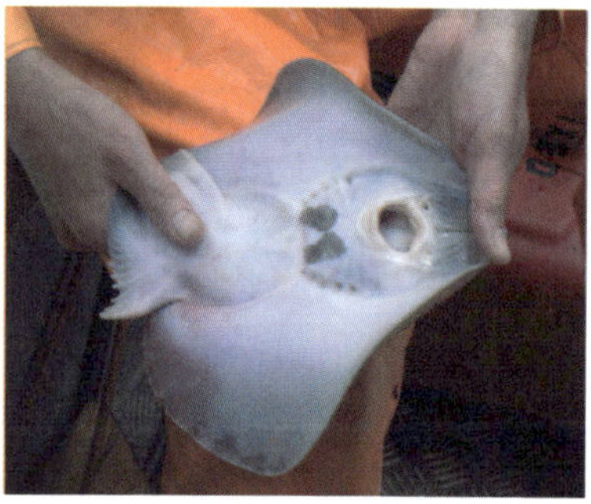

DESCRIPTION The body of the winter skate has a pancake shape. The tail is long and slender. The colouration of the dorsal surface is light brown with many small dark spots. The snout is blunt and has a translucent appearance. The ventral surface is white with irregular pale splotches. The dorsal surface has three or more rows of thorns[7] forming an arrow pattern. Winter skate can grow to a maximum length of about 110 centimetres.[8]

HABITAT The winter skate is found only in the northwest Atlantic Ocean. It ranges from the Gulf of St. Lawrence and the southern coast of Newfoundland, along the Scotian Shelf, and southward to the coast of North Carolina. The winter skate feeds on marine worms, amphipods, bivalve molluscs, and small fishes, especially sand lance and cunner. Predators of winter skate include grey seals and sharks.[9]

RESOURCE USE While there is no directed fishery for winter skate in the Gulf of St. Lawrence,[10] it is caught as bycatch in fisheries targeting groundfish species. The wings (pectoral fins) of skate are considered a delicacy in European countries. The wings are cut into circular pieces in the shape of a scallop, as its flavor is similar to that of scallop.

Phylum Chordata, class Chondrichthyes, order Rajiformes, and family Rajidae, the taxonomic category of cartilaginous fishes called skates and rays.[11]

The thorny skate is found on both hard and soft sea bottoms in the subtidal zone down to a depth of about 200 metres. The thorny skate was assessed by COSEWIC and assigned a status of "special concern" because the species has declined in abundance in the southern Gulf of St. Lawrence and on the Scotian Shelf. The thorny skate has a low reproductive potential, and populations recover slowly.[12]

THORNY SKATE

"Starry skate; Atlantic prickly skate"
Amblyraja radiata

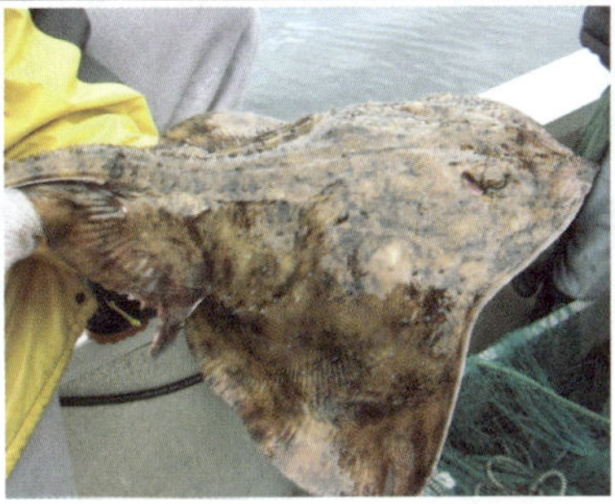

Two specimens of thorny skate collected from the seabed in subtidal waters of Bonne Bay.[13] Note the long dorsal thorns.

DESCRIPTION The body of the thorny skate has a pancake shape. The snout is blunt. There is a row of large thorns along the centre of the back, and large thorns are scattered on the dorsal surface of the pectoral fins, which make up the pancake shape. These thorns may appear eroded in large specimens.[14] The colouration is brownish grey on the dorsal surface with dark blotches. The ventral surface is white or sooty white. Thorny skate may grow to 110 centimetres in length.[15]

HABITAT The thorny skate is found in the western and eastern North Atlantic Ocean. In the western North Atlantic, the thorny skate ranges from Baffin Island and Hudson Bay, the Labrador shelf, the Grand Banks of Newfoundland, the Gulf of St. Lawrence, the Scotian Shelf, and south to the coast of North Carolina. The thorny skate preys upon marine worms, amphipods, shrimp, crab, and small fish such as sand lance. Natural predators of thorny skate are unknown.[16]

RESOURCE USE There is no fishery in the Gulf of St. Lawrence directed at thorny skate,[17] but the species is caught as bycatch in fisheries for groundfish using bottom trawls.[18] The wings of the thorny skate are cut into the shape of scallop meat and marketed as imitation scallop.

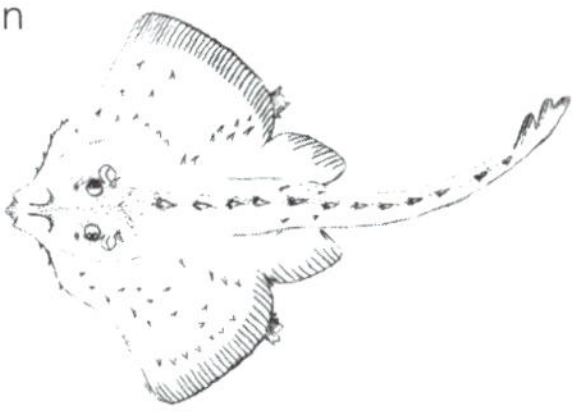

Phylum Chordata, class Chondrichthyes, order Rajiformes, and family Rajidae, the taxonomic category of cartilaginous fishes called skates and rays.[19]

Along with skates, three species of small demersal fishes called "pricklebacks" live off the shoreline in subtidal waters of Bonne Bay: the radiated shanny, the daubed shanny, and the Arctic shanny.[20] Pricklebacks have tiny spines along the dorsal fin, making the back of these fish feel prickly.

The radiated shanny lives amongst the seaweeds and rocks on hard bottom substrate in subtidal waters in the Gulf of St. Lawrence, including Bonne Bay. The radiated shanny spawns during the spring and summer. Females lay eggs in clumps on the sea bottom, and males will protect the egg mass until hatching occurs.[21]

RADIATED SHANNY "Shanny"

Ulvaria subbifurcata

The radiated shanny is a small demersal fish that lives in subtidal waters of Bonne Bay. Note the distinctive black bar under the eye and across the cheek.

DESCRIPTION The body of the radiated shanny is elongate. There is a single, long dorsal fin with many small spines. The single anal fin has two small spines. The caudal fin is rounded, and the colouration is brown with a yellowish belly. There is a dark blotch on the dorsal fin and a black bar which runs downward and backward from the eye. The radiated shanny does not grow to more than 18 centimetres in length.[22]

Phylum Chordata, class Actinopterygii, order Perciformes, and family Stichaeidae, the taxonomic category of small demersal fishes living in subtidal waters, known as "pricklebacks."[23]

HABITAT The radiated shanny is found only in the northwest Atlantic Ocean, from the Strait of Belle Isle south to the coast of Massachusetts. The radiated shanny feeds primarily on marine worms, copepods, amphipods, and especially capelin eggs when available. Predators of the radiated shanny are piscivorous fishes.[24]

RESOURCE USE The radiated shanny is not utilized by people.

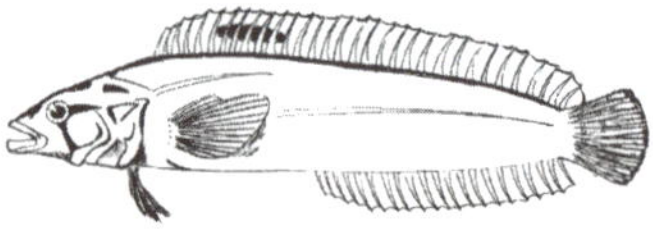

Another prickleback, the daubed shanny, lives in both coastal and continental shelf waters over mud, sand, and hard bottom substrates. The daubed shanny spawns demersal eggs in the winter and spring.

DAUBED SHANNY

"Shanny; Langbarn"

Leptoclinus maculatus

The daubed shanny is a small demersal fish that inhabits the subtidal waters of Bonne Bay.[25]

DESCRIPTION The body of the daubed shanny is elongate, and the head is relatively small. There is a single long dorsal fin with many small spines. The single anal fin has one small spine. The caudal fin is square with dark vertical stripes.[26] The colouration is greyish yellow, and the sides are marked with irregular yellow-brown blotches. The daubed shanny does not grow to more than 20 centimetres in length.[27]

HABITAT The daubed shanny is a circumpolar species of the Northern Hemisphere. In the northwest Atlantic Ocean, the daubed shanny is found in Hudson Bay, along the Labrador coast, in the Gulf of St. Lawrence, and along the coast southward to Cape Cod, Massachusetts. The daubed shanny feeds on marine worms, amphipods, and small benthic crustaceans. The predators of the daubed shanny are piscivorous fishes.[28]

RESOURCE USE The daubed shanny is not utilized by people.

Phylum Chordata, class Actinopterygii, order Perciformes, and family Stichaeidae, the taxonomic category of small demersal fishes living in subtidal waters, known as "pricklebacks."[29]

The alligatorfish lives on muddy and sandy bottoms in coastal and continental shelf waters, including the Gulf of St. Lawrence and the St. Lawrence River estuary. Alligatorfish were collected over the sandy bottom of Deer Brook delta in Bonne Bay.[30] The spawning behavior of the alligatorfish is not well known, but it is postulated that the alligatorfish spawns demersal eggs in the late autumn or early winter.[31]

ALLIGATORFISH "Sea poacher"

Aspidophoroides monopterygius

The alligatorfish is a small demersal fish that inhabits subtidal waters of Bonne Bay.

DESCRIPTION The body of the alligatorfish is elongate and covered by bony, overlapping plates.[32] There is a prominent ridge above each eye. The mouth is small. The pectoral fins are long and fan-like while the caudal fin is small and rounded. There is one dorsal fin and one anal fin. The colouration is dark brown on the back and lighter brown below. There are dark cross bands along the body. The alligatorfish does not grow to more than 18 centimetres in length.[33]

HABITAT The alligatorfish is found only in the western North Atlantic Ocean, ranging from West Greenland and the Labrador coast south to Cape Cod, Massachusetts. The alligatorfish feeds on amphipods, copepods, and mysid-shrimp. Predators of alligatorfish are piscivourous fishes.[35]

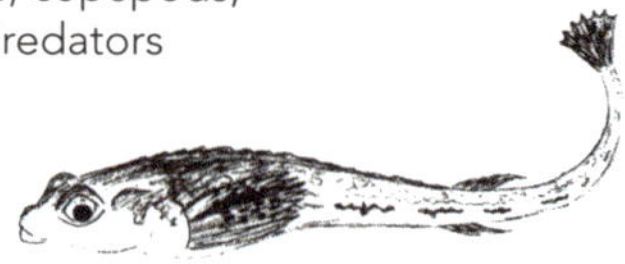

Phylum Chordata, class Actinopterygii, order Scorpaeniformes, and family Agonidae, the taxonomic category of small, bottom-dwelling fishes called "poachers." These fish are related to the sculpins.[34]

RESOURCE USE The alligatorfish is not utilized by people.

Sea ravens live on the rocky and sandy sea bottoms in coastal and continental shelf waters. There may be a resident population of sea raven in Bonne Bay as both adult and juvenile life stages were collected in subtidal waters.[36] The sea raven spawns in late fall or early winter when the female deposits her adhesive eggs in a cluster, often on a finger sponge.[37]

The longhorn sculpin is found in nearshore waters, especially in subtidal waters of bays. There may be a resident population of longhorn sculpin living in Bonne Bay, since both adults and juveniles of this species were collected.[38] Norris Cove is a nursery ground for juvenile longhorn sculpin recently settled

SEA RAVEN "Puff-belly; Sea hen"

Hemitripterus americanus

The sea raven is a demersal fish that lives in subtidal waters of Bonne Bay. When caught, the sea raven may inflate its stomach with air (as seen in the photograph).

DESCRIPTION The sea raven has a large head and large mouth. It has fleshy tabs of skin hanging from the lower jaw and numerous bony knobs around the eyes.[39] The sea raven has rough skin and short spines on the gill covers. There are two dorsal fins: the first has a ragged outline, and the second has a rounded outline. The pectoral fins are fan-like, and the caudal fin is rounded. The colouration is reddish brown, marbled with dark brown. The belly is yellowish brown. Sea raven can grow to 65 centimetres in length.[40]

HABITAT The sea raven is found only in the northwest Atlantic Ocean, ranging from Hamilton Inlet on the Labrador coast and southward to Chesapeake Bay, Maryland. The sea raven preys upon marine worms, bivalve molluscs, marine snails, benthic crustaceans, and fish (e.g. herring and sand lance). Predators of the sea raven are piscivorous fishes.[41]

Phylum Chordata, class Actinopterygii, order Scorpaeniformes, and family Hemitripteridae, the taxonomic category of sculpin-like fishes having a sail-like dorsal fin and a prickly texture of the skin.[42]

RESOURCE USE The sea raven has no commercial value, but it is edible. It is sometimes caught unintentionally by recreational anglers fishing with rod and reel from wharves.

from the plankton. Spawning occurs during the winter months in shallow, rocky subtidal waters. The female lays her eggs in a mass on the sea bottom, often in an empty clam shell or among the branches of finger sponge.[43]

The shorthorn sculpin is found in shallow waters of the Gulf of St. Lawrence. Bonne Bay may have a resident population of shorthorn sculpin as both adults and juveniles were collected.[44] This sculpin spawns in late fall when the female lays her eggs in the crevices of a rocky bottom or amongst seaweeds, and the male guards the eggs until they hatch.

LONGHORN SCULPIN

"Hacklehead; Toadfish"

Myoxocephalus octodecemspinosus

The longhorn sculpin is a demersal fish that lives in subtidal waters of Bonne Bay.

Phylum Chordata, class Actinopterygii, order Scorpaeniformes, and family Cottidae, a taxonomic category of sculpins.[45]

DESCRIPTION The body of the longhorn sculpin is elongate, tapering from a large head to a slender tail. The head is flattened and has numerous spines and bony protuberances. Two long spines near the top of the head give this fish its common name. The longhorn sculpin has two dorsal fins and one anal fin. The tail fin is rounded. It uses its large, fan-like pectoral fins to "walk" over the sea bottom. The colouration can slowly change to match its habitat background. The back is dark olive, the sides are pale yellow, and the body is marked with irregular dark crossbars. The pectoral fins have dark crossbands.[46] The belly is white. Longhorn sculpin can grow to about 45 centimetres in length.[47]

SHORTHORN SCULPIN

"Daddy sculpin"

Myoxocephalus scorpius

The shorthorn sculpin is a demersal fish that lives in subtidal waters of Bonne Bay. Shorthorn sculpin have short spines on the head, hence the common name.

RESOURCE USE There is no commercial fishery for shorthorn sculpin although it is edible. It is often caught unintentionally by recreational anglers fishing with hook and line around wharves.

DESCRIPTION The body shape of the shorthorn sculpin is elongate, tapering from a large head to a slender tail. The uppermost head spines are much shorter than those of the longhorn sculpin.[48] The shorthorn sculpin has a longitudinal ridge with three knobs running along each side of its crown, one knob before the eyes, and one knob behind the eyes. It also has blunt spines on its cheeks. The colouration is dark greenish brown on the back and upper sides with dark bars and mottling. The belly is yellowish. Males have

Note the two long spines protruding from the top of the head, hence the common name.

HABITAT The longhorn sculpin is found only in the western North Atlantic Ocean. It inhabits coastal waters from the northern Gulf of St. Lawrence and eastern Newfoundland south to the Virginia coastline. The longhorn sculpin feeds upon marine worms, crustaceans, bivalve molluscs, and fish, including other sculpins. Longhorn sculpin are preyed upon by spiny dogfish, winter skate, sea raven, and other sculpins.[49]

RESOURCE USE The longhorn sculpin has no commercial value, although it is edible. It is often caught unintentionally by recreational anglers fishing around wharves. The sharp spines of the longhorn sculpin can make it painful to unhook.

Phylum Chordata, class Actinopterygii, order Scorpaeniformes, and family Cottidae.[50]

large, pale spots on the lower sides and belly. The shorthorn sculpin may grow to a maximum length of 80 centimetres.[51]

HABITAT The shorthorn sculpin is found on both sides of the North Atlantic Ocean.[52] In the western Atlantic, it occurs in the Canadian Arctic, Hudson Bay, along the coast of Labrador, and south to the coast of New York. The shorthorn sculpin feeds on marine worms, amphipods, bivalve molluscs, sea urchins, crabs, and shrimp. It will also eat small fish such as juvenile Atlantic herring and Atlantic cod. The predators of shorthorn sculpin include spiny dogfish, winter skate, sea raven, and longhorn sculpins.[53]

GRUBBY "Little sculpin"

Myoxocephalus aenaeus

The grubby is a small demersal fish that lives in subtidal waters of Bonne Bay.

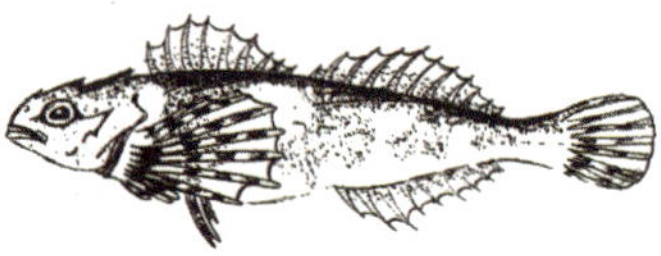

Phylum Chordata, class Actinopterygii, order Scorpaeniformes, and family Cottidae.[56]

DESCRIPTION The body shape of the grubby is "sculpin-like." There is a ridge with two short spines running along the top of the head over each eye. The cheek spines are short.[54] There are two dorsal fins and one anal fin. The caudal fin is rounded, and the pectoral fins are fan-like. The colouration is greenish grey with dark, broken bars on the sides. The belly is pale grey. The grubby is the smallest of the sculpin species found in Bonne Bay. Its maximum length is about 18 centimetres.[55]

HABITAT The grubby is found only in the northwest Atlantic Ocean. It lives in coastal waters and on the continental shelf, ranging from the northern Gulf of St. Lawrence and the east coast of Newfoundland south to the New Jersey coastline. The grubby eats copepods, shrimp, small crabs, bivalve molluscs, and small fish such as sticklebacks. Predators of the grubby are piscivorous fishes such as the spiny dogfish, winter skate, longhorn sculpin, shorthorn sculpin, and sea raven.[57]

RESOURCE USE The grubby is not utilized by people.

The grubby is a small sculpin that can be found in estuaries and in the shallow water of bays along the west coast of Newfoundland. There may be a resident population of grubby in Bonne Bay as both juvenile and adults were collected in the area.[58] Spawning occurs during the winter and spring months. The female deposits her eggs in clusters that adhere to seaweed or rocks on the sea bottom.

Like the fish described above, the Atlantic cod is considered demersal, but cod spend a considerable amount of time feeding in the water column. Atlantic cod were once very abundant on the Grand Banks of Newfoundland, in the Gulf of St. Lawrence, on the Scotian Shelf, and on Georges Bank. Cod live in the subtidal waters of bays and on the continental shelf down to depths of 300

ATLANTIC COD "Codfish; Torsk"

Gadus morhua

There are offshore stocks and bay stocks of Atlantic cod. This female cod in spawning condition was captured in Deer Arm and released unharmed.

DESCRIPTION The body of the Atlantic cod is stout. The head and mouth are relatively large. Cod have three dorsal fins and two anal fins. The caudal fin is almost square. There is a barbel near the tip of the lower jaw. Atlantic cod have a colouration of dark olive green on the back with a lighter olive green or light brown on the sides. The back and sides of cod are speckled with numerous reddish-brown spots. The lateral line is prominently pale white.[59] The belly is a greyish white or white. Atlantic cod that feed primarily on invertebrates (e.g. shrimp) rather than fish (e.g. capelin) may have more reddish-brown or golden-brown pigmentation on the sides and belly.[60] Atlantic cod can grow to 180 centimetres in length and weigh 95 kilograms.[61]

Phylum Chordata, class Actinopterygii, order Gadiformes, and family Gadidae, the taxomonic classification of demersal fishes, called "codfishes."[62]

HABITAT Atlantic cod are found in most coastal waters of the North Atlantic Ocean.[63] In the northwest Atlantic Ocean, cod inhabit coastal waters around Greenland and Baffin Island southward to Cape Hatteras, North Carolina. Cod feed along the sea bottom, eating shrimp, crab, molluscs, and marine worms. But cod will also feed on fish (such as capelin, sand lance, and herring) in the water column. Larval cod feed on plankton such as copepods. Juvenile cod in shallow nursery grounds eat amphipods, mysid-shrimp, and small crabs. Juvenile cod are eaten by piscivorous fishes, including larger cod (cannibalism).[64] Cod are preyed upon by grey seals and harp seals.[65]

RESOURCE USE There has been a fishery for Atlantic cod in the coastal waters of Newfoundland and Labrador for over 450 years.[66] Historically, fishermen caught cod on the Grand Banks using jiggers and baited hooks on longlines.[67] In the middle of the last century, large vessels dragged trawl nets along the seafloor to sweep up cod on the offshore banks.[68] Inshore fishermen used cod traps and gillnets[69] to catch cod that migrated to the coast to feed on capelin. Eventually, the northern cod stock became overfished, and the fishery collapsed in 1992. Rebuilding of the inshore and offshore components of the northern cod stock has been slow.

Traditionally, cod were sold as salted codfish in barrels.[70] With the invention of factory freezer trawlers, cod were frozen in blocks at sea for the later production of breaded fish sticks or fish portions. Today, most Atlantic cod are sold as fresh or frozen fillets. The white flesh of cod flakes easily when cooked and has a mild, tasty flavour.

to 400 metres. There are offshore and inshore stocks of Atlantic cod,[71] and many of the major bays of Newfoundland have a local stock.[72]

Cod move in schools to spawning grounds on the continental shelf. In the Gulf of St. Lawrence, cod spawn during the spring and summer months.[73] Males and females form mating pairs.[74] Eggs and sperm are released into the water. The fertilized eggs are buoyant and float near the surface. Larvae from the hatched eggs are carried by the currents toward shallow nursery grounds. The planktonic larva slowly develops the mouth and fins characteristic of the next life cycle stage. Juvenile cod about six months old will settle to the sea bottom in shallow waters. Cod several years old will join schools of adult fish moving to spawning grounds.

With the collapse of the Grand Banks cod fishery in 1992 and a severe decline in the abundance of Atlantic cod in the Gulf of St. Lawrence several years later, scientists became concerned whether the species itself was at risk of becoming extirpated from the marine waters of Atlantic Canada. The Laurentian North population of Atlantic cod was designated a "species-at-risk" by COSEWIC.[75] Because it would be difficult to avoid the capture of cod as bycatch in other fisheries, the Government of Canada did not add Atlantic cod to the list of species at risk under SARA.

Adapted to the reduced salinities of nearshore coastal waters, Greenland cod are commonly found in fjords and bays. Bonne Bay likely supports a population of Greenland cod as juveniles and adults have been collected there.[76] Spawning occurs during the spring in the brackish waters of estuaries. The demersal eggs of Greenland cod adhere to boulders and cobble on the sea bottom.

Two species of flatfish are also found in the subtidal waters of Bonne Bay: the winter flounder and the windowpane flounder. The winter flounder lives on sand and mud bottoms down to a depth of about 150 metres. Bonne Bay likely supports a population of winter flounder as both adults and juveniles were collected.[77] The winter flounder moves into shallow nearshore waters during the winter months and spawns there in the spring. Winter flounder can sometimes be seen in pre-spawning aggregations near the

GREENLAND COD "Rock cod"
Gadus ogac

The Greenland cod is a demersal fish that lives in subtidal waters of bays and fjords such as Bonne Bay.

DESCRIPTION The body shape of Greenland cod is "cod-like," having a large head, large mouth, three dorsal fins, two anal fins, a square caudal fin, and a barbel on the lower jaw. The Greenland cod has yellowish brown to bronze marbling on its sides. Unlike the Atlantic cod which has a pale-white lateral line, the lateral line of the Greenland cod is indistinct.[78] Greenland cod do not grow as large as Atlantic cod. Its maximum recorded length is 70 centimetres.[79]

Phylum Chordata, class Actinopterygii, order Gadiformes, and family Gadidae, the taxonomic category for cod-like fishes.[80]

HABITAT The Greenland cod is found in both the northeast and northwest Atlantic Ocean. It is abundant along the coast of west Greenland and the Canadian Arctic coast, especially in Hudson Bay. Its range extends from the Hudson Strait, along the Labrador coast, the Gulf of St. Lawrence, and southward to Cape Breton, Nova Scotia. Greenland cod prey upon other fishes, especially capelin. They will also eat amphipods, shrimp, crabs, and marine worms. Predators of Greenland cod are piscivorous fishes and seals.[81]

RESOURCE USE There is no fishery directed at the Greenland cod in the Gulf of St. Lawrence.[82] As Greenland cod are abundant in Hamilton Inlet-Lake Melville in Labrador, an experimental fishery for this "underutilized species" was conducted during 1979-81.[83] However, the harvested fish did not sell well, as the flesh of Greenland cod has black specks of harmless pigment. Consumers prefer the pure white fillet of Atlantic cod.

shoreline during the winter months, giving rise to its common name "winter flounder." Spawning occurs over sand or mud bottoms. The fertilized eggs are adhesive and settle to the bottom singly or in clumps.[84]

The windowpane flounder lives on sandy sea bottoms in subtidal waters, down to a depth of about 50 metres. Both adults and juveniles have been collected in Bonne Bay.[85] Spawning takes place during the spring and early summer. The developing eggs and larvae are planktonic.

WINTER FLOUNDER

"Blackback flounder"

Pseudopleuronectes americanus

Top photo: The winter flounder is a "right-eyed flounder" that lives on a muddy sea bottom in subtidal waters of Bonne Bay. Bottom Photo: A juvenile winter flounder recently settled to the bottom in Bonne Bay. Note that the left eye has migrated to the right side of the fish. (PHOTOGRAPH BY CRAIG PURCHASE)

DESCRIPTION The body shape of the winter flounder is oblong, and the sides of the fish are compressed. The mouth is small, and the lower jaw protrudes slightly. During the demersal stage of its life cycle, the winter flounder lies on its left side. Both eyes are on the right side of the body, the uppermost side when the fish is lying on the sea bottom. The left eye migrates to the right side when the young flounder is still planktonic. The colouration is muddy brown with black mottling on the dorsal surface. The ventral surface (the blind side) is white with slightly translucent edges tinged with yellow pigment. The lateral line is nearly straight.[86] The winter flounder can grow to 65 centimetres in length.[87]

HABITAT The winter flounder is found only in the western North Atlantic Ocean. This flatfish occurs in coastal waters of southern Labrador, throughout the Gulf of St. Lawrence, on the Grand Banks of Newfoundland, on the Scotian Shelf, in the Gulf of Maine, and along the coast southward to Georgia. The winter flounder feeds on marine worms, copepods, small bivalve molluscs, and the eggs of herring and capelin. Winter flounder are preyed upon by piscivorous fishes such as the sea raven; marine mammals such as the harbour seal, harp seal, and grey seal; and birds of prey such as osprey and bald eagles.[90]

Phylum Chordata, class Actinopterygii, order Pleuronectifomes, and family Pleuronectidae, the taxonomic category of right-eyed flounders.[88]

RESOURCE USE In the Gulf region, fishermen catch winter flounder for baiting lobster pots.[89] But along the eastern seaboard of the US, the winter flounder is caught both commercially and recreationally. It has a soft, white flesh and is marketed as fresh or frozen fillets of "lemon sole."

WINDOWPANE FLOUNDER

"Spotted flounder; Sand flounder"

Scophthalmus aquosus

The windowpane flounder is a "left-eyed flounder" that lives on sandy sea bottoms in the shallow subtidal zone. It has been collected in the Deer Brook delta of Bonne Bay.[91]

DESCRIPTION The body shape of the windowpane flounder is oval and the sides of the fish are compressed. Young juveniles are so thin that the body is translucent, akin to a "windowpane." During the demersal stage of its life cycle, this flatfish species lies on its right side. Both eyes are on the left side. The lower jaw protrudes slightly. The caudal fin is rounded.[92] The dorsal fin, pelvic fin, and anal fin form a near continuous margin. The colouration is brownish with dark mottling and white spots on the dorsal, eyed side. The ventral, blind side is white with dark splotches. Windowpane flounder can grow to a maximum length of about 50 centimetres.[93]

HABITAT The windowpane flounder is found only in the western North Atlantic Ocean in shallow coastal waters from the Gulf of St. Lawrence south to Florida. The windowpane flounder feeds on amphipods, mysid-shrimp, and small fishes. The predators of windowpane flounder are piscivorous fishes such as spiny dogfish, thorny skate, and Atlantic cod.[95]

Phylum Chordata, class Actinopterygii, order Pleuronectifomes, and family Scophthalmidae, the taxonomic group of left-eyed flounders.[94]

RESOURCE USE There is no fishery presently directed at windowpane flounder.[96] Because the body of this flounder is so thin, it is difficult to fillet this edible fish.

PELAGIC FISHES IN SUBTIDAL WATERS OF THE BAY

Fishes that spend most of the time swimming in the water column are known as "pelagic" species, to distinguish them from "demersal" species that spend long periods resting on the sea bottom. Pelagic fishes living in subtidal waters of Bonne Bay include the cunner and Acadian redfish. These fishes may spend a significant amount of time off the bottom, feeding in the water column.

CUNNER "Conner, Sea perch; Nipper"

Tautogolabrus adspersus

The cunner is a pelagic fish that inhabits the shallow subtidal zone.

DESCRIPTION The body shape of the cunner resembles that of the freshwater perch. The head of the cunner is pointed. The mouth with thick lips is relatively small. The dorsal, pelvic, and anal fins have spines. The caudal fin is slightly rounded, and the caudal peduncle is wide.[97] The colouration changes with the environmental background, but the body is usually a dull olive green with brown and reddish mottling. The belly is bluish white. The cunner can grow to 43 centimetres in length.[98]

Phylum Chordata, class Actinopterygii, order Perciformes, and family Labridae, the taxonomic group of marine fishes which inhabit tropical, subtropical, and temperate zones of the Atlantic, Pacific, and Indian Oceans. The Labridae family includes coral reef fishes.[99]

HABITAT The cunner is found in the western North Atlantic Ocean, ranging from northern coastal Newfoundland and the Gulf of St. Lawrence south to Chesapeake Bay, Maryland. Cunners can crush the shells of barnacles, blue mussels, and sea urchins and eat the soft tissue. They also eat marine worms, amphipods, and shrimp. Cunners are preyed upon by piscivourous fishes such as Atlantic cod, sea ravens, skates, and sculpins.[100]

RESOURCE USE The cunner has no commercial value, although it is edible. The cunner is fun to catch by angling from piers and whaves.

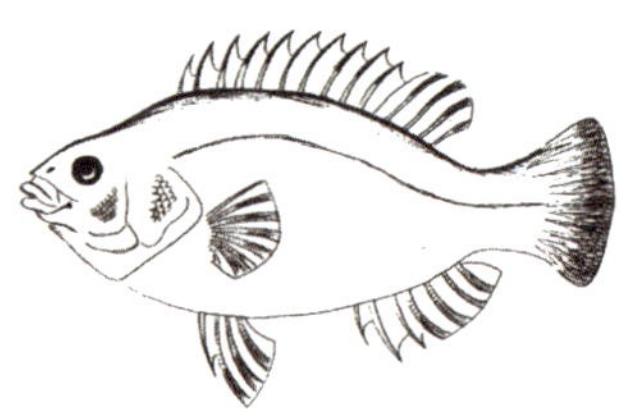

The cunner inhabits the shallow subtidal zone, and schools are commonly seen around wharves and rock outcroppings. The cunner is a resident species of Bonne Bay. Both adult and juvenile cunner have been collected there.[101] Spawning occurs during the summer, and swarms of spawning cunners can often be observed off the wharf in Norris Point in early July. The developing eggs and larvae are planktonic.

ACADIAN REDFISH

"Ocean perch; Rosefish"

Sebastes fasciatus

The Acadian redfish has been collected in subtidal waters of Bonne Bay using gillnets.

DESCRIPTION The body shape of the Acadian redfish resembles that of a freshwater bass, except that it has spines. The gill cover has bony spines, and there is a bony protrusion on the lower jaw.[102] The eyes are large. The colouration is notably orange to red with a brownish cast. Redfish can live for 40 years or more, but are slow growing. Female Acadian redfish grow to about 70 centimetres in length, while males grow to approximately 55 centimetres.[103]

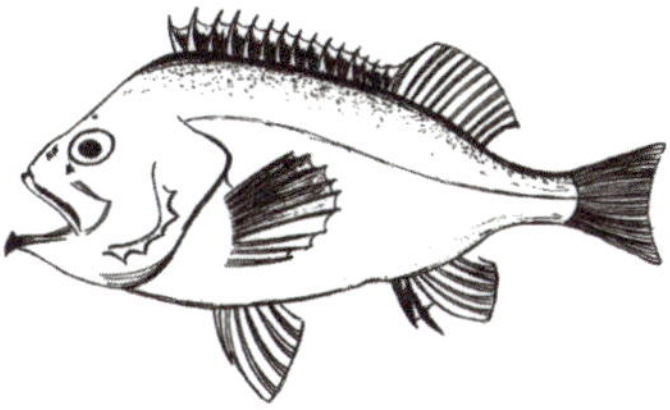

HABITAT The Acadian redfish lives only in the northwest Atlantic Ocean, ranging from west Greenland and Labrador south to the Gulf of Maine. The Acadian redfish feeds in the water column on copepods, krill-shrimp, and small fish. It also feeds near the sea floor on shrimp. Predators of redfish include piscivourous fishes such as Atlantic cod and Greenland halibut.[104]

RESOURCE USE There has been a commercial fishery for redfish in deep waters of the Gulf of St. Lawrence and along the continental slope of the Grand Banks of Newfoundland since the mid-1930s. Redfish are caught using an otter trawl near the sea bottom or a pelagic trawl higher in the water column.[105] The commercial fishery for redfish began with technological advances in fast-freezing aboard trawlers. Frozen blocks of filleted redfish were cut and breaded, then marketed as fish sticks of "ocean perch." Today, redfish are sold as fresh fillets or frozen breaded fillets which are higher value products.

Phylum Chordata, class Actinopterygii, order Scorpaeniformes, and family Sebastidae, the taxonomic grouping of marine rockfishes.[106]

The Acadian redfish inhabits deep-water channels and slopes of the continental shelf in the Northwest Atlantic Ocean. It can also be found in the deep-water bays of Newfoundland and Labrador, such as Bonne Bay. The Acadian redfish is similar in appearance to two other species of redfish: the golden redfish and the deepwater redfish.[107] The population of Acadian redfish living in Bonne Bay is genetically distinguishable from the Acadian redfish living in the Gulf of St Lawrence.[108] Mating occurs in the fall, and the young are born in the summer. The eggs are fertilized internally and develop within the female's body until they are released through the genital pore as free-swimming larvae. The genetic distinctiveness of Bonne Bay redfish indicates that the bay population does not mix and breed with redfish in the Gulf.

Because redfish species grow slowly and produce relatively few young, redfish stocks can be easily overfished. The genetically-distinguishable population of Acadian redfish living in Bonne Bay has been assessed by COSEWIC and assigned the status of "special concern" due to the small geographic range of the population. The area of occupancy in Bonne Bay is estimated at only 70 square kilometres. Acadian redfish can be caught as bycatch by commercial fishermen seining for herring or mackerel in Bonne Bay. The population in Bonne Bay would be threatened by a major oil spill in the bay. The federal government might list the Acadian redfish (Bonne Bay Population) as "special concern" under SARA. DFO would then be required to produce a management plan for maintaining the redfish population in Bonne Bay.[109]

GULF FISHES THAT SPAWN IN BONNE BAY

Some fishes living in the Gulf of St. Lawrence migrate considerable distances to spawn nearshore. Gulf fishes that spawn in Bonne Bay include capelin, American sand lance, lumpfish, Atlantic wolffish, spotted wolffish, ocean pout, and Laval's eelpout.

There are stocks of capelin on the Labrador continental shelf, in the Gulf of St. Lawrence, and on the Grand Banks of Newfoundland. During the summer, schools of capelin migrate inshore to spawn on cobble beaches along the coast, including beaches in Outer Bonne

Bay. Some capelin spawn on coarse sand and gravel bottom substrate in subtidal waters. Pre-spawning males develop ridges of elongated scales along the sides, and larger pectoral and anal fins. Mating pairs of capelin will bury the eggs in the gravel by their body motion. The eggs stick to the gravel until they hatch, and the larvae are carried offshore by the outgoing tide. Most capelin spawn only once, but some females live to spawn a second, third, or even fourth year.[110]

The waters of the Outer Basin of Bonne Bay merge with the Gulf. Some fishes that live in the Gulf of St. Lawrence enter Bonne Bay to spawn.

CAPELIN

"Caplin; Lodde; Whitefish (juvenile capelin)"
Mallotus villosus

A female capelin in spawning condition. Note that some extruded eggs have stuck to the hand.

Phylum Chordata, class Actinopterygii, order Osmeriformes, and family Osmeridae, the taxomonic category for pelagic, smelt-like fishes. The capelin is related to the rainbow smelt.[113]

DESCRIPTION Capelin are long and slender. There are two fins on the back: a dorsal fin in the middle and a smaller adipose fin just in front of the tail.[111] The capelin has no spines. The colouration on the back is olive green, and the sides are silver; the belly is silvery white. The skin over the gills is dark. Capelin can grow to a maximum length of 25 centimetres.[112]

HABITAT The capelin has a circumpolar distribution in the North Atlantic Ocean and North Pacific Ocean and occurs in all Arctic seas, including Hudson Bay.[114] In the northwest Atlantic Ocean, capelin range from Greenland south to the Gulf of Maine. Capelin feed by filtering seawater through their gills, capturing planktonic copepods and krill on gill rakers. Capelin will also eat amphipods, shrimp, and young sand lance.

The capelin is regarded as a "keystone species" in the food web, meaning that it is a major link between the plankton and large predators. Capelin are preyed upon by piscivorous fishes (e.g. the Atlantic salmon, Atlantic cod, and Greenland cod), by baleen whales (e.g. the minke and humpback whale), by seals (e.g. the harp seal), and by seabirds (e.g the Atlantic puffin, the common murre, and the thick-billed murre).[115]

RESOURCE USE Historically, capelin were taken using dip nets and cast nets when they were spawning on the beaches and prepared as homemade food by smoking, pickling, or drying the whole capelin. Capelin were also used as fertilizer in root-vegetable gardens. Capelin were traditionally used as bait in the Atlantic cod longline fishery. These practices are still in use today, but pre-spawning capelin are now caught commercially using purse seines.[116] Female capelin with eggs are processed into a Japanese snack food called "shishamo." The roe is also used in preparing Japanese sushi. Male capelin are processed into fishmeal used in the aquaculture of Atlantic salmon or used in preparing pet food.

At spawning time, the mature male capelin (shown here above a female capelin) has a ridge along each side of the body formed by enlarged lateral line scales. The ridge may help the male hold the female when spawning on a beach.[117]

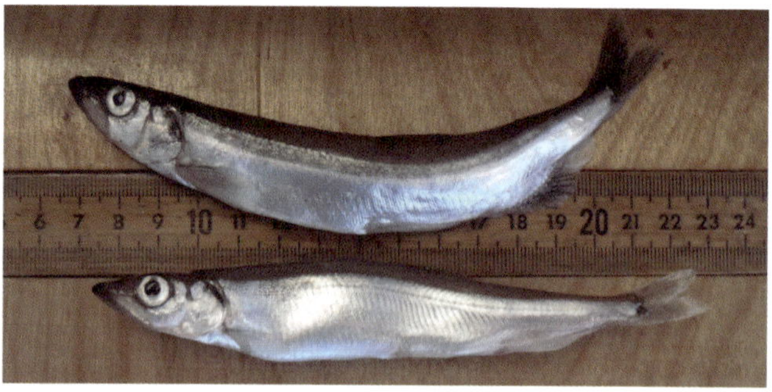

AMERICAN SAND LANCE "Sand-eel"

Ammodytes americanus

The American sand lance lives in coastal waters of the Gulf of St. Lawrence, but enters Bonne Bay to spawn.

DESCRIPTION The American sand lance has an elongate body and a pointed snout. The lower jaw of the mouth projects slightly beyond the upper jaw.[118] Its colouration is iridescent blue green or bronze on the back, gradating to a white belly. Sand lance can grow to a length of 25 centimetres.[119]

HABITAT The American sand lance lives in coastal waters of the Northwest Atlantic Ocean, extending from west Greenland to Labrador and south to the coast of Delaware. The sand lance feeds on plankton, mostly copepods. Sand lance is an important prey item in the diet of many marine fishes (e.g. Atlantic cod), marine mammals, and seabirds. Sea-run brook trout feed on sand lance in Bonne Bay. Sand lance will burrow into sand or gravel on the sea bottom to escape predators.[120]

RESOURCE USE There is no commercial fishery for sand lance in the Gulf of St. Lawrence.[121] In New England, sand lance are used as bait in marine sport fishing.

Phylum Chordata, class Actinopterygii, order Perciformes, and family Ammodytidae, the taxonomic category of slender marine fishes which bury themselves in the sand bottoms of the littoral zone.[122]

Schools of sand lance are often observed in the Gulf of St. Lawrence and on the Grand Banks of Newfoundland. The sand lance spawns on sand bottoms in shallow water during the winter. The eggs stick to sand grains. Both adult and juvenile sand lance have been collected in Bonne Bay,[123] which suggests that sand lance reproduce within the bay.

The lumpfish lives in the Gulf of St. Lawrence and on the continental shelf down to depths of 300 metres. Adult lumpfish migrate toward the coast in the spring in preparation for spawning during the summer. Lumpfish spawn on the bottom amongst seaweeds growing on rocky substrate. The eggs are deposited in a round mass. Having spawned, the female lumpfish moves to deeper water, but the male remains behind to guard the eggs until hatching.[124]

LUMPFISH "Henfish; Lumpsucker"

Cyclopterus lumpus

The lumpfish is a Gulf species that migrates inshore to spawn in subtidal waters of Bonne Bay.[125] (PHOTOGRAPH BY DAVID METHVEN)

Phylum Chordata, class Actinopterygii, order Scorpaeniformes, and family Cyclopteridae.[128]

DESCRIPTION The body shape of lumpfish is nearly spherical. The skin is leathery and without scales. The dorsal fin is encased by a hump. Three rows of wart-like tubercles appear along the sides, and the pelvic fins form a sucker disk, enabling the lumpfish to grip rocks or floating kelp.[126] The colouration can vary from bluish grey to greenish brown. The belly is usually grey white, but turns red in breeding males. Female lumpfish can grow to a length of 60 centimetres, while male lumpfish are smaller than females of the same age.[127]

HABITAT The lumpfish can be found on both the western and eastern sides of the North Atlantic Ocean.[132] In the northwest Atlantic Ocean, lumpfish range from Hudson's Bay and James Bay, along the Labrador coast, in the Gulf of St. Lawrence, on the Grand Banks of Newfoundland, on the Scotian Shelf, and south to the coast of New Jersey. The lumpfish feeds on planktonic crustaceans, jellyfish, and small fish associated with floating seaweed. The lumpfish also feeds on marine worms and shrimp on the sea bottom. Sharks are known predators of lumpfish.[133]

RESOURCE USE In Atlantic Canada, the lumpfish is fished commercially to obtain the roe of pre-spawning females.[129] Lumpfish are caught in gillnets with a mesh[130] designed to capture only the large females. The salted and cured eggs are marketed as inexpensive caviar, an alternative to the scarce caviar made from eggs of the Atlantic sturgeon.[131]

The Atlantic wolffish is found in the Gulf of St. Lawrence, along the east and west coasts of Newfoundland, and on the Grand Banks of Newfoundland. This demersal fish inhabits waters down to 500 metres depth. Scuba divers have observed wolffish living in the crevices of submerged bedrock walls below Newfoundland cliffs, such as the rock walls near Gadds Harbour in Bonne Bay. Atlantic wolffish living offshore may migrate into shallower waters to spawn. Reproduction occurs in the fall, and the female deposits large, cohesive eggs in a clump on the sea bottom. The male will then guard the eggs until they hatch.

Because the abundance of Atlantic wolffish has declined in the waters of Atlantic Canada, the species is now protected under SARA. The Atlantic wolffish is listed under SARA as "special concern," i.e., "particularly sensitive to human activities or natural events."[134] Any fish caught as bycatch should be returned to the water unharmed. DFO has a management plan in place under SARA.[135]

ATLANTIC WOLFFISH

"Catfish; Striped wolffish"

Anarchichas lupus

The Atlantic wolffish is a Gulf species that migrates inshore to spawn. It has been observed living in the crevices of submerged bedrock walls in Bonne Bay. (PHOTOGRAPH BY JENNIFER DAWE)

DESCRIPTION The body shape of the Atlantic wolffish is elongate, and the head is blunt. The mouth has jaws with canine teeth in the front and molar-like teeth in the back. The dorsal fin is long and has spines. The caudal fin is small and rounded, and the pectoral fins are large and fan-like. The pelvic fins are absent, as in all wolffish species.[136] The colouration is dark olive green to purplish brown. Dark vertical bars give rise to its common name "striped wolffish." The belly is dirty white. Atlantic wolffish can grow to a length of 150 centimetres.[137]

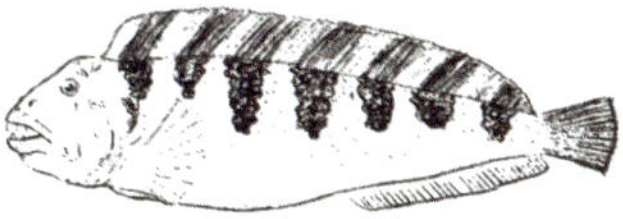

HABITAT The Atlantic wolffish occurs on both sides of the Atlantic Ocean.[138] In the western North Atlantic, it inhabits coastal waters off west Greenland, off Labrador, and along the coast south to Maine. Wolffish use their canine teeth in the front of the mouth to capture fish and crush the shells of sea urchins, crabs, and lobsters. The moliform teeth in the back of the mouth are used to crush the hard shells of bivalve molluscs. Juvenile wolffish are preyed upon by Atlantic cod and other piscivorous fishes. Adult wolffish have few predators.[139]

Phylum Chordata, class Actinopterygii, order Perciformes, and family Anarhichadidae, the taxonomic category of wolffish or "ocean catfish" species.[140]

RESOURCE USE There is no commercial fishery directed at Atlantic wolffish, but this demersal fish is sometimes caught as bycatch in bottom trawls fishing for groundfish. The Atlantic wolffish will enter snow crab pots and lobster traps to eat the bait.[141] The white flesh of the Atlantic wolffish is flavourful. In the past, the Atlantic wolffish caught as bycatch was marketed as fresh fillets.

The spotted wolffish naturally lives deeper than the Atlantic wolffish. Spotted wolffish inhabit the continental slope down to 800 metres depth. Spotted wolffish spawn in late fall or early winter, and the eggs are laid in clusters on the sea bottom. The male provides parental care of the eggs until they hatch.

Spotted wolffish are listed under SARA as "threatened," i.e. "likely to become endangered of extirpation in the waters of Atlantic Canada," if threats to its existence continue. Spotted wolffish unintentionally caught in fishing gear must be returned to the water with minimal harm.[142]

SPOTTED WOLFFISH

"Leopardfish; Spotted catfish"

Anarhichas minor

The spotted wolffish is a Gulf species that has been observed in subtidal waters of Bonne Bay.[143] (PHOTOGRAPH BY JENNIFER DAWE)

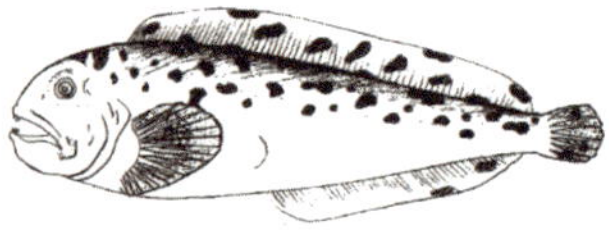

Phylum Chordata, class Actinopterygii, order Perciformes, and family Anarhichadidae, the taxomonic category for wolffish or ocean catfish species.[148]

DESCRIPTION The body shape of the spotted wolffish is similar to that of the Atlantic wolffish, but the colouration is different. The spotted wolffish is dull olive green or brown. The spotted wolffish has black-brown spots on its dorsal fin, anal fin, caudal fin, and upper sides, which are different from the dark stripes of the Atlantic wolffish.[144] The belly is white. Spotted wolffish can measure up to 180 centimetres in length.[145]

HABITAT The spotted wolffish occurs on both sides of the North Atlantic Ocean.[146] In the northwest Atlantic Ocean, the species is found off east and west Greenland, off Labrador, on the Grand Banks of Newfoundland, and ranging south to Cape Cod, Massachusetts. Similar to the Atlantic wolffish, the spotted wolffish feeds on hard-shelled invertebrates. It will also ingest marine worms, seaweeds, and small fish (e.g. sand lance). The spotted wolffish has few predators.[147]

RESOURCE USE The spotted wolffish is not fished intentionally in the waters of Atlantic Canada,[149] but some fish are occasionally taken as bycatch by offshore trawlers. The fish cannot be retained and sold.

Laval's eelpout inhabits subarctic to temperate waters to depths greater than 500 m. This demersal species is present in Bonne Bay, but is rarely encountered by fisherpersons.

The ocean pout inhabits subtidal waters down to depths of 150 metres. The ocean pout spawns in crevices of rocky sea bottoms during the fall months. The female will lay her eggs in a gelatinous mass and continue to guard the eggs until they hatch. Both adult and juvenile specimens of ocean pout have been collected from Bonne Bay, indicating that ocean pout breed in the bay.[150]

LAVAL'S EELPOUT

"Newfoundland eelpout"

Lycodes lavalaei

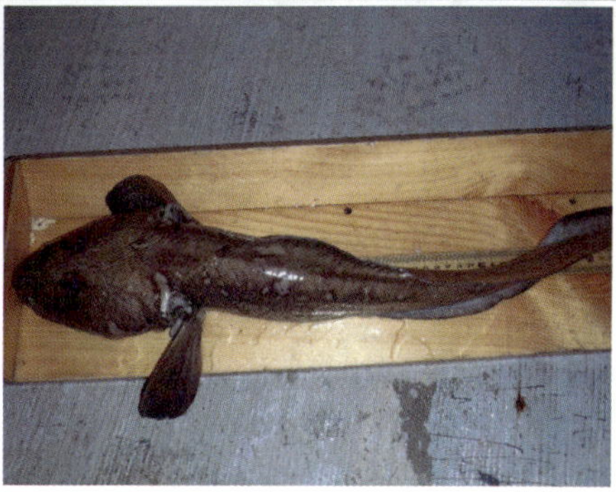

Laval's eelpout is a Gulf species that enters Bonne Bay to spawn. This specimen captured in Bonne Bay has grown to the maximum reported length for the species.

DESCRIPTION The body shape of Laval's eelpout is elongate. The head and mouth are large, and the upper jaw projects over the lower jaw. The long dorsal and anal fins are continuous with the caudal fin. The colouration is brownish grey with black blotches and irregular vertical bands.[151] Laval's eelpout can grow to about 60 centimetres in length.[152]

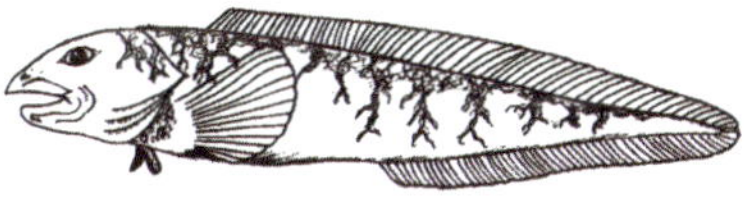

HABITAT Laval's eelpout is found on the continental shelf in the northwest Atlantic Ocean from Labrador southwards to the Gulf of St. Lawrence, including the Grand Banks of Newfoundland. Laval's eelpout feeds over muddy and sandy sea bottoms, eating benthic invertebrates and small fishes. Atlantic cod are known predators of juvenile Laval's eelpout.[153]

RESOURCE USE Laval's eelpout is not utilized by humans. There is no commercial fishery for this species.

Phylum Chordata, class Actinopterygii, order Perciformes, and family Zoarcidae, the taxonomic category for eelpout fishes.[154]

OCEAN POUT

"Eelpout; Laughing jack"
Zoarces americanus

The ocean pout is a Gulf species that enters Bonne Bay to spawn. This juvenile eelpout was collected in Norris Cove of Bonne Bay.

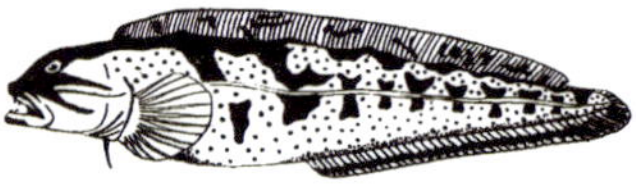

DESCRIPTION The body shape of the ocean pout is elongate. The head is broad; the snout is blunt. The eyes are small and located high on the head. The mouth has a fleshy upper lip.[155] The tail is pointed, and the dorsal fin is continuous with the caudal fin and anal fin. The colouration is muddy yellow to reddish brown. Its belly is white or dull yellow. Pectoral fins are reddish orange. The eelpout can grow to a length of 110 centimetres.[156]

HABITAT The eelpout is found in coastal waters in the northwest Atlantic Ocean from southern Labrador to the New Jersey coast, including the Gulf of St. Lawrence and the Grand Banks of Newfoundland. Ocean pout feed on marine worms, sea urchins, crabs, amphipods, shrimp, mussels, and small fishes. Predators of the ocean pout include harbour seals and piscivorous fishes such as the longhorn sculpin, sea raven, and Atlantic cod.[157]

RESOURCE USE The eelpout is not utilized by humans. There is no fishery for eelpout in the waters of Atlantic Canada.

Phylum Chordata, class Actinopterygii, order Perciformes, and family Zoarcidae, the taxonomic category for eelpout fishes.[158]

GULF FISHES THAT USE BONNE BAY AS A NURSERY

Some Gulf fishes spawn offshore, but their young can be found in subtidal waters of Bonne Bay. The adult fish spawn in the Gulf, and their fertilized eggs drift with the currents towards the coastline. The embryos develop into planktonic fish larvae. The larvae metamorphose into the juvenile stage which eventually settles on the sea bottom in shallow water. Gulf fishes that use Bonne Bay as a nursery ground include yellowtail flounder, white hake, and silver hake.

The yellowtail flounder spawns near the sea bottom in the Gulf, and the fertilized eggs float to the surface where they develop into planktonic larvae. The larvae grow into the shape of a flatfish and then settle to the ocean bottom.[159] Both adult and juvenile specimens of yellowtail flounder were collected in Bonne Bay,[160] suggesting that yellowtail flounder could also spawn in the bay.

YELLOWTAIL FLOUNDER "Rusty dab"

Limanda ferruginea

Yellowtail flounder is a "right-eyed flounder" which spawns in the Gulf, but uses nearshore waters, including Bonne Bay, as a nursery ground. Bottom photo: Note the yellow pigmentation on the underside skin near the tail, hence the common name "yellowtail" flounder.

DESCRIPTION The yellowtail flounder has an oval-shaped body. The sides of the fish are laterally compressed. The mouth is small and the caudal fin is rounded. The left eye migrates to the right side when the young flounder is still planktonic. Both eyes look upward when the fish lies on its left side on the sea bottom. Yellowtail flounder are brownish olive green on the top (eyed) side and white with a yellow colouring on the under (blind) side near the tail. There are numerous rusty spots on the skin. The lateral line is arched above the pectoral fin.[161] Yellowtail flounder can grow to a maximum length of about 65 centimetres.[162]

HABITAT The yellowtail flounder is found on the continental shelf in the northwest Atlantic Ocean from southern Labrador to Chesapeake Bay, Maryland, including the Gulf of St. Lawrence and the Grand Banks of Newfoundland. The yellowtail flounder feeds on marine worms, amphipods, shrimp, and small crabs. They are preyed upon by piscivorous fishes such as winter skate, Atlantic cod, and spiny dogfish.[163]

Phylum Chordata, class Actinopterygii, order Pleuronectifomes, and family Pleuronectidae, the taxonomic category of right-eyed flounders.[164]

RESOURCE USE The yellowtail flounder is a commercially valuable flatfish species. There is a fishery for yellowtail in the southern Gulf of St. Lawrence and on the Grand Banks of Newfoundland conducted by vessels using bottom trawls.[165] The yellowtail flounder has a soft, white flesh and is marketed as frozen fillets.

The white hake is a continental shelf-spawning species which uses the coastal zone as a nursery ground. The spawning time for white hake in the Gulf is summer. Juvenile white hake were collected in shallow subtidal waters of Bonne Bay.[166]

Silver hake spawn over the continental shelf during the summer and fall. Juvenile silver hake settle on inshore nursery grounds, such as in Bonne Bay.

WHITE HAKE "Mud hake"

Urophycis tenuis

The white hake is a Gulf species which spawns offshore, but uses nearshore waters as a nursery ground. Note the long filaments of the pelvic fins positioned near the throat.

DESCRIPTION The body shape of the white hake is elongated. The caudal fin is rounded. The chin has a small barbel. The white hake has two dorsal fins and one anal fin. The pelvic fins have long filamentous rays,[167] and these filaments help these fish feel prey on the sea floor. The colouration of the back and sides is usually reddish or purple brown. The belly is pale grey, yellowish, or white. White hake may grow to 135 centimetres in length.[168]

HABITAT The white hake is found only in the western Atlantic Ocean. It ranges from the Gulf of St. Lawrence and the southern part of the Grand Banks southward to Cape Hatteras, North Carolina. White hake feed over mud sea bottoms, eating shrimp, amphipods, crabs, small fish, and squid.[169]

RESOURCE USE There is a commercial fishery for white hake in deep waters of the southern Gulf of St. Lawrence and the Scotian Shelf.[171] White hake are captured by fishermen using otter trawls, gillnets, and baited longlines.[172] The flesh of the white hake is softer than Atlantic cod. White hake is marketed as fresh or frozen fillets.

Phylum Chordata, class Actinopterygii, order Gadiformes, and family Phycidae, a taxonomic category of hakes.[170]

Yellowtail flounder, white hake, and silver hake spawn in the Gulf of St. Lawrence, but their young can be found in Bonne Bay. The developing larvae of these species drift with the Gulf currents towards the coastline. The juvenile life stage may settle to the bottom in Bonne Bay.

SILVER HAKE "Whiting"

Merluccius bilinearis

This juvenile silver hake was collected in Deer Arm of Bonne Bay.

DESCRIPTION The body of silver hake is slender. There are two dorsal fins. The shape of the anal fin is very similar to the shape of the rear dorsal fin. The lower jaw slightly protrudes beyond the upper jaw.[173] Unlike the white hake, the silver hake does not have a barbel under the chin. The colouration is dark grey with silvery iridescent sides and belly. Silver hake can grow to a maximum size of 76 centimetres.[174]

HABITAT The silver hake is found in continental shelf waters of the northwest Atlantic Ocean, down to depths of about 300 metres. It ranges from the Grand Banks of Newfoundland, the Gulf of St. Lawrence, and the Scotian Shelf, south to waters off South Carolina. Adult silver hake feed on small fishes, while juveniles feed on crustaceans. Juvenile silver hake are preyed upon by other fish such as Atlantic cod. Adult silver hake are eaten by Atlantic halibut.[175]

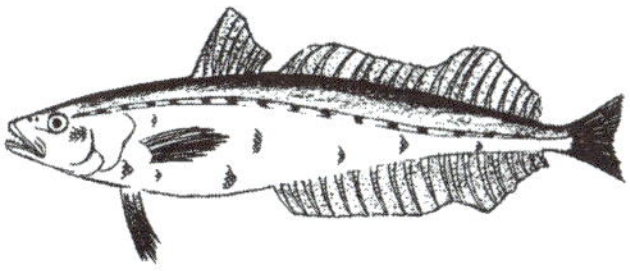

Phylum Chordata, class Actinopterygii, order Gadiformes, and family Merlucciidae, the taxonomic category of cod-like fishes, including most hakes.[176]

RESOURCE USE Presently there is no commercial fishery for silver hake in the Gulf of St. Lawrence.[177] Silver hake are harvested on the Scotian Shelf by vessels using bottom trawls. These fish are marketed as fresh, frozen, or smoked fillets.

GULF FISHES THAT FEED IN BONNE BAY

Migratory fishes that live in the Gulf of St. Lawrence but move into nearshore waters to feed during the summer may enter Bonne Bay. Examples include the Atlantic herring, Atlantic mackerel, spiny dogfish, haddock, and pollock.

Large schools of Atlantic herring are often observed in the Gulf of St. Lawrence and in coastal waters off the east and south coasts of Newfoundland. The northeast Gulf has two spawning stocks of herring: a group that spawns in the spring (April-May) and a group that spawns in the fall (August-September). Atlantic herring display a homing behavior that brings the spawning stock back to the same coastal area. Herring spawn close to the sea bed, and the eggs sink and stick to bottom substrate such as seaweed and rocks. A layer of fertilized eggs several centimetres thick may cover the sea floor. Atlantic herring spawn in St. Paul's Inlet, and the area

Wild Cove Head and waters of Outer Bonne Bay. Migratory fishes of the Gulf of St. Lawrence enter Bonne Bay to feed during the summer.

has special protection under the Fisheries Act.[178] After spawning, Atlantic herring migrate to seasonal feeding areas. Herring may enter Bonne Bay to feed during the summer and fall.

ATLANTIC HERRING

"Sea herring; Sardine (small herring)"
Clupea harengus

The Atlantic herring is a schooling fish living in the Gulf of St. Lawrence that may enter Bonne Bay to feed during the summer.

DESCRIPTION The body shape of the Atlantic herring is deeper than thick. Its scales are large and loosely attached to the body, so they slough off easily when the fish is handled. The lower jaw projects slightly beyond the upper jaw. The caudal fin is forked, and the single dorsal fin is located midway along the body.[179] Atlantic herring have a saw-tooth like keel along the belly. The body is counter shaded (dark on the back and light below) which acts to camouflage the herring in open waters. The back is steel blue with green reflections while the sides and belly are silvery. The Atlantic herring can grow to a length of about 45 centimetres.[180]

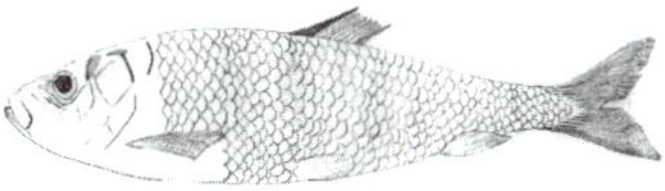

HABITAT The Atlantic herring lives in coastal waters shallower than 200 metres on both sides of the Atlantic Ocean.[181] On the western side, Atlantic herring range from southern Labrador to Cape Hatteras, North Carolina. The herring feeds by filtering seawater through its gills, trapping zooplankton (such as copepods, krill, fish eggs and larvae) on gill rakers. The plankters are then swallowed. The Atlantic herring is preyed upon by marine mammals (minke whales and harbour seals), piscivourous fish (e.g. Atlantic salmon, Atlantic cod, and Acadian redfish), and seabirds.[182]

Phylum Chordata, class Actinopterygii, order Clupeiformes, and family Clupidae, the taxonomic category that includes herrings, shads, sardines, and menhaden.[183]

RESOURCE USE There has been a fishery for Atlantic herring since ancient times. The herring fishery in Europe began circa 500 AD, and the herring fishery in North America began circa 1500 AD when a fishing fleet from France began catching herring in Newfoundland's coastal waters. Today, herring are caught using purse seines, weirs, and gillnets. There is a purse seine fishery[184] for herring in the Gulf,[185] including Bonne Bay.[186] Herring are used for both human consumption and as bait for lobster traps and crab pots. Cut herring are often used to bait the hooks of longlines set for cod. The nutritional benefits of eating herring are well known. Herring is marketed as split and smoked, but is also canned as sardines (small juvenile herring) or kippered snacks.[187] Traditionally, herring was vinegar-cured as Solomon Grundy.

Atlantic mackerel spawn in the southern Gulf around the Magdalen Islands, Prince Edward Island, and off Cape Breton during the summer. Eggs and sperm are released in open waters near the surface. After spawning, mackerel migrate north with the seasonal warming of coastal waters. Schools of Atlantic mackerel may enter Bonne Bay on their feeding migration north toward the Labrador coast.[188]

ATLANTIC MACKEREL

"Tinker (small mackerel)" *Scomber scombrus*

The Atlantic mackerel is a schooling fish living in the Gulf of St. Lawrence that may migrate into Bonne Bay to feed during the late summer.

Phylum Chordata, class Actinopterygii, order Perciformes, and family Scombridae, a classification category that includes pelagic, fast swimming fishes of tropical and temperate oceans, such as tunas.[191]

DESCRIPTION The Atlantic mackerel is streamlined, and the body tapers at the snout and tail. Mackerel have a steel-blue back with dark, wavy bands extending down to the midline of the sides. The lower sides are silvery with iridescence, and the belly is whitish. The Atlantic mackerel has distinctive finlets near the forked tail.[189] The scales are small. Atlantic mackerel can grow to a maximum length of about 55 centimetres.[190]

HABITAT The Atlantic mackerel inhabits coastal waters in the northwestern and eastern Atlantic Ocean.[192] In the northwest Atlantic, its range extends from Labrador south to Cape Hatteras, North Carolina. The Atlantic mackerel is a plankton feeder, eating copepods, fish eggs, and fish larvae. Adult mackerel will also eat small fish, such as juvenile capelin and juvenile herring. Predators of Atlantic mackerel include minke whales and harbour seals, and large seabirds such as gannets. Juvenile mackerel are eaten by Atlantic cod and squid.[193]

RESOURCE USE The Atlantic mackerel has been a commercially important fish for centuries. Historically, mackerel were harvested nearshore using weirs.[194] Today, schooling mackerel are caught in open waters using purse seines. There is a purse seine fishery for mackerel in the Gulf[195] and the Outer Basin of Bonne Bay during the summer and fall months.[196] Mackerel were traditionally marketed as pickled or salted. The Atlantic mackerel must be processed soon after catch as the fish spoils rapidly due to the high oil content of the flesh. Atlantic mackerel are marketed as frozen, dressed, smoked, and canned. Mackerel are used for bait in lobster traps and snow crab pots, and on longline hooks set for Atlantic cod. Mackerel are fished recreationally by rod and reel from wharves and piers.

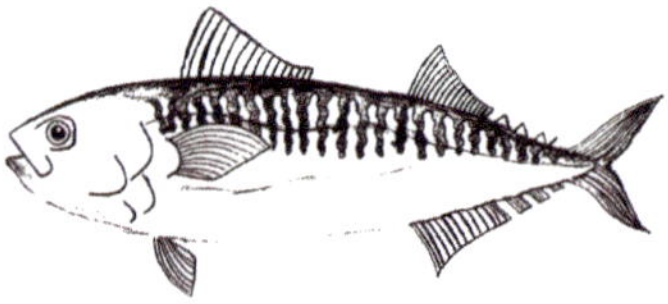

Spiny dogfish overwinter and spawn off the US northeast coast. In the spring, schools of dogfish migrate north to feed in waters off Nova Scotia and southern Newfoundland. The appearance of dogfish in the Gulf is unpredictable, but usually occurs during the warmest summer months. Spiny dogfish leave Gulf waters by late autumn and return south. Because spiny dogfish grow slowly and mature late in the life cycle, this species has a low reproductive rate. Dogfish stocks can be easily overfished. COSEWIC designated spiny dogfish as "special concern" in 2010.[197]

SPINY DOGFISH "Piked dogfish; Spurdog"

Squalus acanthias

The spiny dogfish lives off the US eastern seaboard and migrates north to coastal waters off Nova Scotia and Newfoundland to feed during the summer. This shark species has been observed in the East Arm of Bonne Bay.[198]

DESCRIPTION The spiny dogfish gets its common name from the sharp spines at the leading edge of the two dorsal fins. It does not have an anal fin, the lack of which distinguishes the spiny dogfish from other sharks in the Atlantic Ocean. The colouration of the spiny dogfish is grey over the back and sides, sometimes with a brownish tinge. The belly is white. There are rows of white spots on the back and sides.[199] The spiny dogfish has a maximum length of about 120 centimetres.[200]

HABITAT The spiny dogfish inhabits coastal waters in the western and eastern Atlantic Ocean and in the Pacific Ocean.[201] In the northwest Atlantic, its range extends from Newfoundland south to North Carolina and Virginia. The prey of spiny dogfish includes squid, crab, shrimp, and fish, especially herring and capelin. Spiny dogfish have few predators, except for larger sharks.[202]

Phylum Chordata, class Chondrichthyes, order Squaliformes, and family Squalidae. This taxonomic category includes bottom-dwelling sharks found in all the world's oceans from the Arctic to the Antarctic.[203]

RESOURCE USE Presently there is no fishery directed at spiny dogfish in the Gulf of St. Lawrence,[204] but these small sharks are often caught as bycatch in gillnets or baited line trawls.[205] The belly flap and back of the dogfish are exported to Europe and the fins are sold in Asia. Dogfish bellies are the batter-dipped fried fish in "fish and chips" served in England. Dogfish fins are used in Asian countries to make shark fin soup.

Haddock and pollock are Gulf fishes[206] that are occasionally observed feeding in Outer Bonne Bay.[207] The haddock inhabits coastal waters along both sides of the North Atlantic Ocean.[208] In the northwest Atlantic, haddock range from the Strait of Belle Isle eastward to the Grand Banks and south to Cape Cod. Haddock spawn in the spring on the continental shelf. The haddock preys upon small fish such as sand lance and juvenile herring, but it mainly feeds along the sea bottom on crustaceans such as amphipods, shrimp, and crabs. Offshore stocks of haddock in Atlantic Canada are fished using otter trawls, but gill-nets are also used.[209] Haddock in the Gulf of St. Lawrence and on the Grand Banks were severely overfished by offshore trawlers during the 1950s and 1960s.[210] There has been no apparent rebuilding of haddock stocks on the Grand Banks.[211] Haddock is marketed as fresh and frozen fillets. Traditionally haddock were sold headless, split, and smoked as "Finnan haddie."

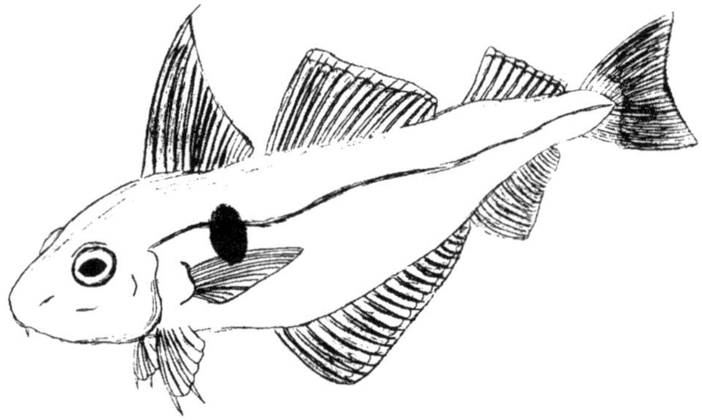

Schools of haddock from the Gulf are sometimes observed feeding in the Outer Basin of Bonne Bay. The haddock has a distinctive dark spot like a "thumbprint" above each pectoral fin and a dark lateral line.[212]

The pollock is found in northern waters of the North Atlantic Ocean. In European coastal waters, the pollock is known as "saithe."[213] In the northwest Atlantic, pollock range from southern Labrador to Cape Cod and are most abundant in coastal waters from Maine to Nova Scotia, but schools may migrate north into the Gulf of St. Lawrence. Pollock spawn in coastal waters during late fall or early winter. The pollock eats smaller fish and crustaceans near the sea bottom and preys upon krill and squid near the sea surface. The inshore fishery for pollock uses gillnets and baited longlines.[214] Schools of pollock in coastal waters may be encircled and caught using purse seines while the offshore fishery for pollock is conducted by large fishing vessels towing pelagic trawl nets. Pollock can be caught near the shoreline by recreational anglers using lures. Marketed as fresh or frozen fillets or processed as breaded portions of "Boston bluefish" or fish sticks, pollock can also be dried and salted, similar to salt codfish.

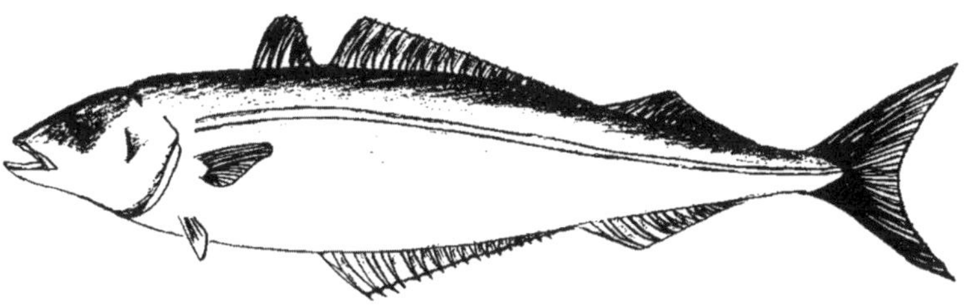

Schools of migrating pollock are sometimes observed feeding in the Outer Basin of Bonne Bay. The pollock has three dorsal fins and two anal fins, similar to its relatives the haddock and the Atlantic cod.[215]

OCEANIC FISHES THAT OCCASIONALLY VISIT BONNE BAY

The last component of the fish fauna of Bonne Bay is the group of highly migratory oceanic fishes of the North Atlantic[216] that may stray into the Gulf of St. Lawrence and occasionally visit Bonne Bay. There have been sightings in Bonne Bay of North Atlantic saury, ocean sunfish, Atlantic bluefin tuna, and swordfish.[217]

The North Atlantic saury is a subtropical oceanic species and is rarely found in northern coastal waters, except when schools stray during the annual northward migration with warming of surface ocean waters during the summer. In some years, Atlantic saury will swim into the southern Gulf of St. Lawrence and may enter Bonne Bay. Atlantic saury spawn in tropical waters during the winter and early spring. The eggs are released near the surface and develop as they drift with the ocean currents.[218]

NORTH ATLANTIC SAURY

"Needlefish; Skipper"

Scomberesox saurus

The North Atlantic saury is an oceanic fish that occasionally strays into the Gulf of St. Lawrence and sometimes into Bonne Bay in late summer. This dead specimen was found on a beach near Norris Point.

Phylum Chordata, class Actinopterygii, order Beloniformes, and family Scomberesocidae, the taxonomic category of surface-dwelling, oceanic fishes which are widely distributed in warm waters of the Atlantic, Pacific, and Indian oceans.[223]

DESCRIPTION The body is elongate and tapered at both ends. The jaws are long and slender with the lower jaw slightly prolonged more than the upper jaw, giving the North Atlantic saury its nickname of "needlefish." There are finlets behind the dorsal fin and the anal fin.[219] The caudal fin is forked. The colouration of the Atlantic saury is olive green on the back with silvery sides. The Atlantic saury can grow to a maximum length of about 50 centimetres.[220]

HABITAT The Atlantic saury is a subtropical species, found in warm surface waters of the Atlantic Ocean.[221] The Atlantic saury eats copepods, krill, and the planktonic eggs and larvae of other fishes. It has a second nickname, "skipper," because it will skip along the surface of the water to escape predators such as tunas, dolphins, and porpoises. In the Gulf of St. Lawrence, the saury may be preyed upon by Atlantic cod.[222]

RESOURCE USE Because its presence in the waters of Atlantic Canada is sporadic, there is no commercial fishery for North Atlantic saury.[224] However, the flesh is tasty.

View of Pinnacle Rock and the Outer Basin of Bonne Bay. Oceanic fishes of the North Atlantic such as ocean sunfish, bluefin tuna, swordfish, and Atlantic saury may stray into the Gulf of St. Lawrence and occasionally visit Bonne Bay.

The ocean sunfish lives in tropical and temperate waters in both the Atlantic and Pacific oceans.[225] It is not a common inhabitant of Atlantic Canadian coastal waters, occurring only as an occasional visitor in the summer months. Sunfish sometimes stray into the Gulf of St. Lawrence and Bonne Bay. The ocean sunfish drifts with ocean currents, but is capable of strong swimming and can display the unusual behavior of swimming lazily on its side near the sea surface.[226]

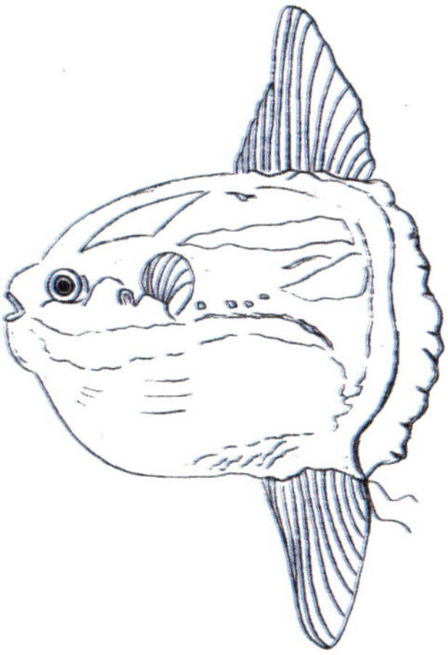

The ocean sunfish is a warm water species of the Atlantic and Pacific Oceans that may stray into the Gulf of St. Lawrence and occasionally appear in the Outer Basin of Bonne Bay. The ocean sunfish has a laterally compressed body and appears to be missing a full tail. The sunfish can grow to more than three metres in length and weigh almost 1500 kilograms.[227]

Another occasional visitor to the Outer Basin of Bonne Bay is the bluefin tuna. Bluefin tuna are found at low latitudes in both the Atlantic Ocean and Pacific Ocean. For bluefin tuna living in the Atlantic Ocean, the main spawning grounds are the Mediterrean Sea and the Gulf of Mexico.[228] After spawning in the Gulf of Mexico, some bluefin tuna will migrate to coastal waters of Atlantic Canada to feed on mackerel, herring, squid, and capelin. Bluefin tuna may be present in the Gulf of St. Lawrence during the summer and might follow schools of prey into Bonne Bay.

The commercial fishery for bluefin tuna in the waters of Atlantic Canada is open between July and November. Bluefin are caught using baited hooks attached to floating longlines. Bluefin tuna are marketed fresh or frozen. Raw bluefin is used in Japanese sashimi, highly favored for its fish oil content and dark red flesh. The bluefin tuna is a prized sports fish,[229] and in Prince Edward Island and Nova Scotia, fishing tournaments for bluefin are held. The fish caught by rod and reel are then sold as part of Canada's commercial fishery quota. A catch-and-release charter sports fishery for bluefin may also be held in the Gulf of St. Lawrence,

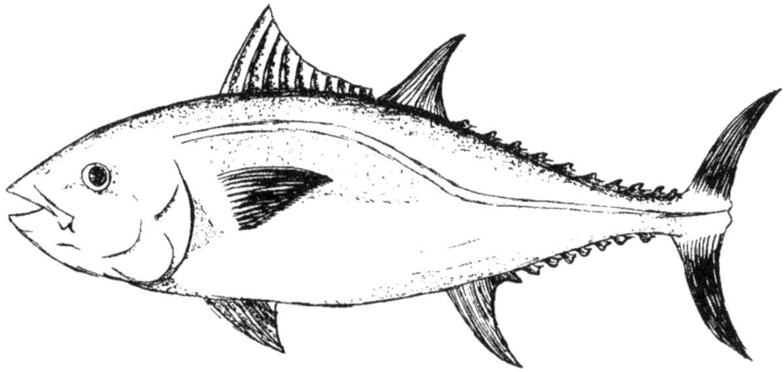

The Atlantic bluefin tuna is an oceanic species that feeds in the Gulf during the summer and may follow schools of prey into the Outer Basin of Bonne Bay. The body of the bluefin tuna is streamlined and nearly round in cross section. Bluefin can grow to 4 metres in length and weigh over 650 kilograms.[230]

if the annual catch quota permits.[231] Due to the severe decline in the abundance of Atlantic bluefin tuna and the low numbers of spawners, this fish was designated by COSEWIC as an endangered species.[232] The bluefin tuna is not protected by SARA.

Like bluefin tuna, swordfish are sometimes observed in the Outer Basin of Bonne Bay. The swordfish is found throughout the tropical and temperate oceans of the world.[233] After spawning in tropical and subtropical waters, the swordfish migrates to northern waters to feed. The fish uses its bill or "sword" to stun or kill prey, which includes squid, mackerel, and saury. Swordfish appear in the waters of Atlantic Canada, including the Grand Banks and the Gulf of St. Lawrence, during the summer and fall months of the year. Swordfish are fished both commercially on the Scotian Shelf and the Grand Banks of Newfoundland and recreationally in coastal waters for sport.[234] In the past, swordfish were caught by harpooning the fish basking on the surface of the ocean, but today swordfish are caught primarily using baited hooks attached to floating longlines. Swordfish are marketed as fresh or frozen fillets.

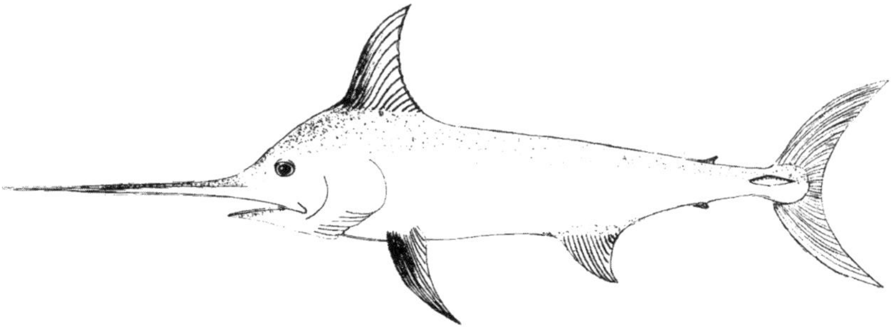

The swordfish is a warm water species of the Atlantic and Pacific Oceans that has been occasionally observed in the Outer Basin of Bonne Bay. The upper jaw bone of the swordfish develops into a long, flat, sword-like rostrum. Swordfish can grow to a length of 4.5 metres (including the "sword") and weigh up to 540 kilograms.[235]

In the past, sea ice in the Gulf of St. Lawrence impeded shipping traffic and required icebreakers to keep the shipping lanes open. (PHOTOGRAPH BY ALAIN FRÉCHET)

A CHANGING MARINE ECOSYSTEM

4

By its very nature, the marine environment is constantly changing. The land, ocean, and atmosphere exchange heat from solar radiation on daily, seasonal, and annual time scales. This heat exchange gives rise to local weather, seasonal warming and cooling, and regional climates. Change in the earth's climatic state occurs naturally on time scales of thousands to millions of years due to small variations in solar radiation warming the planet. Throughout the earth's existence, there have been alternate periods of warm and cool climate. But the current change in the earth's climate is taking place at an unnatural rate. Human activity on earth is affecting the exchange of heat and elements—such as carbon dioxide—between the land, sea, and air. The global average atmospheric temperature is climbing above the range of normal variation.[1]

Nearly everyone recognizes that weather patterns and regional climates are changing. Regions of the earth where high rainfall is normal are experiencing floods more often; desert regions of the earth are experiencing longer periods of drought. The Arctic and Subarctic regions are experiencing greater heating during the summer while the formation of sea ice in the Arctic Ocean during the winter is decreasing. Permafrost is melting in some Arctic lands,[2] and the melting of glaciers is contributing to a rising sea level.

People living in coastal communities are witnessing more extreme coastal flooding during storms. Wharfs and roads along shorelines are being swamped more often by strong onshore winds driving seawater ashore at high tide. In 2010, Hurricane Igor caused over $100 million in damage to infrastructure on the island of Newfoundland. The coastline near Daniel's Harbour, just north of Gros Morne National Park, was seriously eroded by storm lashed waves at high tide. Hurricane Sandy, the "Superstorm" of 2012, was the largest storm recorded to move up the eastern seaboard of the US, causing $16 billion in damage and taking many lives.

A WARMING OCEAN CLIMATE

Like other coastal waters of Canada, the Gulf of St. Lawrence is changing. A prominent environmental feature of the Gulf is the presence of sea ice in winter. International ship traffic through the St. Lawrence Seaway can be halted by thick ice, requiring Canadian Coast Guard icebreakers to keep the shipping lanes open.

There has always been year-to-year variation in the date of freeze-up, the maximum thickness of the sea ice, the extent of the ice cover in the Gulf, and the date of spring thaw. Bonne Bay is normally covered by ice during February and March, but in recent years the formation of landfast ice in the early winter has been delayed.[3] The thickness of the ice layer over Bonne Bay has decreased, and the melting of the ice comes earlier in the spring. In most recent years, the bay has not frozen over during the winter. Warmer winters with less snow have affected people's winter activities, particularly snowmobiling for recreation. While thin sea ice on Bonne Bay is a danger to snowmobilers who attempt to travel across the bay, the change in seasonal ice formation signals an even larger problem.

A warming ocean climate[4] is likely affecting the marine ecosystem of Bonne Bay. The seaweeds and marine animals of the bay are adapted to a cold-temperate environment. If the local oceanographic conditions change too quickly, many species may not be able to tolerate the new extremes in seawater temperature and will decline in abundance or possibly disappear from the bay altogether.

Continued warming of the waters would result in the decline in abundance of some subarctic species and an increase in abundance of temperate species in the bay.[5]

For example, consider the anadromous Arctic char which, in the past, was found in coastal waters along the west coast of Newfoundland.[6] Arctic char inhabit the cold highland lakes of Gros Morne National Park[7] but are absent in surveys of the nearshore waters of Bonne Bay[8] and offshore waters of the Gulf.[9] The waters of Bonne Bay are likely too warm today for Arctic char to tolerate. There is an anadromous Arctic char population at the tip of the Northern Peninsula of Newfoundland (the Arctic char in Parker's Brook, a river that runs into Pistolet Bay),[10] but the Strait of Belle Isle is now considered the southern latitudinal limit of the range of this species.[11]

The presence of sea ice in the Gulf of St. Lawrence during winter is becoming less common. (PHOTOGRAPH BY ALAIN FRÉCHET)

ARCTIC CHAR "Blueback trout"
Salvelinus alpinus

An Arctic char collected from Gilbert Bay, Labrador.[12] There are landlocked Arctic char in highland streams of Gros Morne National Park, but no sea-run Arctic char have been collected in Bonne Bay. The waters of the bay are apparently too warm for this anadromous subarctic fish to tolerate. (PHOTOGRAPH BY DAVID METHVEN)

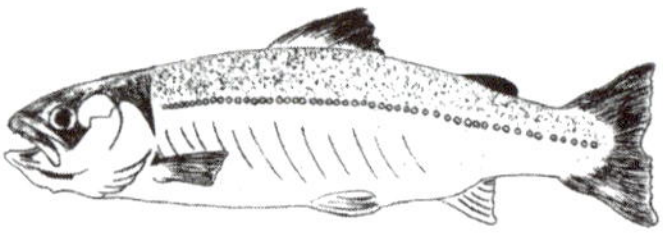

DESCRIPTION The body shape of the Arctic char is spindle-like. The lower jaw protrudes slightly. A dorsal adipose fin is present. The pectoral, pelvic, and anal fins are white along the leading edge, and the caudal fin is slightly forked. Non-spawning char are blue green or bluish on the back, silvery blue on the sides, and whitish on the lower sides and belly. Sea-run char are bright silvery while char in spawning condition are highly coloured. Spawning males have silvery-blue sides with large reddish spots and an orange-red belly.[13]

Phylum Chordata, class Actinopterygii, order Salmoniformes, and family Salmonidae, the taxomonic group of freshwater fishes, known as "salmonids."[15] The Arctic char is among the salmonid species that migrate to the sea to feed and then return to freshwater to spawn and are therefore called anadromous.

HABITAT The Arctic char has a circumpolar distribution in the Northern Hemisphere. Populations of Arctic char in lakes and rivers of North America, northern Europe, northern Asia, Iceland, and Greenland may be landlocked or anadromous if there is passage to the sea. Unlike salmon, Arctic char cannot surmount waterfalls.[14] After several years of growth in rivers or lakes, members of anadromous populations will move downstream into coastal waters to feed for several months during the summer, and these fish do not stray more than a few kilometres from the river mouth. Sea-run char return to freshwater in the fall. Spawning occurs in the natal river.

There are landlocked Arctic char populations in cold highland lakes in the Long Range Mountains of insular Newfoundland.[16] The most southern anadromous Arctic char population can be found in the watershed of Pistolet Bay on the tip of the Northern Peninsula and the area has special protection under the Fisheries Act.[17]

RESOURCE USE The Arctic char is a prized catch for recreational anglers. Trophy-sized char can be 90 centimetres long and weigh 12 kilograms. There is a subsistence food fishery for Arctic char conducted by aboriginal groups in Labrador.

With increased warming of the marine environment, one would expect temperate fishes inhabiting Bonne Bay (e.g. cunner, grubby, and longhorn sculpin) to become more abundant due to improved conditions for survival of their young and faster growth. One might also see more frequent appearances of the occasional summer visitors to Bonne Bay (e.g. the leatherback turtle, loggerhead turtle, ocean sunfish, Atlantic bluefin tuna, swordfish, and North Atlantic saury).

The loss of a species which cannot adapt to changing environmental conditions can have consequences for the stability of the local ecosystem. Each marine species has a role to play in the functioning of that marine ecosystem. A reduction in the number of species in the ecological system, or loss of biodiversity, could mean that the ecological system remaining does not function as previously. For example, the marine ecosystem's efficiency at turning sunlight energy into commercially-important fish biomass may be reduced, and people should be concerned when species are at risk of disappearing from a region of the sea.[18]

OCEAN ACIDIFICATION

A threat to the functioning of the marine ecosystem associated with global warming is "ocean acidification." Since the beginning of the Industrial Revolution, people have been significantly polluting the earth's atmosphere with carbon dioxide (CO_2) by burning coal and oil. Some of this CO_2 has moved from the atmosphere into the earth's ocean, raising the acidity of seawater. This is known as the "second CO_2 problem" with the first CO_2 problem, of course, being the greenhouse effect of carbon dioxide.[19]

The increased acidity of ocean surface waters could prevent many calcareous plankton species such as foramifera and pteropods from forming their tiny shells. In an acidic ocean, these species could no longer exist in the marine food chain. Ocean acidification threatens the future survival of coral reefs, calcareous marine algae, and commercially important bivalve molluscs with shells made of calcium carbonate.

A significantly increased acidity of the marine environment of Bonne Bay could prevent coralline red algae (or "live rock") from forming calcium carbonate stony crusts. Coralline red algae grow on the rocky bottoms of Bonne Bay down to depths of about 15-20 metres where sunlight becomes insufficient to allow growth of these marine algae. Coralline red algae play an important role in the Bonne Bay ecosystem, providing marine animals with shelter from predators. Small fish hide behind the branches of coralline algae and feed on the invertebrates (e.g. polychaete worms,

CORALLINE RED ALGAE

"Live rock" *Lithothamnion sp.*

"Live rock" is the nickname for various species of corraline red algae. Coralline algae species (e.g. *Lithothamnion glaciale*) can grow as a thin layer over rock (left) or grow with branches (right). Both growth forms are found in Bonne Bay.

Phylum Rhodophyta.[20] Coralline red algae have deposits of calcium carbonate in the cell walls.

DESCRIPTION Coralline red algae will encrust rock. Unattached specimens have branches and form compact balls (called "rhodoliths") that may roll on the sea bottom along with strong currents. The colouration of coralline algae is typically pink or reddish. Identification of coralline red algae to species often requires examination with a microscope.

HABITAT Coralline red algae are found in all oceans of the world, growing in the intertidal zone and in subtidal waters down to the depth of maximum penetration of sunlight available for photosynthesis.[21]

RESOURCE USE The calcium carbonate structures formed on the sea bottom by coralline red algae provide many small marine organisms with shelter from predation. Small juvenile Atlantic cod will hide amongst the branches of rhodoliths.[22] Coralline algae are eaten by sea urchins and limpets. These algal species are threatened by "ocean acidification" and would not be able to form their calcium carbonate structures in an acidic ocean.

chitons, and bryozoans) living in the crevices of the live rock. Under extreme conditions of ocean acidification, live rock could no longer exist.

Acidification of the ocean is happening globally, but countries like Canada, which are located at higher latitudes, are particularly at risk. CO_2 moves from the atmosphere into the ocean more easily where the seawater is colder because the gas molecule is more soluble in cold water. The Arctic and Subarctic coastal waters of Canada, including the cold-temperate waters of Bonne Bay, will likely see changes in the marine ecosystem due to ocean acidification sooner than other regions of the earth's oceans.

INVASIVE SPECIES

Human activity can inadvertently introduce non-native species to a local ecosystem. The flushing of ballast water by tankers transporting goods across the North Atlantic Ocean is an example. Tankers loading cargo in European ports take on seawater for ballast. This ballast water has marine plankton from the eastern North Atlantic. If that seawater is flushed by tankers when entering North American ports, non-native plankton are introduced into North American coastal waters. Invasive species have arrived in US coastal waters by this route, and a particularly problematic example is the European green crab.[23]

The European green crab was introduced to coastal waters of the northeastern US several decades ago, most likely by tankers from Europe flushing ballast water which held green crab larvae. The green crab has moved northward from the Gulf of Maine to the coastal waters of Nova Scotia with the general warming of the ocean. The green crab is a concern since it competes with economically valuable crustacean species such as lobster for both food and habitat. A predator of bivalve molluscs (such as the soft shell clam and the blue mussel), the green crab digs up eelgrass beds in its hunt for prey. This invasive species has recently appeared in the coastal waters of western and southern Newfoundland. It has been discovered in St. Georges Bay, just to the south of Bonne Bay.[24] In 2011, the carapace (exoskeleton shed during moulting) of a green crab was found along the beach near Norris Cove. Live green crabs were observed in the intertidal zone of Bonne Bay a year later.

EUROPEAN GREEN CRAB

Carcinus maenas

The European green crab is an invasive species now living in nearshore waters of Bonne Bay.

Phylum Anthropoda, class Malacostraca, order Decapoda, and family Portunidae.[26]

DESCRIPTION The European green crab has four pairs of walking legs (last pair flattened but not paddle-shaped) and two claws of similar size. Its colouration is bright green or dark green above and yellowish below. Adult females are red orange below. The European green crab can be distinguished from other crabs by the five notch points along the edge of the carapace on each side, located between the eye and the widest part of the shell. The green crab grows to a maximum size of about 9 centimetres carapace width.[25]

HABITAT The native habitat of the European green crab is the intertidal zone of British and northern European coastal waters. It was inadvertantly introduced (likely at the larval stage in ballast water flushed by tankers) to the coastal waters of the US eastern seaboard, Brazil, Panama, the Suez Canal, Australia, and Hawaii. The European green crab has spread north from New England waters to the Bay of Fundy and to Newfoundland waters.[27] This crab species is a voracious predator of mussels and clams. It burrows into the mud sediment of eelgrass beds in search of clams and damages the seagrass. As eelgrass beds are an important habitat for juvenile fishes, the destruction of eelgrass habitat caused by the green crab is of concern to fisheries managers.

RESOURCE USE The meat of the European crab is edible, but presently is not considered marketable.

Another invasive species that can affect the usual functioning of the marine ecosystem of the Gulf of St. Lawrence and the productivity of Gulf fisheries is the "Lacy crust." "Lacy crusts" is a taxonomic group of tiny marine animals called bryozoans that settle on rocks, submerged wood, seaweeds, and sea grasses. Individual bryozoans join together in colonies that resemble a white lace.[28] If there are too many encrusting colonies of bryozoans on a kelp blade (i.e. the brown seaweeds of the order Laminariales), the invader can weaken the seaweed and reduce its growth rate.[29] Loss of kelp would have a negative effect on the habitat of many juvenile fishes in nearshore waters. Lacy crusts have been found on kelp along the west coast of Newfoundland, including Bonne Bay. [30]

LACY CRUSTS "Coffin box"

Membranipora membranacea

Numerous colonies of the bryozoan species *Membranipora membranacea* encrusting a kelp. The colonies resemble patches of white lace, hence the common name. This invasive species has been found in nearshore waters of Bonne Bay. (PHOTOGRAPH BY PATRICK GAGNON)

DESCRIPTION This bryozoan species is only about 0.5 millimetres in length and lives within a coffin-box-like chamber that it secretes, hence the nickname "coffin box." Individual bryozoans join together to form colonies that encrust solid marine substrates. These colonies may be several centimetres in size and appear as patches of white lace.

HABITAT "Lacy crust" bryozoans can be found on nearly all types of marine bottom substrate (e.g. rocks, shells, wood pilings, seaweeds, and sea grasses) with the exception of sand and mud sea bottoms.[31] Bryozoans feed on microscopic plankton filtered from seawater using ciliated tentacles. Bryozoans reproduce by shedding eggs that develop into planktonic larvae. The larvae settle on suitable substrate and metamorphose into polyp-like zooids.[33] Individuals bud asexually to form a colony.

"Lacy crusts" is a taxonomic group of bryozoans (animal phylum Bryozoa) which form crusts on solid marine substrates.[32]

RESOURCE USE Lacy crust bryozoans are bio-fouling organisms. Bio-fouling of man-made structures has a negative effect on continued efficient use. For example, a ship's hull severely fouled by barnacles and seaweed has an increased drag through the water which reduces ship speed. Wood-boring marine worms weaken wharf pilings. However, all bio-fouling organisms, including lacy crust bryozoans, have ecosystem value as part of the marine food chain.[34]

MARINE WILDLIFE AT RISK OF DISAPPEARING FROM BONNE BAY

Commercial fishing since the middle of the last century has depleted a third of all the fish stocks on earth. Overfishing the top predators in a marine ecosystem (such as tunas, sharks, and cods) can change the food chain dynamics and the equilibrium of the entire ecosystem.[35]

There are several marine reptile, mammal, and fish species living in the Gulf of St. Lawrence, including Bonne Bay, which are at risk of disappearing due to fishing activity. There has been no commercial hunting of whales in Canadian coastal waters for several decades, except for aboriginal subsistence hunts for bowhead, beluga, and narwhal.[36] However, sea turtles, whales, and seals can become entangled in commercial fishing gear and drown.

The harbour porpoise is relatively abundant along Canada's east coast, but the species was assessed by COSEWIC and assigned a status of "special concern" in 2006. The main reason for concern is the susceptibility of the harbour porpoise to entanglement in fishing gear, especially gillnets.

Harbour porpoise are sometimes unintentionally caught in gillnets set for fish. This young porpoise was returned to the water unharmed.

And there are several species of fish which are in danger of disappearing from the Gulf and Bonne Bay due to fishing activities. The fish fauna of Bonne Bay includes the Laurentian North population of Atlantic cod designated by COSEWIC as "endangered" of becoming extirpated.

The fish fauna of Bonne Bay includes Atlantic cod from the Laurentian North population designated by COSEWIC as "endangered." However, Atlantic cod are not protected under Canada's Species at Risk Act.

Two wolffish species living in Bonne Bay that are threatened by fishing activity are the Atlantic wolffish and the spotted wolffish. These two species are not targeted by fishers, but rather are caught as bycatch in the lobster fishery, the snow crab fishery, and groundfish fisheries. Wolffish will enter a lobster pot or crab pot to eat the bait intended to attract the decapod crustaceans. In past years, fishers were allowed to keep wolffish to eat personally or sell, as the flesh of wolffish is firm and tasty. However, due to the decline in the number of wolffish in certain marine areas, the Government of Canada has protected Atlantic wolffish, spotted wolffish, and northern wolffish under Canada's Species at Risk Act (SARA), and fishers should return wolffish bycatch to the water alive.[37] There is some flexibility in SARA and DFO regulations which allow Atlantic wolffish unintentionally caught to be landed. However, spotted wolffish and northern wolffish must be released from fishing gear with minimal harm.[38]

The genetically distinctive population of Acadian redfish living in the East Arm of Bonne Bay[39] is designated by COSEWIC as "special concern." Redfish are sometimes caught unintentionally in a gillnet set for cod or in a purse seine set for herring in the East Arm. Fish species listed as "species-at-risk" often have a biological characteristic that make them susceptible to population decline: a specialized habitat or diet, a limited geographic range, or a large body size that makes capture by humans easier. In the case of Bonne Bay's redfish population, it is the small geographic range. The local redfish population is apparently confined to the area (about 70 km^2) of the East Arm of Bonne Bay.

An Atlantic wolffish unintentionally caught in a lobster trap set in Bonne Bay. The Atlantic wolffish, spotted wolffish, and northern wolffish are protected under Canada's Species at Risk Act. (PHOTOGRAPH BY JENNIFER DAWE)

The genetically distinctive population of Acadian redfish living in the East Arm of Bonne Bay is designated by COSEWIC as "special concern." Redfish are sometimes unintentionally caught in gillnets set by commercial fishermen for cod in Bonne Bay.

Angling for Atlantic salmon in Deer Brook. The Atlantic salmon is a prized sport fish, famous for its fighting ability when hooked on an artificial fly cast by rod and reel.

STEWARDSHIP OF BONNE BAY

5

Bonne Bay exists today in a near-natural state, except for the impact of fishing on the marine ecosystem of the bay[1] and localized pollution of nearshore waters by oil spills and sewage discharge from houses without septic tanks.[2] Oil pollution, in the form of unintentional leaks of gasoline from pleasure boats and diesel oil in bilge water discharged from fishing boats, is a common problem in coastal waters.

RESPONSIBLE RECREATIONAL FISHING

One can enjoy the unspoiled nature of Bonne Bay by simply walking along the shoreline or engaging in recreational boating or fishing. Atlantic salmon pass through Bonne Bay on their return to natal spawning grounds in either the Lomond River or Deer Brook. Fly fishermen cast for them as the fish journey upstream.

Parks Canada is responsible for monitoring the abundance of Atlantic salmon and brook trout for which recreational fishing is permitted in Gros Morne National Park.[3] Park employees will periodically construct a counting fence across the mouth of a river to monitor the upstream and downstream migrations of these anadromous fishes.

The federal Department of Fisheries and Oceans Canada (DFO) is responsible for the management of Atlantic salmon throughout Newfoundland and Labrador. The recreational fishery for Atlantic salmon can be closed by DFO if low water levels prevent salmon from moving up the rivers to spawn.

A fish counting fence at Deer Brook constructed by Parks Canada personnel to monitor the upstream and downstream migrations of Atlantic salmon and sea-run brook trout.

A large salmon in the holding box of the counting fence at Deer Brook operated by Parks Canada to monitor the number of salmon returning from the sea to spawn in Deer Brook. (PHOTOGRAPH BY CRAIG PURCHASE)

Deer Brook is sometimes closed to recreational fishing when low water levels and warm temperatures stress migrating salmon. When rain returns water levels to normal, the salmon will move up the brook to spawn.

RESPONSIBLE COMMERCIAL FISHING

The viability of coastal fishing communities is dependent on the health of fisheries resources, and Fisheries and Oceans Canada has the mandate of maintaining the productivity of Canada's fisheries. Recent progressive changes in federal government fisheries management policy have given coastal communities a voice in the management of marine resources upon which they depend. Throughout the world today, fishing communities and conservation groups are working with municipal governments, provincial governments, and federal governments to establish local stewardship of coastal fisheries resources.[4] This local stewardship approach has the potential to work particularly well for local stocks of finfish and shellfish species that do not migrate.

The Canadian Coast Guard vessel *Cape Fox* in Bonne Bay. The vessel is used for fisheries patrol as well as search and rescue missions.

The people of coastal communities will adopt a stewardship attitude toward the marine environment if they are convinced the local marine resources are their own, for example the lobster stock and snow crab stock in Bonne Bay.[5] Lobster fishermen living in Norris Point and Woody Point know from experience that Bonne Bay lobsters rarely move outside the bay. That local knowledge is based on years of fishers' observation of the catch rates of lobster pots placed along the outside boundary of the bay. As the lobsters in Bonne Bay apparently do not move outside the bay, these harvesters therefore have a vested interest in promoting a sustainable local fishery.

On the other hand, coastal community-based stewardship of a fishery resource is less encouraged if the fish stock migrates long distances and crosses a fishery management zone. Consider for example the migrating schools of Atlantic mackerel that enter Bonne Bay to feed. A fisherman using a seine net to catch mackerel in Bonne Bay knows that if he doesn't catch the school in Bonne Bay, the migrating school will likely be caught by other fishers further along the mackerel migration path. This impediment to fisheries conservation is known as "the fisherman's dilemma." However, for local stocks of non-migratory finfish and shellfish in bays and estuaries, conservation can contribute significantly to achieving a sustainable fishery. A "sustainable fishery" in this context is where the local harvest is balanced by the ability of the local stock to replenish itself biologically.[6]

A temporary moratorium on fishing snow crab in Bonne Bay was an initiative led by fisherpersons living in Norris Point and Woody Point.[7] Establishment of a lobster conservation area in Trout River Bay on the southwestern boundary of Gros Morne National Park was initiated by local harvesters, another example of stewardship of a local shellfish stock.[8] Lobster conservation initiatives undertaken with local support include closed fishing areas, lobster size limits, and the release of reproductive female lobsters.[9]

Marine life is lost with the destruction of marine habitat. The diversity of fishes found in Bonne Bay is directly related to the wide range of habitats available to support marine life in the bay.[10] Conserving the shallow nursery grounds of marine fishes requires the prevention of pollution along the shoreline of the bay. Lobsters live in the same habitat as many fish species in these waters. Therefore, protection of fish habitat in Bonne Bay will also protect lobster grounds.

Protecting the marine ecosystem from pollution is the responsibility of the Federal Government of Canada. But people who utilize Bonne Bay for commercial fishing, recreational fishing, pleasure boating, and subsistence harvesting of seafood also have a responsibility to help protect the marine ecosystem. The Federal Fisheries Act[11] prohibits the harmful alteration or destruction of fish habitat. Fisheries and Oceans Canada supports community-based efforts to conserve and restore fish habitats in both marine and freshwater environments.

Bonne Bay is a spawning ground and nursery ground for Atlantic cod.[12] LEFT PHOTO: Student Jennifer Dawe holding a female Atlantic cod in spawning condition collected from Deer Arm of Bonne Bay. The fish was released alive and unharmed.[13] RIGHT PHOTO: Juvenile Atlantic cod collected from nearshore waters of Norris Cove in the East Arm.

Protecting the nearshore waters of Bonne Bay will help rebuild Gulf of St. Lawrence fish stocks which use Bonne Bay as a breeding ground and nursery ground. In the case of Atlantic cod, a good fishery depends upon the survival of cod larvae in the plankton as well as the survival of young cod after settlement to the sea bottom. The survival of juvenile cod living near the seafloor depends on the availability of food and shelter. Juvenile cod occupy a range of habitats in Bonne Bay as young cod can be found in nearshore waters living amongst various seaweed species and over different types of sea bottom. Cod would benefit from protection of the entire shoreline of Bonne Bay from human-induced disturbance and pollution.

Both commercial and recreational fishers can help conserve the marine resources of Bonne Bay by adhering to fishing regulations and avoiding the loss of fishing gear that could entangle fish and marine mammals.[14]

ENSURING LOCAL FOOD SECURITY

Conservation of the fisheries resources of Bonne Bay helps ensure the food security of adjacent coastal communities. "Food security" refers to economically available local foods that are nutritious and meet the cultural preferences of local people.[15] Locally-produced foods are nutritious and promote good health, especially for growing young people.[16] Seafood is rich in omega-3 fatty acids, compounds known to reduce the risk of cardiovascular disease in older people. Wild berries contain vitamins and antioxidants that promote human health, especially vision.[17]

Historically, food production by coastal people followed a seasonal pattern. The harvest of fish from the sea and vegetables from subsistence gardens in the summer was followed by the hunting of game and picking of wild berries in the fall. Hares were trapped in winter, and seals were hunted on sea ice in the early spring.

Food harvested from the sea included seaweeds (e.g. kelp), shellfish (e.g. scallops, mussels, shrimp, lobster, snow crab) and fish (e.g. cod, mackerel, herring, salmon). Cod was the main fish harvested for over 200 years. The production of salt cod was historically important before modern refrigeration, but continues today in relatively small amounts.[18]

Drying salted cod hung near lobster traps stored on a wharf. Cod too small for filleting are dressed and salted for preservation. Boiled salt cod served with hard bread is a popular meal during the winter months. (PHOTOGRAPH BY BY ARNAULT LE BRIS)

Recipes for heritage foods such as cod-head chowder and fried cod tongues and sounds (the swim bladder) are still available.[19]

Subsistence gardening of root vegetables, hunting for game meat (moose and snowshoe hare), angling for fish (cod, salmon, trout), and berry-picking are still today important aspects of life for people living in coastal Newfoundland communities.[20] The eider duck and other sea ducks, two species of seabird (the thick-billed murr and the common murr, locally known as "turr"[21]), and one species of marine mammal (the harp seal) can still be legally hunted. Hunting is not permitted within the boundaries of Gros Morne National Park, except with special permit.[22] But lands adjacent to the Park have good hunting. Wild berries gathered from heaths, barrens, woods, and rocky headlands of the coastline include crowberry (locally known as blackberry), alpine bilberry (blueberry), partridgeberry (lingonberry or redberry), and cloudberry (bakeapple). The berries are used in pies, tarts, and jams.

People who grow their own vegetables and consume foods harvested from the land and the sea are less dependent on transported goods and are therefore more food-secure. Traditional foods are an important component of the diet of the people of the Bonne Bay region even today. Research has shown that the social and human health of coastal communities is closely linked with residents maintaining their traditional diet of nutritious local foods.[23]

Traditional harvest of food from the land includes berry picking. Cloudberry, locally known as bakeapple, is an Arctic plant[24] that grows in bogs throughout Gros Morne National Park region. The berry is boiled and eaten with sugar and cream during the winter. (PHOTOGRAPH BY BY ARNAULT LE BRIS)

SUSTAINABLE RECREATIONAL USE

Stewardship of the environment of Bonne Bay and the surrounding Gros Morne National Park is instilled in people when they experience firsthand the wonders of nature, as during recreational boating, sailing, and kayaking on Bonne Bay. Hiking the highlands in the Park provides one with spectacular views of the bay and the Gulf of St. Lawrence.

Pleasure boating on Bonne Bay instills stewardship of the bay and the surrounding lands of Gros Morne National Park.

Experiencing nature by kayaking on Bonne Bay.

Ecotourism is important to the economies of the coastal communities adjacent to the Park. Some residents maintain a livelihood by working in both the commercial fishing industry and the ecotourism industry. "Fishing-tourism" is a new development in the travel industry where visitors learn about the local fishing industry, talk with fisher persons, and perhaps even take a trip on a fishing boat.[25]

MARINE SCIENCE EDUCATION PROMOTES STEWARDSHIP

Public knowledge about the environment is the foundation of stewardship of nature. The public education programs held annually at the Bonne Bay Marine Station[26] help to inform people about the marine life of Bonne Bay. The station has a marine science education program directed toward grade school students and tourists. People learn about the many species of seaweed and marine animals present in the bay, that many of these species are commercially and recreationally valuable and contribute to local food security, and that Bonne Bay is an

important nursery ground for many Gulf of St. Lawrence fishes.

The Marine Station has a public aquarium with live displays of several shellfish and fish species described in this book.

The Marine Station offers a base from which to gather information needed for the sustainable use of the marine resources of Bonne Bay. For example, recent research has been conducted on commercially important lobsters and snow crab in Bonne Bay.[27]

In recent years, the mandate of the Marine Station has been expanded beyond research and teaching to include interaction with the general public through events such as Oceans Day, Celebrate the Sea Day, and the Trails, Tales and Tunes Festival. The Festival has been held in the spring annually since 2007. There are music workshops, interpretive walks, hikes, dinners, and boat tours.[28]

The Bonne Bay Marine Station is located on the waterfront of the coastal community of Norris Point. (PHOTOGRAPH BY CRAIG PURCHASE)

Students discovering the diversity of fishes living in Bonne Bay. The author (kneeling in centre of photo) identifies the fish species caught in a beach seine for students enrolled in a field course at the Bonne Bay Marine Station. (PHOTOGRAPH BY DAVID METHVEN) RIGHT PHOTO: Course instructor Dr. David Methven explains the characteristic features of the winter skate to CURRA principal investigator Dr. Barbara Neis.

The bald eagle nests in the Park but feeds on flatfish in the shallow waters of Bonne Bay. (PHOTOGRAPH BY ARNAULT LE BRIS)

CONNECTIVITY OF ECOSYSTEMS OF THE PARK AND THE SEA

The ecosystems of Gros Morne National Park, Bonne Bay, and the Gulf of St. Lawrence meet at the shoreline. These ecosystems are interconnected. For example, anadromous fish (Atlantic salmon, brook trout, and rainbow smelt) and catadromous fish (American eel and ninespine stickleback) migrate between freshwaters of the Park and marine waters of Bonne Bay and the Gulf. Birds of prey nest in the Park and prey upon marine fish in shallow waters of the bay. Shorebirds feed in the intertidal zone.

The marine ecosystem of Bonne Bay and the terrestrial ecosystem of Gros Morne National Park meet at the shoreline. A bull moose[29] watches the photographer. (PHOTOGRAPH BY ARNAULT LE BRIS)

A woodland caribou[30] walks across the Lomond River delta.

This book has been written to provide the public with information from recent research on the marine wildlife in the Gros Morne National Park region. As public knowledge is the foundation of stewardship, it is hoped that the book will encourage continued stewardship of the terrestrial and freshwater environments of Gros Morne National Park and the adjacent marine waters of Bonne Bay and the Gulf of St. Lawrence.

View from Gadds Harbour at sunset looking toward the Outer Basin of Bonne Bay. The sun is setting behind Pinnacle Rock .(PHOTOGRAPHS BY ARNAULT LE BRIS)

NOTEPAD

Actions people can take as stewards of Bonne Bay include:

☒ JOIN THE GROS MORNE OCEAN BEACH WATCH PROGRAM

Volunteers in the Gros Morne Ocean Beach Watch program monitor the shoreline of Bonne Bay for pollution caused by the dumping of garbage and oil spills. They record observations of dead birds, beached marine mammals, non-native species (e.g. the European green crab), and any other unusual occurrences. This community-based, volunteer observer program has been developed by Gros Morne National Park in partnership with the Bonne Bay Marine Station and the CURRA project.

☒ PREVENT DOMESTIC WASTE POLLUTION OF NEARSHORE WATERS

Untreated sewage from homes without septic tanks that flows into Bonne Bay allows toxic bacteria to grow in marine waters. Mussels, scallops, and clams filtering the polluted seawater become unfit for human consumption.[31] Nutrient pollution of the bay can result from household kitchen and laundry soaps, agricultural fertilizers, and effluent from fish plants. Phosphate and nitrate from these sources can initiate blooms of plankton in the bay. The seawater can become depleted of oxygen when the bloom dies out and decays. Anoxic waters will kill fish which cannot escape to more oxygenated waters.

☒ PREVENT OIL POLLUTION OF THE BAY

Oil spills from ships are a common problem in coastal waters.[32] Oil spills are especially harmful to seabirds swimming on the ocean surface and to fishes living in the tidal zone where the oil washes onto the shore. The toxic hydrocarbons in oil spills can kill planktonic fish eggs and larvae and juvenile fish living in shallow coastal waters.

There is a potential threat of oil pollution from oil and gas development in the Gulf of St. Lawrence. A hydrocarbon field in the Gulf known as Old Harry is thought to contain oil deposits twice as large as the Hibernia project off the southeast coast of Newfoundland. Steps must be taken to minimize the risk of a major oil spill, as occurred in the Gulf of Mexico in 2010. A major oil spill even in a distant sea can have an impact on Newfoundland's marine wildlife. The first oiled seabird rescued during the Gulf of Mexico disaster was a northern gannet from Eastern Canada.[33]

☒ PRACTICE RESPONSIBLE USE OF THE RESOURCES OF THE BAY

People who utilize the bay for commercial fishing, recreational fishing, subsistence harvesting of seafood, and pleasure boating have a responsibility to conduct activities in a sustainable manner. Conserving the brook trout and Atlantic salmon for recreational fishing in the rivers and streams of Gros Morne National Park requires protecting the waters of Bonne Bay from pollution and fish habitat destruction. Juvenile fish habitat along the shoreline is likely to suffer negative effects from disturbance during human activities. Protecting the natural shoreline of Bonne Bay will help rebuild Gulf of St. Lawrence fish stocks that use Bonne Bay as a nursery ground.

CHAPTER NOTES

CHAPTER 1

1 Burzynski and Marceau, *Rocks Adrift*, 57. Further information about Gros Morne National Park as a World Heritage Site is available online at http://whc.unesco.org/

2 Burzynski, *Gros Morne*, 1-3.

3 Rogerson, "Geological Evolution," 5-35.

4 *The National Parks Act* is available online at: http://laws-lois.justice.gc.ca/eng/acts/N-14.01/page-16.html. Further information on Gros Morne National Park is available online at http://www.grosmorne.ca.

5 Hild, *Geology*, 74.

6 Hild, *Geology*, 1-256.

7 Rogerson, "Geological Evolution," 5-35.

8 Burton, *Fish and Wildlife*, 338-356.

9 Gardner Pinfold Consultants, *Economic Value*, 70.

10 Dickie and Trites, "Gulf of St. Lawrence,"405-413.

11 Fréchet, *Changes*, 1-30; Benoît, Darbyson, and Swain, *An Atlas*, 1-185.

12 Fréchet, *Changes*, 1-30; Benoît, Darbyson, and Swain, *An Atlas*, 1-185.

13 Syvitski, Burrell, and Skei, Fjords, 1-379; Karleskint, Turner, and Small, *Introduction to Marine Biology*, 324-328.

14 Shaw, "Submarine Moraines," 115-134.

15 Richards and deYoung, *Analysis*, 1-41.

16 Parsons, "Management," 19-34; Guénette and Alder, "Lessons," 51-78. More information on federal government management of Canada's coastal waters is available online at http://www.dfo-mpo.gc.ca

17 Burzynski, *Gros Morne*, 185-187.

18 Russell and McKee, "Oral histories," 1-18. The Bonne Bay Marine Station in Norris Point is a not-for-profit organization jointly operated by Memorial University of Newfoundland and the Gros Morne Co-operating Association. The Marine Station was built with funds provided by the Atlantic Canada Opportunities Agency (ACOA) and the Newfoundland and Labrador Provincial Government and was officially opened on 6 September 2002. The Station had its beginnings in 1969 when Memorial University established a research station to study the biological productivity of the Gulf of St. Lawrence. Graduate students from Memorial University began studies of the marine ecology of Bonne Bay in the 1980s, and field courses for undergraduate students began at the Station in the 1990s.

19 Rogers, "Examining the local lobster" 1-184; Temple, *Opportunities*, 1-60. http://www.curra.ca/documents/Sustainable_Lobster_Fishery_Report_December_21_2010_Final_for_Web.pdf.

CHAPTER 2

1 Karleskint, Turner, and Small, *Introduction to Marine Biology*, 23-26; Burton, *Fish and Wildlife*, 56; Kaiser et al., *Marine Ecology*, 12.

2 Karleskint, Turner, and Small, *Introduction to Marine Biology*, 26-27; Kaiser et al., *Marine Ecology*, 8.

3 Karleskint, Turner, and Small, *Introduction to Marine Biology*, 136-138; Kaiser et al., *Marine Ecology*, 76-78.

4 Karleskint, Turner, and Small, *Introduction to Marine Biology*, 23-24; Kaiser et al., *Marine Ecology*, 36-42.

5 Karleskint, Turner, and Small, *Introduction to Marine Biology*, 141-148; Gosner, *A Field Guide*, 25-52.

6 Karleskint, Turner, and Small, *Introduction to Marine Biology*, 138.

7 Ibid., 145-147.

8 Hooper, *Bonne Bay Marine Resources*, 1-127; Currie et al., *The Nearshore Fish Fauna*, 60-66.

9 Gosner, *A Field Guide*, 36; Proctor and Lynch, *A Field Guide*, 2.

10 Gosner, *A Field Guide*, 35; Proctor and Lynch, *A Field Guide*, 2.

11 Gosner, *A Field Guide*, 34.

12 Karleskint, Turner, and Small, *Introduction to Marine Biology*, 375-380.

13 Gosner, *A Field Guide*, 34-35.

14 Karleskint, Turner, and Small, *Introduction to Marine Biology*, 375-379.

15 Gosner, *A Field Guide*, 33.

16 Ibid., 33.

17 Karleskint, Turner, and Small, *Introduction to Marine Biology*, 149.

18 Ibid., 149.

19 Karleskint, Turner, and Small, *Introduction to Marine Biology*, 148-155; Gosner, *A Field Guide*, 52-53.

20 Gosner, *A Field Guide*, 52.

21 Schneider, Norris, and Gregory, "Predictive Analysis," 71-78.

22 Gosner, *A Field Guide*, 52; Proctor and Lynch, *A Field Guide*, 98.

23 Karleskint, Turner, and Small, *Introduction to Marine Biology*, 152-153.

24 Ibid., 148.

25 Ibid., 152.

26 Karleskint, Turner, and Small, *Introduction to Marine Biology*, 152; Gosner, *A Field Guide*, 24.

27 Karleskint, Turner, and Small, *Introduction to Marine Biology*, 335.

28 Ibid., 154-155, 335-338.

29 Karleskint, Turner, and Small, *Introduction to Marine Biology*, 162-163; Kaiser et al., *Marine Ecology*, 128-140.

30 Gosner, *A Field Guide*, 69.

31 Karleskint, Turner, and Small, *Introduction to Marine Biology*, 173.

32 Gosner, *A Field Guide*, 92; Karleskint, Turner, and Small, *Introduction to Marine Biology*, 170-173.

33 Gosner, *A Field Guide*, 92-93.

34 Colpron, Edinger, and Neis, "Mapping the Distribution," 1-15.

35 Ibid., 1-15.

36 Colpron, Edinger, and Neis, "Mapping the Distribution," 1-15; Baillon et al., "Deep Cold-Water Corals," 1-10.

37 Karleskint, Turner, and Small, *Introduction to Marine Biology*, 162-225; Gosner, *A Field Guide*, 55-275; Gosner, *Guide to Identification*, 1-693.

38 Karleskint, Turner, and Small, *Introduction to Marine Biology*, 162-225; Gosner, *A Field Guide*, 55-275; Gosner, *Guide to Identification*, 1-693.

39 Gosner, *A Field Guide*, 261.

40 Ibid., 253.

41 Ibid., 258.

42 Ibid., 262.

43 Benoît, Darbyson, and Swain, *An Atlas*, 1-185.

44 Gosner, *A Field Guide*, 142-144; Karleskint, Turner, and Small, *Introduction to Marine Biology*, 195-198.

45 Karleskint, Turner, and Small, *Introduction to Marine Biology*, 195-198; Gosner, *A Field Guide*, 142-161.

46 Benoît, Darbyson, and Swain, *An Atlas*, 1-185.

47 Hooper, *Bonne Bay Marine Resources*, 1-267.

48 Kearley, *Here's the Catch*, 151.

49 Gosner, *A Field Guide*, 146; Department of Fisheries and Aquaculture, *Seafood Industry Year in Review*, 1-29.

50 Muus and Nielsen, *Sea Fish*, 294-295.

51 Benoît, Darbyson, and Swain, *An Atlas*, 1-185.

52 Hooper, *Bonne Bay Marine Resources*, 1-267.

53 Gosner, *A Field Guide*, 146.

54 Department of Fisheries and Aquaculture, *Seafood Industry Year in Review*, 1-29.

55 Karleskint, Turner, and Small, *Introduction to Marine Biology*, 202-203.

56 Gosner, *A Field Guide*, 205-206.

57 Karleskint, Turner, and Small, *Introduction to Marine Biology*, 202-208; Gosner, *A Field Guide*, 199-253; Benoît, Darbyson, and Swain, *An Atlas*, 1-185.

58 Dadswell, "Some Notes,"374-377.

59 Benoît, Darbyson, and Swain, *An Atlas*, 1-185.

60 Department of Fisheries and Aquaculture, *Seafood Industry Year in Review*, 1-29.

61 Department of Fisheries and Aquaculture, *Seafood Industry Year in Review*, 1-29. When the Newfoundland fishery for snow crab began in 1967, the species was known as spider crab or queen crab. The name was replaced by "snow crab" after a ruling by the US Food and Drug Administration that all seafood products from crab of the genus *Chinoecetes* must bear the trade name of "snow crab."

62 Neville, "Effects of a Fishing Moratorium," 1-84.

63 Gosner, *A Field Guide*, 244-245; Karleskint, Turner, and Small, *Introduction to Marine Biology*, 205-2086.

64 Gosner, *A Field Guide*, 246-247.

65 Ibid., 246-247.

66 Benoît, Darbyson, and Swain, *An Atlas*, 1-185.

67 Gosner, *A Field Guide*, 245.

68 Ibid., 245.

69 Benoît, Darbyson, and Swain, *An Atlas*, 1-185.

70 Seiden, Wilke, and Schneider, *Lobster Sustainability*, 1-12.

71 Gosner, *A Field Guide*, 239.

72 Burton, *Fish and Wildlife*, 396.

73 Benoît, Darbyson, and Swain, *An Atlas*, 1-185.

74 Temple, *Opportunities*, 1-60; Rogers, "Examining the Local Lobster," 1-184.

75 Gosner, *A Field Guide*, 239; Muus and Nielsen, *Sea Fish*, 286-287.

76 Karleskint, Turner, and Small, *Introduction to Marine Biology*, 226-300.

77 Barton, *Bond's Biology of Fishes*, 1-891; Moyle and Cech, *Fishes, an Introduction to Ichthyology* 1-612.

78 Scott and Scott, *Atlantic Fishes of Canada*, 522-523.

79 Karleskint, Turner, and Small, *Introduction to Marine Biology*, 276-300.

80 Karleskint, Turner, and Small, *Introduction to Marine Biology*, 226-253; Moyle and Cech, *Fishes, an Introduction to Ichthyology*, 1-612.

81 Robins and Ray, *A Field Guide*, 1-354.

82 Karleskint, Turner, and Small, *Introduction to Marine Biology*, 229-224; Moyle and Cech, *Fishes, an Introduction to Ichthyology* 1-612.

83 Scott and Scott, *Atlantic Fishes of Canada*, 129-134; Collette and Klein-MacPhee, *Bigelow and Schroeder's Fishes*, 174-179.

84 Collette and Klein-MacPhee, *Bigelow and Schroeder's Fishes*, 174-179; Karleskint, Turner, and Small, *Introduction to Marine Biology*, 235-250.

85 Karleskint, Turner, and Small, *Introduction to Marine Biology*, 235-236.

86 Barton, *Bond's Biology of Fishes*, 35-44.

87 Scott and Scott, *Atlantic Fishes of Canada*, 129-134; Collette and Klein-MacPhee, *Bigelow and Schroeder's Fishes*, 174-179.

88 Karleskint, Turner, and Small, *Introduction to Marine Biology*, 254-262; Burton, *Fish and Wildlife*, 400.

89 Proctor and Lynch, *A Field Guide*, 68-71.

90 Karleskint, Turner, and Small, *Introduction to Marine Biology*, 257.

91 Canada's federal legislation called the Species at Risk Act (SARA) was enacted in 2002. The regulations in the Act are designed to prevent plants and animals living in Canada from disappearing because of human activity. Under SARA, a species is considered "endangered" if it could soon be exterminated in Canada. A species is "threatened" if it is likely to become exterminated if nothing is done to reverse man-made threats to its existence. A species is designated "special concern" if its status could soon change to "threatened"

or "endangered." The Committee on the Status of Endangered Wildlife in Canada (COSEWIC) is the national body of scientists that provides advice to the Canadian Federal Government about the current risks to a species and whether the species should be given protection under SARA. More information is available online at http://www.cosewic.gc.ca/eng/sct6/sct6_6_e.cfm. Provincial legislation, entitled the Newfoundland and Labrador Endangered Species Act (NL ESA), was enacted in 2001. The regulations of the NL ESA are aimed at protecting plants and animals indigenous to the province. Marine fish species at risk would be protected under federal legislation rather than provincial legislation. The Species Status Advisory Committee (SSAC) is a provincial body of scientists that provides advice to the Government of Newfoundland and Labrador about protecting species at risk of extinction or extirpation within the province. More information is available online at http://www.env.gov.nl.ca/env/wildlife/endangeredspecies/index.html

92 COSEWIC, *Leatherback Turtle*, 1-25.

93 Proctor and Lynch, *A Field Guide*, 68-69.

94 COSEWIC, *Loggerhead Sea Turtle*, 1-75.

95 Proctor and Lynch, *A Field Guide*, 70.

96 Wayne Ledwell, personal communication, December 2012.

97 Lein, Fawcett, and Staniforth, *Wet and Fat*, 23-29; Ledwell, *Whales and Dolphins*, 36-43; Proctor and Lynch, *A Field Guide*, 70-71.

98 Karleskint, Turner, and Small, *Introduction to Marine Biology*, 276-298; Burton, *Fish and Wildlife*, 186-206; Lein, Fawcett, and Staniforth, *Wet and Fat*, 7.

99 Proctor and Lynch, *A Field Guide*, 150-151; Ledwell, *Whales and Dolphins*, 20-23.

100 Lein, Fawcett, and Staniforth, *Wet and Fat*, 24; Ledwell, *Whales and Dolphins*, 40.

101 Lein, Fawcett, and Staniforth, *Wet and Fat*, 13.

102 Dickinson and Sanger, *Twentieth-Century Shore-Station Whaling*, 1-273.

103 Lein, Fawcett, and Staniforth, *Wet and Fat*, 7; Ledwell, *Whales and Dolphins*, 36-43.

104 COSEWIC, *Humpback Whale*, 1-32.

105 Lein, Fawcett, and Staniforth, *Wet and Fat*, 32-35; Ledwell, *Whales and Dolphins*, 24-27.

106 COSEWIC, *Fin Whale*, 1-37.

107 Lein, Fawcett, and Staniforth, *Wet and Fat*, 13.

108 Ledwell, *Whales and Dolphins*, 16.

109 Hilborne, et al., *State of the World's Fisheries*, 359-399.

110 Lein, Fawcett, and Staniforth, *Wet and Fat*, 13.

111 Reeves, "The Origins and Character," 71-106.

112 Lein, Fawcett, and Staniforth, *Wet and Fat*, 23-29; Ledwell, *Whales and Dolphins*, 36-43.

113 Lein, Fawcett, and Staniforth, *Wet and Fat*, 48-51; Ledwell, *Whales and Dolphins*, 44-49.

114 COSEWIC, *North Atlantic Right Whale*, 1-28.

115 Lein, Fawcett, and Staniforth, *Wet and Fat*, 58-63; Ledwell, *Whales and Dolphins*, 32-35; Proctor and Lynch, *A Field Guide*, 148-149.

116 Lein, Fawcett, and Staniforth, *Wet and Fat*, 58-63; Ledwell, *Whales and Dolphins*, 32-35; Proctor and Lynch, *A Field Guide*, 148-149.

117 Lein, Fawcett, and Staniforth, *Wet and Fat*, 62.

118 Ledwell, *Whales and Dolphins*, 34.

119 Ibid., 16.

120 Lein, Fawcett, and Staniforth, *Wet and Fat*, 44-47; Ledwell, *Whales and Dolphins*, 20-23.

121 COSEWIC, *Blue Whale*, 1-32.

122 Ledwell, *Whales and Dolphins*, 104.

123 Proctor and Lynch, *A Field Guide*, 192; Lein, Fawcett, and Staniforth, *Wet and Fat*, 74.

124 Lein, Fawcett, and Staniforth, *Wet and Fat*, 74.

125 Lein, Fawcett, and Staniforth, *Wet and Fat*, 74-75; Ledwell, *Whales and Dolphins*, 102-105; Procter and Lynch, *A Field Guide*, 192-194.

126 Proctor and Lynch, *A Field Guide*, 160-177.

127 Lein, Fawcett, and Staniforth, *Wet and Fat*, 86-89; Ledwell, *Whales and Dolphins*, 76-79; COSEWIC, *Beluga Whale*, 1-70.

128 Lein, Fawcett, and Staniforth, *Wet and Fat*, 64-67; Ledwell, *Whales and Dolphins*, 62-67; COSEWIC, *Killer Whale*, 1-65.

129 Karleskint, Turner, and Small, *Introduction to Marine Biology*, 291-297.

130 Proctor and Lynch, *A Field Guide*, 184-193.

131 Ledwell, *Whales and Dolphins*, 105; Lesage et al., "Bycatch of Harbour Porposies," 67-78.

132 COSEWIC, *Harbour Porpoise*, 1-32.

133 Karleskint, Turner, and Small, *Introduction to Marine Biology*, 277-282.

134 Lein, Fawcett, and Staniforth, *Wet and Fat*, 110-113.

135 Ibid., 102-107.

136 Ibid., 118-125.

137 Ibid., 102-104.

138 Ibid., 102-104.

139 Lacoste and Stenson, "Winter distribution," 805-811.

140 Chassot et al., "Role of predation by harp seals," 279–297.

141 Sergeant, *Harp Seals, Man and Ice*, 1-153.

142 Fisheries and Oceans Canada (DFO) is the federal department responsible for managing the hunting of seals based on conservation principles. DFO sets a harvest level that ensures the health of the seal populations. Hunters receive training on the best practices for humane harvesting of seals. Not following the humane killing process would be a violation of the federal Marine Mammal Regulations. Sealers may not kill newly born pups or adult seals on whelping or breeding patches.

143 Cairns, Chapdelaine, and Montevecchi, "Prey Exploitation by Seabirds," 277-291.

144 Burton, *Fish and Wildlife*, 223.

145 Karleskint, Turner, and Small, *Introduction to Marine Biology*, 263-273.

146 Threlfall, "Seabirds," 467-508; Montevecchi and Tuck, *Newfoundland Birds*, 1-273; Warkentin and Newton, *Birds of Newfoundland*, 1-237.

147 Burton, *Fish and Wildlife*, 261-263.

148 Warkentin and Newton, *Birds of Newfoundland*, 1-237.

149 More information on marine birds at risk of extinction or extirpation is available online at: http://www.env.gov.nl.ca/env/wildlife/endangeredspecies/Piping_Plover_Information_Sheet.pdf and http://www.env.gov.nl.ca/env/wildlife/endangeredspecies/Eskimo_Curlew_Information_Note.pdf and http://www.sararegistry.gc.ca/species/speciesDetails_e.cfm?sid=687.

150 Roger Tory Peterson, *A Field Guide*, 120.

151 Karleskint, Turner, and Small, *Introduction to Marine Biology*, 263.

152 Darroch Whitaker, personal communication, June 2012.

153 Proctor and Lynch, *A Field Guide*, 114-123.

154 Burton, *Fish and Wildlife*, 314; Proctor and Lynch, *A Field Guide*, 114-123.

155 COSEWIC, *Ivory Gull*, 1-42.

156 Burton, *Fish and Wildlife*, 315.

157 Proctor and Lynch, *A Field Guide*, 130-145; Warkentin and Newton, *Birds of Newfoundland*, 83-143.

158 Cairns, Chapdelaine, and Montevecchi, "Prey exploitation," 277-291.

159 Proctor and Lynch, *A Field Guide*, 144-145.

160 Pritchard, "What is an estuary?" 3-5.

161 Richards, "Wind-forced Dynamics," 1-111; Richards and deYoung, *Analysis*, 1-41.

162 Richards, "Wind-forced Dynamics," 1-111.

163 Steele, "Marine Ecology and Zoogeography," 422.

164 Karleskint, Turner, and Small, *Introduction to Marine Biology*, 77-81.

165 McKnight, *Physical Geography*, 99.

CHAPTER 3: PART I

1 Moyle and Cech, *Fishes, an Introduction to Ichthyology*, 1-612; Barton, *Bond's Biology of Fishes*, 1-891.

2 Snelgrove, *Discoveries*, 1-270.

3 Barton, *Bond's Biology of Fishes*, 702.

4 Elliott and Hemingway, *Fishes in Estuaries*, 1-636.

5 Able and Fahay, *Ecology of Estuarine Fishes*, 1-566.

6 Haedrich and Hall, "Fishes and estuaries," 55-63; Haedrich, "Estuarine fishes," 183-207.

7 Hooper, *Bonne Bay Marine Resources*, 267. Currie, et al., *The Nearshore Fish Fauna of Bonne Bay*, 1-66.

8 Scott and Scott, *Atlantic Fishes of Canada*, 1-730; Nozères et al., *Identification Guide*, 1-243.

9 Currie, et al., *The Nearshore Fish Fauna of Bonne Bay*, 1-66.

10 Bruce, Schneider, and Wroblewski, *The Habitats of 0-group*, 1-41.

11 Barton, *Bond's Biology of Fishes*, 1-891.

12 COSEWIC, *Atlantic Salmon*, 1-136.

13 Young salmon raised in hatcheries are grown to market size in sea cages for human consumption. Salmon aquaculture operations present risks to wild Atlantic salmon populations. Salmon in crowded sea cages are prone to infection by parasites and disease, which can be passed onto wild salmon migrating past the sea cages. Hatchery raised salmon escaping from sea cages can mate with wild salmon and negatively impact the genetic diversity of the wild salmon populations. Greenberg, *Four Fish*, 1-284.

14 Anderson, *The Rivers of Labrador*, 1-389.

15 Nozères et al., *Identification Guide*, 45.

16 Scott and Scott, *Atlantic Fishes of Canada*, 129-134; Scott and Crossman, *Freshwater Fishes of Canada*, 192-197; Collette and Klein-MacPhee, *Bigelow and Schroeder's Fishes*, 174-179.

17 Scott and Scott, *Atlantic Fishes of Canada*, 129-134; Scott and Crossman, *Freshwater Fishes of Canada*, 192-197; Collette and Klein-MacPhee, *Bigelow and Schroeder's Fishes*, 174-179.

18 Muus and Nielsen, *Sea Fish*, 100-103.

19 Klemetsen et al., "Atlantic salmon," 1-59.

20 Caputo, "Marine Migratory Behaviour of Brook Trout," (forthcoming).

21 Currie, et al., *The Nearshore Fish Fauna of Bonne Bay*, 1-66.

22 Scott and Scott, *Atlantic Fishes of Canada*, 141-145; Scott and Crossman, *Freshwater Fishes of Canada*, 208-213; Collette and Klein-MacPhee, *Bigelow and Schroeder's Fishes*, 179-181.

23 Scott and Scott, *Atlantic Fishes of Canada*, 141-145; Scott and Crossman, *Freshwater Fishes of Canada*, 208-213; Collette and Klein-MacPhee, *Bigelow and Schroeder's Fishes*, 179-181.

24 Scott and Scott, *Atlantic Fishes of Canada*, 141-145; Scott and Crossman, *Freshwater Fishes of Canada*, 208-213; Collette and Klein-MacPhee, *Bigelow and Schroeder's Fishes*, 179-181.

25 Nozères et al., *Identification Guide*, 43.

26 Scott and Scott, *Atlantic Fishes of Canada*, 150-154; Scott and Crossman, *Freshwater Fishes of Canada*, 310-317; Collette and Klein-MacPhee, *Bigelow and Schroeder's Fishes*, 166-170.

27 Scott and Scott, *Atlantic Fishes of Canada*, 150-154; Scott and Crossman, *Freshwater Fishes of Canada*, 310-317; Collette and Klein-MacPhee, *Bigelow and Schroeder's Fishes*, 166-170.

28 Scott and Scott, *Atlantic Fishes of Canada*, 150-154; Scott and Crossman, *Freshwater Fishes of Canada*, 310-317; Collette and Klein-MacPhee, *Bigelow and Schroeder's Fishes*, 166-170.

29 Muus and Nielsen, *Sea Fish*, 305-307; Benoît, Darbyson and Swain, *An Atlas*, 1-185.

30 Nozères et al., *Identification Guide*, 55.

31 Scott and Scott, *Atlantic Fishes of Canada*, 338-341; Scott and Crossman, *Freshwater Fishes of Canada*, 665-668; Collette and Klein-MacPhee, *Bigelow and Schroeder's Fishes*, 314-316.

32 Scott and Scott, *Atlantic Fishes of Canada*, 338-341; Scott and Crossman, *Freshwater Fishes of Canada*, 665-668; Collette and Klein-MacPhee, *Bigelow and Schroeder's Fishes*, 314-316.

33 Muus and Nielsen, *Sea Fish*, 157.

34 Scott and Scott, *Atlantic Fishes of Canada*, 338-341; Scott and Crossman, *Freshwater Fishes of Canada*, 665-668; Collette and Klein-MacPhee, *Bigelow and Schroeder's Fishes*, 314-316.

35 Currie, et al., *The Nearshore Fish Fauna of Bonne Bay*, 1-66.

36 Nozères et al., *Identification Guide*, 18.

37 Ibid., 18.

38 Scott and Scott, *Atlantic Fishes of Canada*, 281-283; Scott and Crossman, *Freshwater Fishes of Canada*, 646-649; Collette and Klein-MacPhee, *Bigelow and Schroeder's Fishes*, 242-245; Nozères et al., *Identification Guide*, 18.

39 Dr. Tom Knight, personal communication, June 2010; Scott and Crossman, *Freshwater Fishes of Canada*, 105-108.

40 Scott and Crossman, *Freshwater Fishes of Canada*, 646-649.

41 Benoît, Darbyson, and Swain, *An Atlas*, 1-185.

42 Scott and Scott, *Atlantic Fishes of Canada*, 281-283; Scott and Crossman, *Freshwater Fishes of Canada*, 646-649; Collette and Klein-MacPhee, *Bigelow and Schroeder's Fishes*, 242-245; Nozères et al., *Identification Guide*, 18.

43 Dr. Darroch Whitaker, personal communication, June 2012.

44 Nozères et al., *Identification Guide*, 47.

45 Scott and Crossman, *Freshwater Fishes of Canada*, 120-128; Scott and Scott, *Atlantic Fishes of Canada*, 105-108; Collette and Klein-MacPhee, *Bigelow and Schroeder's Fishes*, 118-125.

46 Scott and Crossman, *Freshwater Fishes of Canada*, 120-128; Scott and Scott, *Atlantic Fishes of Canada*, 105-108; Collette and Klein-MacPhee, *Bigelow and Schroeder's Fishes*, 118-125.

47 Scott and Crossman, *Freshwater Fishes of Canada*, 120-128; Scott and Scott, *Atlantic Fishes of Canada*, 105-108; Collette and Klein-MacPhee, *Bigelow and Schroeder's Fishes*, 118-125.

48 Muus and Nielsen, *Sea Fish*, 307-307

49 Benoît, Darbyson, and Swain, *An Atlas*, 1-185.

50 Barton, *Bond's Biology of Fishes*, 1-891.

51 Hooper, *Bonne Bay Marine Resources*, 267.

52 COSEWIC, *American Eel*, 1-71.

53 Collette and Klein-MacPhee, *Bigelow and Schroeder's Fishes*, 321.

54 Dr. Tom Knight, personal communication, June 2010.

55 Dr. Darroch Whitaker, personal communication, June 2012.

56 Nozères et al., *Identification Guide*, 96.

57 Scott and Crossman, *Freshwater Fishes of Canada*, 624-629; Scott and Scott, *Atlantic Fishes of Canada*, 75-79; Collette and Klein-MacPhee, *Bigelow and*

Schroeder's Fishes, 93-95.

58 Scott and Crossman, *Freshwater Fishes of Canada*, 624-629; Scott and Scott, *Atlantic Fishes of Canada*, 75-79; Collette and Klein-MacPhee, *Bigelow and Schroeder's Fishes*, 93-95; Nozères et al., *Identification Guide*, 96.

59 Scott and Crossman, *Freshwater Fishes of Canada*, 624-629; Scott and Scott, *Atlantic Fishes of Canada*, 75-79; Collette and Klein-MacPhee, *Bigelow and Schroeder's Fishes*, 93-95.

60 Muus and Nielsen, *Sea Fish*, 303-307.

61 Benoît, Darbyson, and Swain, *An Atlas*, 1-185.

62 Melanson and Campbell, "Near-shore Fish Populations," 487-500.

63 Dr. Tom Knight, personal communication, June 2010.

64 Nozères et al., *Identification Guide*, 58.

65 Scott and Crossman, *Freshwater Fishes of Canada*, 671-674; Scott and Scott, *Atlantic Fishes of Canada*, 343-346; Collette and Klein-MacPhee, *Bigelow and Schroeder's Fishes*, 319-321.

66 Muus and Nielsen, *Sea Fish*, 158.

67 Scott and Crossman, *Freshwater Fishes of Canada*, 671-674; Scott and Scott, *Atlantic Fishes of Canada*, 343-346; Collette and Klein-MacPhee, *Bigelow and Schroeder's Fishes*, 319-321; Nozères et al., *Identification Guide*, 58.

68 Scott and Crossman, *Freshwater Fishes of Canada*, 671-674; Scott and Scott, *Atlantic Fishes of Canada*, 343-346; Collette and Klein-MacPhee, *Bigelow and Schroeder's Fishes*, 319-321.

CHAPTER 3: PART II:

1 Story, Kirwin, and Widdowson, *Dictionary of Newfoundland English*, 23.

2 Story, Kirwin, and Widdowson, *Dictionary of Newfoundland English*, 297.

3 Currie et al., *The Nearshore Fish Fauna of Bonne Bay*, 1-66.

4 Nozères et al., *Identification Guide*, 110.

5 Scott and Scott, *Atlantic Fishes of Canada*, 427-429; Collette and Klein-MacPhee, *Bigelow and Schroeder's Fishes*, 481-483.

6 Muus and Nielsen, *Sea Fish*, 210.

7 Scott and Scott, *Atlantic Fishes of Canada*, 427-429; Collette and Klein-MacPhee, *Bigelow and Schroeder's Fishes*, 481-483.

8 Scott and Scott, *Atlantic Fishes of Canada*, 427-429; Collette and Klein-MacPhee, *Bigelow and Schroeder's Fishes*, 481-483.

9 Nozères et al., *Identification Guide*, 89.

10 Scott and Scott, *Atlantic Fishes of Canada*, 522-523; Collette and Klein-MacPhee, *Bigelow and Schroeder's Fishes*, 369-371.

11 Scott and Scott, *Atlantic Fishes of Canada*, 522-523; Collette and Klein-MacPhee, *Bigelow and Schroeder's Fishes*, 369-371.

12 Scott and Scott, *Atlantic Fishes of Canada*, 522-523; Collette and Klein-MacPhee, *Bigelow and Schroeder's Fishes*, 369-371.

13 Story, Kirwin, and Widdowson, *Dictionary of Newfoundland English*, 23.

14 Nozères et al., *Identification Guide*, 56.

15 Scott and Scott, *Atlantic Fishes of Canada*, 341-343; Scott and Crossman,

Freshwater Fishes of Canada, 669-671; Collette and Klein-MacPhee, *Bigelow and Schroeder's Fishes*, 316-318.

16 Scott and Scott, *Atlantic Fishes of Canada*, 341-343; Scott and Crossman, *Freshwater Fishes of Canada*, 669-671; Collette and Klein-MacPhee, *Bigelow and Schroeder's Fishes*, 316-318.

17 Scott and Scott, *Atlantic Fishes of Canada*, 341-343; Scott and Crossman, *Freshwater Fishes of Canada*, 669-671; Collette and Klein-MacPhee, *Bigelow and Schroeder's Fishes*, 316-318.

18 Scott and Scott, *Atlantic Fishes of Canada*, 341-343; Scott and Crossman, *Freshwater Fishes of Canada*, 669-671; Collette and Klein-MacPhee, *Bigelow and Schroeder's Fishes*, 316-318.

19 Currie et al., *The Nearshore Fish Fauna of Bonne Bay*, 1-66.

20 Scott and Scott, *Atlantic Fishes of Canada*, 337.

21 Nozères et al., *Identification Guide*, 57.

22 Scott and Scott, *Atlantic Fishes of Canada*, 335-338; Scott and Crossman, *Freshwater Fishes of Canada*, 658-660; Collette and Klein-MacPhee, *Bigelow and Schroeder's Fishes*, 312-314.

23 Scott and Scott, *Atlantic Fishes of Canada*, 335-338; Scott and Crossman, *Freshwater Fishes of Canada*, 658-660; Collette and Klein-MacPhee, *Bigelow and Schroeder's Fishes*, 312-314.

24 Scott and Scott, *Atlantic Fishes of Canada*, 335-338; Scott and Crossman, *Freshwater Fishes of Canada*, 658-660; Collette and Klein-MacPhee, *Bigelow and Schroeder's Fishes*, 312-314.

25 Currie et al., *The Nearshore Fish Fauna of Bonne Bay*, 1-66.

26 Scott and Scott, *Atlantic Fishes of Canada*, 350-352; Collette and Klein-MacPhee, *Bigelow and Schroeder's Fishes*, 324-326.

27 Scott and Scott, *Atlantic Fishes of Canada*, 350-352; Collette and Klein-MacPhee, *Bigelow and Schroeder's Fishes*, 324-326.

28 Scott and Scott, *Atlantic Fishes of Canada*, 350-352; Collette and Klein-MacPhee, *Bigelow and Schroeder's Fishes*, 324-326; Muus and Nielsen, *Sea Fish*, 159-163.

29 Scott and Scott, Atlantic Fishes of Canada, 350-352; Collette and Klein-MacPhee, Bigelow and Schroeder's Fishes, 324-326.

CHAPTER 3: PART III:

1 Barton, *Bond's Biology of Fishes*, 701-704.

2 Nozères et al., *Identification Guide*, 1-243.

3 Currie et al., *The Nearshore Fish Fauna of Bonne Bay*, 1-66; Nozères et al., *Identification Guide*, 1-243.

4 Currie et al., *The Nearshore Fish Fauna of Bonne Bay*, 1-66.

5 COSEWIC, *Winter Skate*, 1-41.

6 Currie et al., *The Nearshore Fish Fauna of Bonne Bay*, 1-66.

7 Nozères et al., *Identification Guide*, 5.

8 Scott and Scott, *Atlantic Fishes of Canada*, 49-51; Collette and Klein-MacPhee, *Bigelow and Schroeder's Fishes*, 70-72.

9 Scott and Scott, *Atlantic Fishes of Canada*, 49-51; Collette and Klein-MacPhee, *Bigelow and Schroeder's Fishes*, 70-72.

10 Benoît, Darbyson, and Swain, *An Atlas*, 1-185.

11 Scott and Scott, *Atlantic Fishes of Canada*, 49-51; Collette and Klein-MacPhee, *Bigelow and Schroeder's Fishes*, 70-72.

12 COSEWIC, *Thorny Skate*, 1-75.

13 Currie et al., *The Nearshore Fish Fauna of Bonne Bay*, 1-66.

14 Nozères et al., *Identification Guide*, 2.

15 Scott and Scott, *Atlantic Fishes of Canada*, 51-53; Collette and Klein-MacPhee, *Bigelow and Schroeder's Fishes*, 62-64.

16 Scott and Scott, *Atlantic Fishes of Canada*, 51-53; Collette and Klein-MacPhee, *Bigelow and Schroeder's Fishes*, 62-64.

17 Benoît, Darbyson, and Swain, *An Atlas*, 1-185.

18 Muus and Nielsen, *Sea Fish*, 303-312; Kearley, *Here's the Catch*, 149-152.

19 Scott and Scott, *Atlantic Fishes of Canada*, 51-53; Collette and Klein-MacPhee, *Bigelow and Schroeder's Fishes*, 62-64.

20 Hooper, *Bonne Bay Marine Resources*, 1-267; Currie et al., *The Nearshore Fish Fauna of Bonne Bay*, 1-66.

21 Scott and Scott, *Atlantic Fishes of Canada*, 424-426; Collette and Klein-MacPhee, *Bigelow and Schroeder's Fishes*, 479-481.

22 Scott and Scott, *Atlantic Fishes of Canada*, 424-426; Collette and Klein-MacPhee, *Bigelow and Schroeder's Fishes*, 479-481.

23 Scott and Scott, *Atlantic Fishes of Canada*, 424-426; Collette and Klein-MacPhee, *Bigelow and Schroeder's Fishes*, 479-481.

24 Scott and Scott, *Atlantic Fishes of Canada*, 424-426; Collette and Klein-MacPhee, *Bigelow and Schroeder's Fishes*, 479-481.

25 Hooper, *Bonne Bay Marine Resources*, 1-267.

26 Nozères et al., *Identification Guide*, 106.

27 Scott and Scott, *Atlantic Fishes of Canada*, 420-421; Collette and Klein-MacPhee, *Bigelow and Schroeder's Fishes*, 476-477.

28 Scott and Scott, *Atlantic Fishes of Canada*, 420-421; Collette and Klein-MacPhee, *Bigelow and Schroeder's Fishes*, 476-477.

29 Scott and Scott, *Atlantic Fishes of Canada*, 420-421; Collette and Klein-MacPhee, *Bigelow and Schroeder's Fishes*, 476-477.

30 Currie et al., *The Nearshore Fish Fauna of Bonne Bay*, 1-66.

31 Arbour et al., "Aspects of the Ecology," 353-363.

32 Nozères et al., *Identification Guide*, 76.

33 Scott and Scott, *Atlantic Fishes of Canada*, 514-515; Collette and Klein-MacPhee, *Bigelow and Schroeder's Fishes*, 361-362.

34 Scott and Scott, *Atlantic Fishes of Canada*, 514-515; Collette and Klein-MacPhee, *Bigelow and Schroeder's Fishes*, 361-362.

35 Scott and Scott, *Atlantic Fishes of Canada*, 514-515; Collette and Klein-MacPhee, *Bigelow and Schroeder's Fishes*, 361-362.

36 Currie et al., *The Nearshore Fish Fauna of Bonne Bay*, 1-66.

37 Gosner, *A Field Guide*, 65.
38 Currie et al., *The Nearshore Fish Fauna of Bonne Bay*, 1-66.
39 Nozères et al., *Identification Guide*, 72.
40 Scott and *Scott, Atlantic Fishes of Canada*, 496-498; Collette and Klein-MacPhee, *Bigelow and Schroeder's Fishes*, 359-361.
41 Scott and *Scott, Atlantic Fishes of Canada*, 496-498; Collette and Klein-MacPhee, *Bigelow and Schroeder's Fishes*, 359-361.
42 Scott and *Scott, Atlantic Fishes of Canada*, 496-498; Collette and Klein-MacPhee, *Bigelow and Schroeder's Fishes*, 359-361.
43 Gosner, *A Field Guide*, 65.
44 Currie et al., *The Nearshore Fish Fauna of Bonne Bay*, 1-66.
45 Scott and Scott, *Atlantic Fishes of Canada*, 502-504; Collette and Klein-MacPhee, *Bigelow and Schroeder's Fishes*, 351-353.
46 Nozères et al., *Identification Guide*, 71.
47 Scott and Scott, *Atlantic Fishes of Canada*, 502-504; Collette and Klein-MacPhee, *Bigelow and Schroeder's Fishes*, 351-353.
48 Nozères et al., Identification Guide, 69.
49 Scott and Scott, *Atlantic Fishes of Canada*, 502-504; Collette and Klein-MacPhee, *Bigelow and Schroeder's Fishes*, 351-353.
50 Scott and Scott, *Atlantic Fishes of Canada*, 507-509; Collette and Klein-MacPhee, *Bigelow and Schroeder's Fishes*, 353-356.
51 Scott and Scott, *Atlantic Fishes of Canada*, 507-509; Collette and Klein-MacPhee, *Bigelow and Schroeder's Fishes*, 353-356.
52 Muus and Nielsen, *Sea Fish*, 173-174.
53 Scott and Scott, *Atlantic Fishes of Canada*, 507-509; Collette and Klein-MacPhee, *Bigelow and Schroeder's Fishes*, 353-356.
54 Nozères et al., *Identification Guide*, 70.
55 Scott and Scott, *Atlantic Fishes of Canada*, 500-502; Collette and Klein-MacPhee, *Bigelow and Schroeder's Fishes*, 349-351.
56 Scott and Scott, *Atlantic Fishes of Canada*, 500-502; Collette and Klein-MacPhee, *Bigelow and Schroeder's Fishes*, 349-351.
57 Scott and Scott, *Atlantic Fishes of Canada*, 500-502; Collette and Klein-MacPhee, *Bigelow and Schroeder's Fishes*, 349-351.
58 Currie et al., *The Nearshore Fish Fauna of Bonne Bay*, 1-66.
59 Nozères et al., *Identification Guide*, 16.
60 Wroblewski, Neis,l and Gosse, "Inshore Stocks," 411-432.
61 Scott and Scott, *Atlantic Fishes of Canada*, 266-270; Collette and Klein-MacPhee, *Bigelow and Schroeder's Fishes*, 228-235.
62 Scott and Scott, *Atlantic Fishes of Canada*, 266-270; Collette and Klein-MacPhee, *Bigelow and Schroeder's Fishes*, 228-235.
63 Muus and Nielsen, *Sea Fish*, 120-123.
64 Scott and Scott, *Atlantic Fishes of Canada*, 266-270; Collette and Klein-MacPhee, *Bigelow and Schroeder's Fishes*, 228-235.
65 Chouinard et al., "Covariation," 1991-2000; Chassot et al., "Role of Predation," 279-297.

66 Benoît, Darbyson, and Swain, *An Atlas*, 1-185; Rose, *Cod*, 1-591; Murray et al., "Mapping Cod," 581-598.

67 Muus and Nielsen, *Sea Fish*, 303-304; Kearley, *Here's the Catch*, 150

68 Muus and Nielsen, *Sea Fish*, 309; Kearley, *Here's the Catch*, 151.

69 Muus and Nielsen, *Sea Fish*, 306.

70 Ibid., 317.

71 Le Bris et al., "Evidence for Alternative Migratory Behaviours," doi: 10.1093/icesjms/fst068.

72 Wroblewski, Neis, and Gosse, "Inshore Stocks," 411-432; Rose, *Cod*, 1-591.

73 Le Bris et al., "Evidence for Alternative Migratory Behaviours,"doi: 10.1093/icesjms/fst068.

74 Rowe, et al., "Nonrandom Mating," 219-226.

75 COSEWIC, *Atlantic Cod*, 1-105; Greenberg, *Four Fish*, 1-284.

76 Currie et al., *The Nearshore Fish Fauna of Bonne Bay*, 1-66.

77 Currie et al., *The Nearshore Fish Fauna of Bonne Bay*, 1-66.

78 Nozères et al., *Identification Guide*, 17.

79 Scott and Scott, *Atlantic Fishes of Canada*, 270-271; Scott and Crossman, *Freshwater Fishes of Canada*, 646-649.

80 Scott and Scott, *Atlantic Fishes of Canada*, 270-271; Scott and Crossman, *Freshwater Fishes of Canada*, 646-649.

81 Scott and Scott, *Atlantic Fishes of Canada*, 270-271; Scott and Crossman, *Freshwater Fishes of Canada*, 646-649.

82 Benoît, Darbyson, and Swain, *An Atlas*, 1-185.

83 Harvey Best, personal communication, June 2012.

84 Scott and Scott, *Atlantic Fishes of Canada*, 554-557; Collette and Klein-MacPhee, *Bigelow and Schroeder's Fishes*, 579-585.

85 Currie et al., *The Nearshore Fish Fauna of Bonne Bay*, 1-66.

86 Nozères et al., *Identification Guide*, 36.

87 Scott and Scott, *Atlantic Fishes of Canada*, 554-557; Collette and Klein-MacPhee, *Bigelow and Schroeder's Fishes*, 579-585.

88 Scott and Scott, *Atlantic Fishes of Canada*, 554-557; Collette and Klein-MacPhee, *Bigelow and Schroeder's Fishes*, 579-585.

89 Benoît, Darbyson, and Swain, *An Atlas*, 1-185.

90 Scott and Scott, *Atlantic Fishes of Canada*, 554-557; Collette and Klein-MacPhee, *Bigelow and Schroeder's Fishes*, 579-585.

91 Currie et al., *The Nearshore Fish Fauna of Bonne Bay*, 1-66.

92 Nozères et al., *Identification Guide*, 39.

93 Scott and Scott, *Atlantic Fishes of Canada*, 539-540; Collette and Klein-MacPhee, *Bigelow and Schroeder's Fishes*, 548-550.

94 Scott and Scott, *Atlantic Fishes of Canada*, 539-540; Collette and Klein-MacPhee, *Bigelow and Schroeder's Fishes*, 548-550.

95 Scott and Scott, *Atlantic Fishes of Canada*, 539-540; Collette and Klein-MacPhee, *Bigelow and Schroeder's Fishes*, 548-550.

96 Benoît, Darbyson, and Swain, *An Atlas*, 1-185.

97 Nozères et al., *Identification Guide*, 53.
98 Scott and Scott, *Atlantic Fishes of Canada*, 398-398; Collette and Klein-MacPhee, *Bigelow and Schroeder's Fishes*, 457-466.
99 Scott and Scott, *Atlantic Fishes of Canada*, 398-398; Collette and Klein-MacPhee, *Bigelow and Schroeder's Fishes*, 457-466.
100 Scott and Scott, *Atlantic Fishes of Canada*, 398-398; Collette and Klein-MacPhee, *Bigelow and Schroeder's Fishes*, 457-466.
101 Currie et al., *The Nearshore Fish Fauna of Bonne Bay*, 1-66.
102 Nozères et al., *Identification Guide*, 79.
103 Scott and Scott, *Atlantic Fishes of Canada*, 482-487; Collette and Klein-MacPhee, *Bigelow and Schroeder's Fishes*, 334-338.
104 Scott and Scott, *Atlantic Fishes of Canada*, 482-487; Collette and Klein-MacPhee, *Bigelow and Schroeder's Fishes*, 334-338.
105 Muus and Nielsen, *Sea Fish*, 310-311; Kearley, *Here's the Catch*, 151-152.
106 Scott and Scott, *Atlantic Fishes of Canada*, 482-487; Collette and Klein-MacPhee, *Bigelow and Schroeder's Fishes*, 334-338.
107 Muus and Nielsen, *Sea Fish*, 165-168.
108 Valentin, "Structure des Populations," 1-212.
109 COSEWIC, *Acadian Redfish*, 1-80.
110 Scott and Scott, *Atlantic Fishes of Canada*, 145-150; Collette and Klein-MacPhee, *Bigelow and Schroeder's Fishes*, 163-166.
111 Nozères et al., *Identification Guide*, 42.
112 Scott and Scott, *Atlantic Fishes of Canada*, 145-150; Collette and Klein-MacPhee, *Bigelow and Schroeder's Fishes*, 163-166.
113 Scott and Scott, *Atlantic Fishes of Canada*, 145-150; Collette and Klein-MacPhee, *Bigelow and Schroeder's Fishes*, 163-166.
114 Muus and Nielsen, *Sea Fish*, 98.
115 Scott and Scott, *Atlantic Fishes of Canada*, 145-150; Collette and Klein-MacPhee, *Bigelow and Schroeder's Fishes*, 163-166.
116 Benoît, Darbyson, and Swain, *An Atlas*, 1-185; Muus and Nielsen, *Sea Fish*, 308; Kearley, *Here's the Catch*, 152-153.
117 Scott and Scott, *Atlantic Fishes of Canada*, 145-150; Collette and Klein-MacPhee, *Bigelow and Schroeder's Fishes*, 163-166.
118 Nozères et al., *Identification Guide*, 50.
119 Scott and Scott, *Atlantic Fishes of Canada*, 438-440; Collette and Klein-MacPhee, *Bigelow and Schroeder's Fishes*, 498-501.
120 Scott and Scott, *Atlantic Fishes of Canada*, 438-440; Collette and Klein-MacPhee, *Bigelow and Schroeder's Fishes*, 498-501.
121 Benoît, Darbyson, and Swain, *An Atlas*, 1-185.
122 Scott and Scott, *Atlantic Fishes of Canada*, 438-440; Collette and Klein-MacPhee, *Bigelow and Schroeder's Fishes*, 498-501.
123 Currie et al., *The Nearshore Fish Fauna of Bonne Bay*, 1-66.
124 Scott and Scott, *Atlantic Fishes of Canada*, 518-520; Collette and Klein-MacPhee, *Bigelow and Schroeder's Fishes*, 363-367.

125 Hooper, *Bonne Bay Marine Resources*, 1-267.

126 Nozères et al., *Identification Guide*, 84.

127 Scott and Scott, *Atlantic Fishes of Canada*, 518-520; Collette and Klein-MacPhee, *Bigelow and Schroeder's Fishes*, 363-367.

128 Scott and Scott, *Atlantic Fishes of Canada*, 518-520; Collette and Klein-MacPhee, *Bigelow and Schroeder's Fishes*, 363-367.

129 Benoît, Darbyson, and Swain, *An Atlas*, 1-185.

130 Muus and Nielsen, *Sea Fish*, 305.

131 Ibid., 78-79.

132 Muus and Nielsen, Sea Fish, 180-181.

133 Scott and Scott, *Atlantic Fishes of Canada*, 518-520; Collette and Klein-MacPhee, *Bigelow and Schroeder's Fishes*, 363-367.

134 COSEWIC, *Atlantic Wolffish*, 1-21.

135 Kulka, Hood, and Huntington, *Recovery Strategy*, 1-103.

136 Nozères et al., *Identification Guide*, 112.

137 Scott and Scott, *Atlantic Fishes of Canada*, 432-434; Collette and Klein-MacPhee, *Bigelow and Schroeder's Fishes*, 485-494.

138 Muus and Nielsen, Sea Fish, 211-212.

139 Scott and Scott, *Atlantic Fishes of Canada*, 432-434; Collette and Klein-MacPhee, *Bigelow and Schroeder's Fishes*, 485-494.

140 Scott and Scott, *Atlantic Fishes of Canada*, 432-434; Collette and Klein-MacPhee, *Bigelow and Schroeder's Fishes*, 485-494.

141 Benoît, Darbyson, and Swain, An Atlas, 1-185.

142 COSEWIC, *Spotted Wolffish*, 1-22; Kulka, Hood, and Huntington, *Recovery Strategy*, 1-103; Dawe and Neis, "Species at Risk in Canada," 405-413.

143 Hooper, *Bonne Bay Marine Resources*, 1-267.

144 Nozères et al., *Identification Guide*, 113.

145 Scott and Scott, *Atlantic Fishes of Canada*, 434-436; Collette and Klein-MacPhee, *Bigelow and Schroeder's Fishes*, 494-496.

146 Muus and Nielsen, Sea Fish, 212-213.

147 Scott and Scott, *Atlantic Fishes of Canada*, 434-436; Collette and Klein-MacPhee, *Bigelow and Schroeder's Fishes*, 494-496.

148 Scott and Scott, *Atlantic Fishes of Canada*, 434-436; Collette and Klein-MacPhee, *Bigelow and Schroeder's Fishes*, 494-496.

149 Benoît, Darbyson, and Swain, *An Atlas*, 1-185.

150 Currie et al., *The Nearshore Fish Fauna of Bonne Bay*, 1-66.

151 Nozères et al., *Identification Guide*, 119.

152 Scott and Scott, *Atlantic Fishes of Canada*, 408; Collette and Klein-MacPhee, *Bigelow and Schroeder's Fishes*, 467.

153 Scott and Scott, *Atlantic Fishes of Canada*, 408; Collette and Klein-MacPhee, *Bigelow and Schroeder's Fishes*, 467.

154 Scott and Scott, *Atlantic Fishes of Canada*, 408; Collette and Klein-MacPhee, *Bigelow and Schroeder's Fishes*, 467.

155 Nozères et al., *Identification Guide*, 125.

[156] Scott and Scott, *Atlantic Fishes of Canada*, 412-414; Collette and Klein-MacPhee, *Bigelow and Schroeder's Fishes*, 470-474.

[157] Scott and Scott, *Atlantic Fishes of Canada*, 412-414; Collette and Klein-MacPhee, *Bigelow and Schroeder's Fishes*, 470-474.

[158] Scott and Scott, *Atlantic Fishes of Canada*, 412-414; Collette and Klein-MacPhee, *Bigelow and Schroeder's Fishes*, 470-474.

[159] Scott and Scott, *Atlantic Fishes of Canada*, 550-552; Collette and Klein-MacPhee, *Bigelow and Schroeder's Fishes*, 572-576.

[160] Currie et al., *The Nearshore Fish Fauna of Bonne Bay*, 1-66.

[161] Nozères et al., *Identification Guide*, 38.

[162] Scott and Scott, *Atlantic Fishes of Canada*, 550-552; Collette and Klein-MacPhee, *Bigelow and Schroeder's Fishes*, 572-576.

[163] Scott and Scott, *Atlantic Fishes of Canada*, 550-552; Collette and Klein-MacPhee, *Bigelow and Schroeder's Fishes*, 572-576.

[164] Scott and Scott, *Atlantic Fishes of Canada*, 550-552; Collette and Klein-MacPhee, *Bigelow and Schroeder's Fishes*, 572-576.

[165] Benoît, Darbyson, and Swain, *An Atlas*, 1-185.

[166] Currie et al., *The Nearshore Fish Fauna of Bonne Bay*, 1-66.

[167] Nozères et al., *Identification Guide*, 25.

[168] Scott and Scott, *Atlantic Fishes of Canada*, 293-296; Collette and Klein-MacPhee, *Bigelow and Schroeder's Fishes*, 258-261.

[169] Scott and Scott, *Atlantic Fishes of Canada*, 293-296; Collette and Klein-MacPhee, *Bigelow and Schroeder's Fishes*, 258-261.

[170] Scott and Scott, *Atlantic Fishes of Canada*, 293-296; Collette and Klein-MacPhee, *Bigelow and Schroeder's Fishes*, 258-261; Nozères et al., *Identification Guide*, 25.

[171] Benoît, Darbyson, and Swain, *An Atlas*, 1-185.

[172] Muus and Nielsen, *Sea Fish*, 308-310; Kearley, *Here's the Catch*, 149-152.

[173] Nozères et al., *Identification Guide*, 24.

[174] Scott and Scott, *Atlantic Fishes of Canada*, 278-280; Collette and Klein-MacPhee, *Bigelow and Schroeder's Fishes*, 219-222.

[175] Scott and Scott, *Atlantic Fishes of Canada*, 278-280; Collette and Klein-MacPhee, *Bigelow and Schroeder's Fishes*, 219-222.

[176] Scott and Scott, *Atlantic Fishes of Canada*, 278-280; Collette and Klein-MacPhee, *Bigelow and Schroeder's Fishes*, 219-222.

[177] Benoît, Darbyson, and Swain, *An Atlas*, 1-185.

[178] Anderson et al., *Marine Areas with Special Protection*, (forthcoming).

[179] Nozères et al., *Identification Guide*, 46.

[180] Scott and Scott, *Atlantic Fishes of Canada*, 114-118; Collette and Klein-MacPhee, *Bigelow and Schroeder's Fishes*, 141-156.

[181] Muus and Nielsen, Sea Fish, 87-90.

[182] Scott and Scott, *Atlantic Fishes of Canada*, 114-118; Collette and Klein-MacPhee, *Bigelow and Schroeder's Fishes*, 141-156.

[183] Scott and Scott, *Atlantic Fishes of Canada*, 114-118; Collette and

Klein-MacPhee, *Bigelow and Schroeder's Fishes*, 141-156.

184 Muus and Nielsen, *Sea Fish*, 308; Kearley, *Here's the Catch*, 152-153.

185 Benoît, Darbyson, and Swain, *An Atlas*, 1-185.

186 Paterson, *Study on the Small Pelagic Fisheries*, 1-66.

187 Muus and Nielsen, *Sea Fish*, 316-319.

188 Scott and Scott, *Atlantic Fishes of Canada*, 452-455; Collette and Klein-MacPhee, *Bigelow and Schroeder's Fishes*, 523-529.

189 Nozères et al., Identification Guide, 51.

190 Scott and Scott, *Atlantic Fishes of Canada*, 452-455; Collette and Klein-MacPhee, *Bigelow and Schroeder's Fishes*, 523-529.

191 Scott and Scott, *Atlantic Fishes of Canada*, 452-455; Collette and Klein-MacPhee, *Bigelow and Schroeder's Fishes*, 523-529.

192 Muus and Nielsen, *Sea Fish*, 237-239.

193 Scott and Scott, *Atlantic Fishes of Canada*, 452-455; Collette and Klein-MacPhee, *Bigelow and Schroeder's Fishes*, 523-529.

194 Muus and Nielsen, *Sea Fish*, 308.

195 Benoît, Darbyson, and Swain, *An Atlas*, 1-185; Kearley, *Here's the Catch*, 153.

196 Paterson, *Study on the Small Pelagic Fisheries*, 1-66.

197 COSEWIC, *Spiny Dogfish*, 1-50.

198 Hooper, *Bonne Bay Marine Resources*, 1-267.

199 Nozères et al., *Identification Guide*, 10.

200 Scott and Scott, *Atlantic Fishes of Canada*, 35-37; Collette and Klein-MacPhee, *Bigelow and Schroeder's Fishes*, 54-57.

201 Muus and Nielsen, *Sea Fish*, 54-55.

202 Scott and Scott, *Atlantic Fishes of Canada*, 35-37; Collette and Klein-MacPhee, *Bigelow and Schroeder's Fishes*, 54-57.

203 Scott and Scott, *Atlantic Fishes of Canada*, 35-37; Collette and Klein-MacPhee, *Bigelow and Schroeder's Fishes*, 54-57.

204 Benoît, Darbyson, and Swain, *An Atlas*, 1-185.

205 Kearley, *Here's the Catch*, 149-150.

206 Nozères et al., *Identification Guide*, 21.

207 Hooper, *Bonne Bay Marine Resources*, 1-267.

208 Muus and Nielsen, *Sea Fish*, 126-127.

209 Benoît, Darbyson, and Swain, *An Atlas*, 1-185.

210 Anderson, "Millions of Fish," 128-139.

211 Rose, *Cod*, 541.

212 Scott and Scott, *Atlantic Fishes of Canada*, 274-276; Collette and Klein-MacPhee, *Bigelow and Schroeder's Fishes*, 235-242.

213 Muus and Nielsen, *Sea Fish*, 132-133.

214 Benoît, Darbyson, and Swain, *An Atlas*, 1-185.

215 Scott and Scott, *Atlantic Fishes of Canada*, 286-288; Collette and Klein-MacPhee, *Bigelow and Schroeder's Fishes*, 247-252; Nozères et al., *Identification Guide*, 22.

216 Muus and Nielsen, *Sea Fish*, 1-340; Proctor and Lynch, *A Field Guide*, 1-221.

217 Hooper, *Bonne Bay Marine Resources*, 1-267.

218 Scott and Scott, *Atlantic Fishes of Canada*, 310-312; Collette and Klein-MacPhee, *Bigelow and Schroeder's Fishes*, 285-287.

219 Nozères et al., *Identification Guide*, 48.

220 Scott and Scott, *Atlantic Fishes of Canada*, 310-312; Collette and Klein-MacPhee, *Bigelow and Schroeder's Fishes*, 285-287.

221 Muus and Nielsen, *Sea Fish*, 152-153.

222 Scott and Scott, *Atlantic Fishes of Canada*, 310-312; Collette and Klein-MacPhee, *Bigelow and Schroeder's Fishes*, 285-287.

223 Scott and Scott, *Atlantic Fishes of Canada*, 310-312; Collette and Klein-MacPhee, *Bigelow and Schroeder's Fishes*, 285-287.

224 Benoît, Darbyson, and Swain, *An Atlas*, 1-185.

225 Muus and Nielsen, *Sea Fish*, 276-277.

226 Scott and Scott, *Atlantic Fishes of Canada*, 571-573; Collette and Klein-MacPhee, *Bigelow and Schroeder's Fishes*, 604-607.

227 Muus and Nielsen, *Sea Fish*, 276-277.

228 Ibid., 240-241.

229 Coad, *Guide to the Marine Sport Fishes*, 1-307.

230 Collette and Klein-MacPhee, *Bigelow and Schroeder's Fishes*, 531-536; Muus and Nielsen, *Sea Fish*, 240-241.

231 Benoît, Darbyson, and Swain, *An Atlas*, 1-185.

232 COSEWIC, *Bluefin Tuna*, 1-30.

233 Muus and Nielsen, *Sea Fish*, 246-247.

234 Coad, *Guide to the Marine Sport Fishes*, 1-307.

235 Scott and Scott, *Atlantic Fishes of Canada*, 463-467; Collette and Klein-MacPhee, *Bigelow and Schroeder's Fishes,* 509-514; Muus and Nielsen, *Sea Fish*, 246-247.

CHAPTER 4

1 Hutchings et al., *Sustaining Canadian Marine Biodiversity*, 1-315.

2 Office of the Auditor General of Canada. *Adapting to Climate Impacts*.

3 The historical average date of ice formation on Bonne Bay is 5 February, and the average date of ice melting in the spring is 9 April. Richards, "Wind-forced Dynamics in Bonne Bay," 1-111.

4 Hutchings et al., *Sustaining Canadian Marine Biodiversity*, 1-315.

5 Barton, *Bond's Biology of Fishes*, 624-633.

6 Scott and Scott, *Atlantic Fishes of Canada*, 139.

7 Rombough, Barbour, and Kerekes, "Life History and Taxonomic Status," 1537-1541.

8 Currie et al., *The Nearshore Fish Fauna of Bonne Bay*, 1-60.

9 Nozères et al., *Identification Guide*, 1-243.

10 Anderson et al., *Marine Areas*, 9.

11 The Strait of Belle Isle is an oceanographic boundary separating the cold-temperate seawater of the Gulf from the subarctic seawater of coastal Labrador. As expected given the location of Bonne Bay, the fish fauna of the bay is a combination of temperate fishes living at their northern limit of cold water tolerance and subarctic fishes near their southern limit of warm water tolerance.

12 Wroblewski et al., "The Fish Fauna of Gilbert Bay," 575-587.

13 Scott and Scott, *Atlantic Fishes of Canada*, 137-141; Scott and Crossman, *Freshwater Fishes of Canada*, 201-207.

14 Gomez-Uchida, Knight, and Ruzzante, "Interaction of Landscape," 4854-4869.

15 Scott and Scott, *Atlantic Fishes of Canada*, 137-141; Scott and Crossman, *Freshwater Fishes of Canada*, 201-207.

16 Rombough, Barbour, and Kerekes, "Life History and Taxonomic Status," 1537-1541.; Gomez-Uchida, Knight, and Ruzzante, "Interaction of Landscape," 4854-4869.

17 Anderson et al., *Marine Areas*, 9.

18 Snelgrove, *Discoveries of the Census of Marine Life*, 1-270.

19 Anthropogenic carbon dioxide in the atmosphere enters the sea through the air-sea interface. Gaseous CO2 entering the surface of the ocean will acidify the seawater, since CO2 plus water form carbonic acid. The ecological problem is that marine calcareous organisms will have a difficult time forming external body layers of calcium carbonate if the seawater is too acidic. Calcium carbonate will dissolve in acidic seawater. Bivalve molluscs will not be able to form their shells in acidic waters.

People concerned about climate change and the marine environment should be aware of the ocean acidification problem. People can reduce their "carbon footprint" by burning less fossil fuel which produces carbon dioxide, and slow this threat to the marine ecosystem.

For further information see: Hutchings et al., Sustaining Canadian Marine Biodiversity, 1-315.

20 Gosner, A Field Guide, 48; Karleskint, Turner, and Small, *Introduction to Marine Biology*, 142-143.

21 Gosner, A Field Guide, 48; Karleskint, Turner, and Small, *Introduction to Marine Biology*, 142-143.

22 Copeland et al., "Marine Habitat Mapping," 1-13.

23 Gosner, *A Field Guide*, 247.

24 Matheson and Gagnon, "Effects of Temperature," 49-56.

25 Gosner, *A Field Guide*, 247.

26 Ibid., 247.

27 Gosner, *A Field Guide*, 247; Matheson and Gagnon, "Effects of Temperature," 49-56.

28 Gosner, *A Field Guide*, 110-120.

29 Caines and Gagnon, "Population Dynamics," 1817-1832.

30 Caines and Gagnon, "Population Dynamics," 1817-1832.

31 Gosner, *A Field Guide*, 118; Karleskint, Turner, and Small, *Introduction to Marine Biology*, 210.

32 Gosner, *A Field Guide*, 118; Karleskint, Turner, and Small, *Introduction to Marine Biology*, 210.

33 Gosner, *A Field Guide*, 111.

34 Karleskint, Turner, and Small, *Introduction to Marine Biology*, 221.

35 Fréchet, *Changes in Biological Characteristics*, 1-30.

36 Reeves, "The Origins and Character," 71-106; Dickinson and Sanger, *Twentieth-Century Shore-Station Whaling*, 1-273.

37 Dawe and Neis, "Species at Risk in Canada," 405-413.

38 Dawe and Neis, "Species at Risk in Canada," 405-413.

39 Valentin, "Structure des Populations," 1-212.; COSEWIC, *Deepwater Redfish/Acadian Redfish*, 1-80.

CHAPTER 5

1 Martinez-Murillo and Haedrich, "A Perspective on Newfoundland's Fisheries Ecosystem," 13-32; Fréchet, *Changes in Biological Characteristics*, 1-30.

2 Hooper, *Bonne Bay Marine Resources*, 1-267.

3 Fishing regulations for Gros Morne National Park are available online at http://www.pc.gc.ca/pn-np/nl/grosmorne/activ/peche-fishi ng.aspx.

4 Gutiérrez, Hilborn, and Defeo, "Leadership," 386-389; Gray, *Participation*, 1-363.

5 Rogers, "Examining the Local Lobster," 184p; Neville, "Effects of a Fishing Moratorium," 84p.

6 Charles, *Sustainable Fishery Systems*, 1-370.

7 Neville, "Effects of a Fishing Moratorium," 1-84.

8 Ennis, "Closed Areas as a Conservation Strategy," 11-20.

9 Seiden, Wilke, and Schneider, *Lobster Sustainability Measures*, 1-12.

10 Hooper, *Bonne Bay Marine Resources*, 1975; Bruce, Schneider, and Wroblewski, *The Habitats of 0-Group*, 1-41.

11 Information on the Fisheries Act is available online at http://laws-lois.justice.gc.ca/eng/acts/F-14/.

12 Currie et al., *The Nearshore Fish Fauna of Bonne Bay*, 1-66; Bruce, Schneider, and Wroblewski, *The Habitats of 0-Group*, 1-41.

13 An example of what people can do to help rebuild the cod fishery is to return "mother cod" to the water if these large spawners are caught in the recreational/food fishery. CURRA Community partner Intervale Associates has produced Atlantic Cod placemats and distributed these placemats to family-style restaurants across the Province of NL, promoting discussions about cod recovery with people of all ages. The central message of the placemat is that all of us can help. A YouTube video on rebuilding cod stocks produced by Intervale Associates is available online at http://www.curra.ca/videos_cod_dvd.htm.

14 The Canadian Code of Conduct for Responsible Fishing Operations has been developed and adopted by commercial fishing organizations across

Canada. Information on the Code of Conduct is available online at: http://www.dfo-mpo.gc.ca/fm-gp/policies-politiques/cccrfo-cccppr-eng.htm.

15 Lowitt, *A Community Food Security Assessment*, 1-38.

16 Harris and Shepherd, "Food Security," 129-144.

17 Turner, Parrish, and Solberg, "Food Security in Coastal Communities," 1-12.

18 Rose, *Cod*, 288; Kurlansky, *Cod*, 237-238.

19 Kurlansky, *Cod*, 237-238.

20 Solberg, Canning, and Buehler, "Changing Patterns," 161-175.

21 Montevecchi, Chaffey, and Burke, "Hunting for Security," 99-113.

22 Special hunting permits for culling moose in Gros Morne National Park were issued in 2011 and 2012, as these animals normally protected within the Park became too abundant and were overgrazing the woodlands. Dr. Tom Knight, personal communication, June 2011. More information on hunting moose in GMNP is available online at http://www.pc.gc.ca/eng/pn-np/nl/grosmorne/index.aspx.

23 Turner, Parrish, and Solberg, "Food Security in Coastal Communities," 1-12.; Lowitt, *A Community Food Security Assessment*, 1-38.

24 Scott and Black, *Wildflowers*, 64-65; Boland, *Trees and Shrubs*, 246-247.

25 CURRA, *Working Better Together*, 2012.

26 For more information regarding the public events at the Bonne Bay Marine Station and visitor hours for viewing the aquarium, one can visit the website http://www.bonnebay.ca/.

27 Rogers, "Examining the Local Lobster," 184p; Neville, "Effects of a Fishing Moratorium," 1-84.

28 Information on the local radio station Voice of Bonne Bay is available online at: http://www.curra.ca/community_radio.htm

29 Burton, *Fish and Wildlife*, 135; Burzinski, *Gros Morne*, 73-74.

30 Burzinski, *Gros Morne*, 66-69.

31 Anderson et al., *Marine Areas*, 38-39.

32 Office of the Auditor General of Canada. *Oil Spills from Ships*, 1-37.

33 Foss, "Coming Home to Roost," 2-3; Dr. Bill Monetvecchi, personal communication, June 2011.

BIBLIOGRAPHY

Able, K.W. and M.P. Fahay. *Ecology of Estuarine Fishes: Temperate Waters of the Western North Atlantic.* Baltimore: John Hopkins University Press, 2010.

Andersen, R. "Millions of Fish." *Canadian Issues.* 3.1 (1980): 128-139.

Anderson, T.C. *The Rivers of Labrador.* Canadian Special Publication of Fisheries and Aquatic Sciences 81, 1985.

Anderson, T.C., S.D. Lambert, J.M. Simms, and T. Taylor-Walsh. *Marine Areas with Special Protection, Newfoundland and Labrador.* Canadian Manuscript Report of Fisheries and Aquatic Sciences 2507, 2000.

Arbour, J.H., P. Avendano, and J.A. Hutchings. "Aspects of the Ecology and Life History of Alligatorfish *Aspidophoroides monopterygius.*" *Environmental Biology of Fishes* 87 (2010): 353-363.

Baillon, S., J.F. Hamel, V.E. Wareham, and A. Mercier. "Deep Cold-water Corals as Nurseries for Fish Larvae." *Frontiers in Ecology and the Environment* (2012):1-10. doi: 10.1890/120022.

Barton, M. *Bond's Biology of Fishes*, 3rd ed. Belmont, CA: Thompson Higher Education, 2007.

Benoit, H.P., E. Darbyson, and D.P. Swain. *An Atlas of the Geographic Distribution of Marine Fish and Invertebrates in the Southern Gulf of St. Lawrence Based on Annual Bottom-trawl Surveys (1971-2002).* Canadian Data Report of Fisheries and Aquatic Sciences 1112, 2003.

Boland, T. *Trees and Shrubs of Newfoundland and Labrador: Field Guide.* Portugal Cove-St. Philip's, NL: Boulder Publications, 2011.

Bruce, J.E.B., D.C. Schneider, and J.S. Wroblewski. *The Habitats of 0-group Juvenile Atlantic Cod in Bonne Bay, a Fjord Within Gros Morne National Park,* Newfoundland. Community-University Research for Recovery Alliance (CURRA) Project Report. St. John's: Memorial University, 2010. http://www.curra.ca/documents/Bruce_et_al-CURRA-7June2010.pdf.

Burton, L. DeVere. *Fish and Wildlife: Principles of Zoology and Ecology*, 3rd ed. Clifton Park, NY: Delmar, 2010.

Burzynski, M. *Gros Morne National Park.* St. John's: Breakwater Books, 1999.

Burzynski, M. and A. Marceau, eds. *Rocks Adrift: The Geology of Gros Morne National Park.* Rocky Harbour, NL: Gros Morne Co-operating Association, 1990.

Caines, S. and P. Gagnon. "Population Dynamics of the Invasive Bryozoans *Membranipora membranacea* Along a 450-km Latitudinal Range in the Subarctic Northwestern Atlantic." *Marine Biology* 159 (2012: 1817-1832.

Cairns, D.K., G. Chapdelaine, and W.A. Montevecchi. "Prey Exploitation by Seabirds in the Gulf of St. Lawrence." In *The Gulf of St. Lawrence: Small Ocean or Big Estuary?* Edited by J.C. Therriault. *Canadian Special Publication of Fisheries and Aquatic Sciences* 113 (1991): 277-291.

Caputo, M. "Migratory behaviour of Brook Charr (*Salvelinus fontinalis*) in Gros Morne National Park, Newfoundland, and the Potential for Co-management of the Recreational Fishery." M.Sc. thesis, Memorial University of Newfoundland, (forthcoming).

Charles, A.T. *Sustainable Fishery Systems*. Oxford: Blackwell Science, 2001.

Chouinard, G.A., D.P. Swain, M.O. Hammill, and G.A. Poirier. "Covariation Between Grey Seal (*Halichoerus grypus*) Abundance and Natural Mortality of Cod (*Gadus morhua*) in the Southern Gulf of St. Lawrence." *Canadian Journal of Fisheries and Aquatic Sciences* 62 (2005): 1991-2000.

Chassot E., D. Duplisea, M. Hammill, A. Caskenette, N. Bousquet, Y. Lambert, and G. Stenson. "Role of Predation by Harp Seals *Pagophilus groenlandicus* in the Collapse and Non-recovery of Northern Gulf of St. Lawrence Cod *Gadus morhua*." *Marine Ecology Progress Series* 379 (2009): 279–297.

Coad, B.W. *Guide to the Marine Sport Fishes of Atlantic Canada and New England*. Toronto: University of Toronto Press, 1992.

Collette, B. and G. Klein-MacPhee, eds. *Bigelow and Schroeder's Fishes of the Gulf of Maine*, 3rd Ed. Washington: Smithsonian Institution Press, 2002.

Colpron, E., E. Edinger, and B. Neis. "Mapping the Distribution of Deep-sea Corals in the Northern Gulf of St. Lawrence Using Both Scientific and Local Ecological Knowledge." Canadian Science Advisory Secretariat Research Document 2010/047 (2010):1-15.

Copeland, A., E. Edinger, R. Devillers, T. Bell, P. LeBlanc, and. J. Wroblewski. "Marine Habitat Mapping in Support of Marine Protected Area Management in a Subarctic Fjord: Gilbert Bay, Labrador, Canada." *Journal of Coastal Conservation* (2011). doi: 10.1007/s 11852-011-0172-1.

COSEWIC. COSEWIC Assessment and Status Report on the Atlantic Wolffish Anarhichas lupus in Canada. Committee on the Status of Endangered Wildlife in Canada. Ottawa, 2000. http://www.sararegistry.gc.ca/species/species Details_e.cfm?sid=652.

-----. *COSEWIC Assessment and Update Status Report on the Leatherback Turtle* Dermochelys coriacea *in Canada*. Committee on the Status of Endangered Wildlife in Canada. Ottawa, 2001. http://www.sararegistry.gc.ca/species/speciesDetails_e.cfm?sid=274.

-----. *COSEWIC Assessment and Status Report on the Spotted Wolffish* Anarhichas minor *in Canada*. Committee on the Status of Endangered Wildlife in Canada. Ottawa, 2001. http://www.sararegistry.gc.ca/species/species Details_e.cfm?sid=669.

-----. *COSEWIC Assessment and Update Status Report on the Blue Whale* Balaenoptera musculus *in Canada*. Committee on the Status of Endangered Wildlife in Canada. Ottawa, 2002. http://www.sararegistry.gc.ca/species/speciesDetails_e.cfm?sid=717.

-----. *COSEWIC Assessment and Update Status Report on the North Atlantic Right Whale* Eubalaena glacialis *in Canada*. Committee on the Status of

Endangered Wildlife in Canada. Ottawa, 2003. http://www.sararegistry.gc.ca/species/speciesDetails_e.cfm?sid=135.

-----. *COSEWIC Assessment and Update Status Report on the Beluga Whale* Delphinapterus leucas *in Canada.* Committee on the Status of Endangered Wildlife in Canada. Ottawa, 2004. http://www.sararegistry.gc.ca/species/speciesDetails_e.cfm?sid=102.

-----. *COSEWIC Assessment and Update Status Report on the Fin Whale* Balaenoptera physalus *in Canada.* Committee on the Status of Endangered Wildlife in Canada. Ottawa, 2005. http://www.sararegistry.gc.ca/species/speciesDetails_e.cfm?sid=874.

-----. *COSEWIC Assessment and Status Report on the Winter Skate* Leucoraja ocellata *in Canada.* Committee on the Status of Endangered Wildlife in Canada. Ottawa, 2005. http://www.sararegistry.gc.ca/species/speciesDetails_e.cfm?sid=854.

-----. *COSEWIC Assessment and Update Status Report on the American Eel* Anguilla rostrata *in Canada.* Committee on the Status of Endangered Wildlife in Canada. Ottawa, 2006. http://www.sararegistry.gc.ca/species/speciesDetails_e.cfm?sid=891.

-----. *COSEWIC Assessment and Update Status Report on the Harbour Porpoise* Phocoena phocoena *Northwest Atlantic Population in Canada.* Committee on the Status of Endangered Wildlife in Canada. Ottawa, 2006. http://www.sararegistry.gc.ca/species/speciesDetails_e.cfm?sid=147.

-----. *COSEWIC Assessment and Update Status Report on the Ivory Gull* Pagophila eburnea *Northwest Atlantic Population in Canada.* Committee on the Status of Endangered Wildlife in Canada. Ottawa, 2006. http://www.sararegistry.gc.ca/species/speciesDetails_e.cfm?sid=50.

-----. *COSEWIC Assessment and Update Status Report on the Killer Whale* Orcinas orca *in Canada.* Committee on the Status of Endangered Wildlife in Canada. Ottawa, 2008. http://www.sararegistry.gc.ca/species/speciesDetails_e.cfm?sid=598.

-----. *COSEWIC Assessment and Status Report on the Atlantic Cod* Gadus morhua *in Canada.* Committee on the Status of Endangered Wildlife in Canada. Ottawa, 2010. http://www.sararegistry.gc.ca/species/speciesDetails_e.cfm?sid=764.

-----. *COSEWIC assessment and status report on the Atlantic Salmon* Salmo salar *(Nunavik population, Labrador population, Northeast Newfoundland population, South Newfoundland population, Southwest Newfoundland population, Northwest Newfoundland population, Quebec Eastern North Shore population, Quebec Western North Shore population, Anticosti Island population, Inner St. Lawrence population, Lake Ontario population, Gaspé-Southern Gulf of St. Lawrence population, Eastern Cape Breton population, Nova Scotia Southern Upland population, Inner Bay of Fundy population, Outer Bay of Fundy population) in Canada.* Committee on the Status of Endangered Wildlife in Canada. Ottawa, 2010. http://www.sararegistry.gc.ca/document/default_e.cfm?documentID=2258.

-----. *COSEWIC Assessment and Status Report on the Deepwater Redfish/ Acadian Redfish Complex* Sebastes mentella *and* Sebastes fasciatus, *in Canada.* Committee on the Status of Endangered Wildlife in Canada. Ottawa, 2010. http://www.sararegistry.gc.ca/species/speciesDetails_e.cfm?sid=1097.

-----. *COSEWIC Assessment and Update Status Report on the Loggerhead Sea Turtle* Caretta caretta *in Canada.* Committee on the Status of Endangered Wildlife in Canada. Ottawa, 2010. http://www.sararegistry.gc.ca/species/species Details_e.cfm?sid=1090.

-----. *COSEWIC Assessment and Status Report on the Spiny Dogfish* Squalus acanthias, *Atlantic Population, in Canada.* Committee on the Status of Endangered Wildlife in Canada. Ottawa, 2010. http://www.sararegistry.gc.ca/species/ speciesDetails_e.cfm?sid=1102.

-----. *COSEWIC Assessment and Status Report on the Bluefin Tuna* Thunnus thynnus *in Canada.* Committee on the Status of Endangered Wildlife in Canada. Ottawa, 2011. http://www.sararegistry.gc.ca/species/speciesDetails _e.cfm?sid=1148.

-----. *COSEWIC Assessment and Update Status Report on the Humpback Whale* Megaptera novaeangliae *in Canada.* Committee on the Status of Endangered Wildlife in Canada. Ottawa, 2011. http://www.sararegistry.gc.ca/species/ speciesDetails_e.cfm?sid=160.

-----. *COSEWIC Assessment and Status Report on the Thorny Skate* Amblyraja radiata *in Canada.* Committee on the Status of Endangered Wildlife in Canada. Ottawa, 2012. http://www.registrelep-sararegistry.gc.ca/default_e.cfm.

CURRA. *Working Better Together: Fisheries and Tourism in Newfoundland and Labrador.* 2012. http://www.curra.ca/reports.htm.

Currie, J.J., J.S. Wroblewski, D.A. Methven, and R.G. Hooper. *The Nearshore Fish Fauna of Bonne Bay, a Fjord within Gros Morne National Park, Newfoundland.* Community-University Research for Recovery Alliance (CURRA) Project Report. St. John's: Memorial University, 2009. http://www.curra.ca/ documents/Currie%20et%20al%20CURRA%20Report%20Sept09.pdf.

Dadswell, M.J. "Some Notes on Shoaling Behavior and Growth of *Mysis gaspensis* (Mysidacea) in a Small Newfoundland Estuary." *Canadian Journal of Zoology* 53 (1975): 374-377.

Dawe, J. and B. Neis. "Species at Risk in Canada: Lessons Learned from the Listing of Three Species of Wolffish." *Marine Policy* 36 (2012): 405-413.

Department of Fisheries and Aquaculture. *Seafood Industry Year in Review 2010.* St. John's: Government of Newfoundland and Labrador, 2011.

Dickie, L.M. and R.W. Trites. "The Gulf of St. Lawrence." *In Ecosystems of the World. No. 26. Estuaries and Enclosed Seas.* Edited by B.H. Ketchum, 403-426. Amsterdam-Oxford-New York: Elsevier Scientific Publishing Company, 1983.

Dickinson, A.B. and C.W. Sanger. *Twentieth-Century Shore-Station Whaling in Newfoundland and Labrador.* Montreal: McGill-Queen's University Press, 2005.

Elliott, M. and K.L. Hemingway, eds. *Fishes in Estuaries*. Oxford: Blackwell Science, 2002.

Ennis G.P. "Closed Areas as a Conservation Strategy in the Newfoundland Lobster Fishery." *Biodiversity* 12 (2011): 11-20.

Foss, K. 2011. "Coming Home to Roost: How the Gulf of Mexico Oil Spill is Impacting Canadian Birds." *Memorial University's Research Magazine* Winter/Spring (2011): 2-3.

Fréchet, A. *Changes in Biological Characteristics of the Fisheries of the Gulf of St. Lawrence (NAFO Divisions 4RST)* since 1960. Research Document 2005/088 (2005).

Gardner Pinfold Consultants, Inc. *Economic Value of Wild Atlantic Salmon*. Halifax, N.S., 2011.

Gomez-Uchida, D., T.W. Knight, and D.E. Ruzzante. "Interaction of Landscape and Life History Attributes on Genetic Diversity, Neutral Divergence and Gene Flow in a Pristine Community of Salmonids." *Molecular Ecology* 18 (2009): 4854-4869.

Gosner, K.L. *Guide to Identification of Marine and Estuarine Invertebrates: Cape Hatteras to the Bay of Fundy*. New York: Wiley-Interscience, 1971.

Gosner, K.L. *A Field Guide to the Atlantic Seashore: Invertebrates and Seaweeds of the Atlantic Coast from the Bay of Fundy to Cape Hatteras*. Boston: Houghton Mifflin, 1978.

Gray, T.S. *Participation in Fisheries Governance*. Berlin: Springer, 2005.

Greenberg, P. *Four Fish: The Future of the Last Wild Food*. New York: Penguin, 2010.

Guénette, S. and J. Alder. "Lessons from Marine Protected Areas and Integrated Ocean Management Initiatives in Canada." *Coastal Management* 35 (2007): 51-78.

Gutiérrez, N.L., R. Hilborn, and O. Defeo. "Leadership, Social Capital and Incentives Promote Successful Fisheries." *Nature* 470 (2011): 386-389.

Haedrich, R.L. "Estuarine Fishes." In *Ecosystems of the World. No. 26. Estuaries and Enclosed Seas*. Edited by B.H. Ketchum, 183-207. Amsterdam-Oxford-New York: Elsevier Scientific Publishing Company, 1983.

Haedrich, R.L. and C.A.S. Hall. "Fishes and Estuaries." *Estuaries* 19.5 (1976): 55-63.

Harris, C.E. and C. Shepherd. "Food Security, Learning and Culture: Bridging the Responsibility Gap in Public Schools." In *Resetting the Kitchen Table: Food Security, Culture, Health and Resilience in Coastal Communities*. Edited by C.C. Parrish, N.J. Turner, and S.M. Solberg, 129-144. New York: Nova Science Publishers, 2007.

Hilborn, R., T.A. Branch, B. Ernst, A. Magnusson, C.V. Minte-Vera, M.D. Scheuerrel, and J.L. Valero. "State of the World's Fisheries." *Annual Review of Environment and Resources* 28 (2003): 359-399.

Hild, M.H. *Geology of Newfoundland: Touring through Time at 48 Scenic*

Sites. Portugal Cove-St. Phillips: Boulder Publications, 2012.

Hooper, R. *Bonne Bay Marine Resources: An Ecological and Biological Assessment*. Contract Report for Parks Canada, 1975.

Hooper, R.G., G.R. South, and A. Whittick. "Ecological Aspects of the Phytobenthos of the Island of Newfoundland." In *The Shore Environment*. Edited by J.H. Price, D.E.G. Irvine, and W.F. Farnham, 395-423. London: Academic Press, 1980.

Horn, M.H, K.L.M. Martin, and M.A. Chotkowski, eds. *Intertidal Fishes: Life in Two Worlds*. London: Academic Press, 1999.

Hutchings, J.A., I.M. Côté, J.J. Dodson, I.A. Fleming, S. Jennings, N.J. Mantua, R.M. Peterman, B.E. Riddell, A.J. Weaver, and D.L. VanderZwaag. *Sustaining Canadian Marine Biodiversity: Responding to the Challenges Posed by Climate Change, Fisheries, and Aquaculture*. Expert panel report prepared for the Royal Society of Canada, Ottawa, 2012.

Kaiser, M.J., M.J. Attrill, S. Jennings, D.N. Thomas, D.K.A. Barnes, A.S. Brierley, J.G. Hiddink, H. Kaartokallio, N.V.C. Polunin, and D.G. Raffaelli. *Marine Ecology: Processes, Systems, and Impacts*, 2nd ed. Oxford: Oxford University Press, 2011.

Karleskint, G. Jr., R. Turner, and J.W. Small, Jr. *Introduction to Marine Biology*. 2nd ed. Belmont, CA: Thompson Higher Education, 2006.

Kearley, W. *Here's the Catch: The Fish We Harvest from the Northwest Atlantic*. Portugal Cove-St. Phillip's, NL: Boulder Publications, 2012.

Klemetsen A., P.-A. Amundsen, J. B. Dempson, B. Jonsson, N. Jonsson, M. F. O'Connell, and E. Mortensen. "Atlantic Salmon *Salmo salar* L., Brown Trout *Salmo trutta* L. and Arctic Charr *Salvelinus alpinus* L.: A Review of Aspects of Their Life Histories." *Ecology of Freshwater Fish* 12 (2003): 1-59.

Kulka, D., C. Hood, and J. Huntington. *Recovery Strategy for Northern Wolffish (*Anarhichas denticulatus*) and Spotted Wolffish (*Anarhichas minor*), and Management Plan for Atlantic Wolffish (*Anarhichas lupus*) in Canada*. St. John's: Fisheries and Oceans Canada, 2007.

Kurlansky, M. *Cod: A Biography of the Fish that Changed the World*. Toronto: Knopf, 1997.

Lacoste, K.N. and G.B. Stenson. "Winter Distribution of Harp Seals (*Phoca groenlandica*) off Eastern Newfoundland and Southern Labrador." *Polar Biology* 23 (2000): 805-811.

Le Bris. A., A. Fréchet, P.S. Galbraith, and J.S. Wroblewski. "Evidence for Alternative Migratory Behaviors in the Northern Gulf of St. Lawrence Population of Atlantic Cod (*Gadus morhua*)." *ICES Journal of Marine Science*. doi: 10.1093/icesjms/fst068.

Lesage, V., J. Keays, S. Turgeon, and S. Hurtubise. "Bycatch of Harbour Porpoises (*Phocoena phocoena*) in Gillnet Fisheries of the Estuary and Gulf of St. Lawrence, Canada, 2000-02." *Journal of Cetacean Research and Management* 8 (2006): 67-78.

Ledwell, W. *Whales and Dolphins of Newfoundland and Labrador*. Portugal

Cove-St. Philip's, NL: Boulder Publications, 2005.

Lien, J., L.Fawcett, and S. Staniforth. *Wet and Fat: Whales and Seals of Newfoundland and Labrador*. St. John's: Breakwater Books, 1985.

Lowitt, K. *A Community Food Security Assessment of the Bonne Bay Region*. Community-University Research for Recovery Alliance (CURRA) Project Report. St. John's: Memorial University, 2009. http://www.curra.ca/reports.htm

Martinez-Murillo, M. and R.L. Haedrich. "A Perspective on Newfoundland's Fisheries Ecosystem Using Size-based Food-web Relationships." In *Resetting the Kitchen Table: Food Security, Culture, Health and Resilience in Coastal Communities*. Edited by C.C. Parrish, N.J. Turner and S.M. Solberg, 13-32. New York: Nova Science Publishers, 2007.

Matheson, K. and P. Gagnon. "Effects of Temperature, Body Size, and Chela Loss on Competition for a Limited Food Resource Between Indigenous Rock Crab (*Cancer irroratus* Say) and Recently Introduced Green Crab (*Carcinus maenas* L.)." *Journal of Experimental Marine Biology and Ecology* 428 (2012): 49-56.

McKnight, T.L. *Physical Geography: A Landscape Appreciation*. Upper Saddle River, N.J.: Prentice-Hall, 1987.

Melanson, R.L. and C.E. Campbell. "Near-shore Fish Populations Within St. Paul's Inlet, an Estuarine System in Western Newfoundland." *Northeastern Naturalist* 19 (2012): 487-500.

Montevecchi, W. and L. Tuck. *Newfoundland Birds: Exploitation, Study, Conservation*. Cambridge, MA: Nuttall Ornithological Club No. 21, 1987.

Montevecchi, W.A., H. Chaffey, and C. Burke. "Hunting for Security: Changes in the Exploitation of Marine Birds in Newfoundland and Labrador." In *Resetting the Kitchen Table: Food Security, Culture, Health and Resilience in Coastal Communities*. Edited by C.C. Parrish, N.J. Turner, and S.M. Solberg, 99-113. New York: Nova Science Publishers, 2007.

Moyle, P.B. and J.J. Cech, Jr. *Fishes: An Introduction to Ichthyology*, 4th ed. Upper Saddle River, NJ: Prentice-Hall, 2000.

Murray, G., D. Bavington, and B. Neis. "Local Ecological Knowledge, Science, Participation and Fisheries Governance in Newfoundland and Labrador: A Complex, Contested and Changing Relationship." In *Participation in Fisheries Governance*. Edited by T. S. Gray, 269-290. Berlin: Springer, 2005.

Murray, G., B. Neis, C.T. Palmer, and D.C. Schneider. "Mapping Cod: Fisheries Science, Fish Harvesters' Ecological Knowledge and Cod Migration in the Gulf of St. Lawrence." *Human Ecology* 36 (2008):581-598.

Muus, B.J. and J. G. Nielsen. *Sea Fish*. Hedehusene, DK: Scandinavian Fishing Year Book, 1999.

Myers, R. and B. Worm. "Rapid Worldwide Depletion of Predatory Fish Communities." *Nature* 423 (2003): 280-283.

Neville, V. "Effects of a fishing moratorium on snow crab *Chionoecetes opilio* in Bonne Bay, Newfoundland and its Future Implications for the Local Fishery." B.Sc. (Honours) thesis, Memorial University of Newfoundland, 2011.

Nozères, C., D. Archambault, P.-M. Chouinard, J. Gauthier, R. Miller, E. Parent, P. Schwab, L. Savard, and J.-D. Dutil. *Identification Guide for Marine Fishes of the Estuary and Northern Gulf of St. Lawrence and Sampling Protocols Used During Trawl Surveys Between 2004 and 2008*. Canadian Technical Report of Fisheries and Aquatic Sciences 2866, 2010.

Office of the Auditor General of Canada. *Report of the Commissioner of the Environment and Sustainable Development to the House of Commons, Chapter 1 Oil Spills from Ships*. Minister of Public Works and Government Services Canada. Ottawa, 2010.

-----. *Report of the Commissioner of the Environment and Sustainable Development to the House of Commons, Chapter 3 Adapting to Climate Impacts*. Minister of Public Works and Government Services Canada. Ottawa, 2010.

Parsons, L.S. "Management of Marine Fisheries in Canada." *Canadian Bulletin of Fisheries and Aquatic Sciences* 225 (1993): 1-763.

Paterson, B. *Study on the Small Pelagic Fisheries for Herring and Mackerel on the West Coast of Newfoundland*. 2013. http://www.curra.ca.

Peterson, R.T. *A Field Guide to the Birds of Central and Eastern North America*. Boston: Houghton Mifflin, 1980.

Pritchard, D.W. "What is an Estuary: Physical Viewpoint." In *Estuaries* 83. Edited by G.H. Laufff, 3-5. Washington: American Association for the Advancement of Science, 1967.

Proctor, N.S. and P.J. Lynch. *A Field Guide to North Atlantic Wildlife*. New Haven and London: Yale University Press, 2005.

Reeves, R.R. "The Origins and Character of Aboriginal Subsistence Whaling: A Global Review." *Mammal Review* 32 (2002): 71-106.

Richards, C. "Wind-forced Dynamics in Bonne Bay, Newfoundland." M.Sc. thesis, Memorial University of Newfoundland, 2005.

Richards, C. and B. deYoung. *Analysis of Physical Oceanographic Data from Bonne Bay, September 2002 – September 2004*. Physics and Physical Oceanography Data Report 2004-1. Department of Physics and Physical Oceanography. St. John's: Memorial University of Newfoundland, 2004.

Robins, C.R. and G.C. Ray. *A Field Guide to Atlantic Coast Fishes*. Boston: Houghton Mifflin, 1986.

Rogers, K. "Examining the Local Lobster (*Homarus americanus*) Stock of Bonne Bay, Newfoundland: Utilizing an Interdisciplinary Approach." M.Sc. thesis, Memorial University of Newfoundland, 2010.

Rogerson, R.J. 1983. "Geological Evolution." In *Biogeography and Ecology of the Island of Newfoundland*. Edited by G.R. South, 5-35. The Hague: Dr. W. Junk Publishers, 1983.

Rombough, P.J., S.E. Barbour and J.J. Kerekes. "Life History and Taxonomic Status of an Isolated Population of Arctic Char, *Salvelinus alpines*, from Gros Morne National Park, Newfoundland." *Journal of the Fisheries Research Board of Canada* 35 (1978): 1537-1541.

Rose, G.A. *Cod: The Ecological History of the North Atlantic Fisheries.* St. John's: Breakwater Books, 2007.

Rowe, S., J.A. Hutchings, and J.E. Skjaeraasen. "Nonrandom Mating in a Broadcast Spawner: Mate Size Influences Reproductive Success in Atlantic Cod (*Gadus morhua*)." *Canadian Journal of Fisheries and Aquatic Sciences* 64 (2007): 219-226.

Russell, E. and E. McKee. "Oral Histories of the Bonne Bay Marine Station." *Western Shorefast: A Joint Newsletter of the Bonne Bay Marine Station and the Community-University Research for Recovery Alliance* 3 (2010): 1-18. http://www.curra.ca/documents/Newsletter_Western_Shorefast-Issue_3_for_Email.pdf

Schneider D.C., Norris M.J., and Gregory R.S. "Predictive Analysis of Scale-dependent Habitat Association: Juvenile Cod (*Gadus* spp.) in Eastern Newfoundland." *Estuarine, Coastal and Shelf Science* 79 (2008): 71-78.

Scott, P.J. and D. Black. *Wildflowers of Newfoundland and Labrador*. Portugal Cove-St. Philip's: Boulder Publications, 2008.

Scott, W.B. and E.J. Crossman. *Freshwater Fishes of Canada*. St. Andrew's, NB: Fisheries Research Board of Canada, 1973.

Scott, W.B. and M.G. Scott. *Atlantic Fishes of Canada*. Toronto: University of Toronto Press, 1988.

Seiden, J., K. Wilke, and D. Schneider. *Lobster Sustainability Measures in Newfoundland: Are They Effective*. 2012. http://www.curra.ca/documents/LobstersummaryJennicaSeiden.pdf

Sergeant, D.E. "Harp Seals, Man and Ice." *Canadian Special Publications of Fisheries and Aquatic Sciences* 114 (1991): 1-153.

Shaw, J. "Submarine Moraines in Newfoundland Coastal Waters: Implications for the Deglaciation of Newfoundland and Adjacent Areas." *Quaternary International* 99–100 (2003): 115–134.

Snelgrove, P.V.R. *Discoveries of the Census of Marine Life: Making Ocean Life Count*. New York: Cambridge University Press, 2010.

Solberg, S.M., P. Canning, and S. Buehler. "Changing Patterns of Household Food Consumption in Rural Communities of Atlantic Canada." In *Resetting the Kitchen Table: Food Security, Culture, Health and Resilience in Coastal Communities*. Edited by C.C. Parrish, N.J. Turner, and S.M. Solberg, 161-175. New York: Nova Science Publishers, 2007.

South, G.R. *Common Seaweeds of Newfoundland: A Guide for the Layman*. St. John's: Joint Publication by Oxen Pond Botanic Park and Marine Sciences Research Laboratory, 1975.

South, G.R. "Benthic Marine Algae." In *Biogeography and Ecology of the Island of Newfoundland*. Edited by G.R. South, 385-420. The Hague: Dr W. Junk Publishers, 1983.

South, G. R. and R. G. Hooper. *A Catalogue and Atlas of the Benthic Marine Algae of the Island of Newfoundland*. Memorial University of Newfoundland, Occasional Papers in Biology, 1980.

Steele, D.H. "Marine Ecology and Zoogeography." In *Biogeography and Ecology of the Island of Newfoundland*. Edited by G.R. South, 421-465. The Hague: Dr W. Junk Publishers, 1983.

Story, G.M., W.J. Kirwin, and J.D.A. Widdowson. *Dictionary of Newfoundland English*, 2nd ed. Toronto: University of Toronto Press, 1990.

Syvitski, J.P.M., D.C. Burrell, and J.M. Skei. *Fjords: Processes and Products*. Berlin: Springer-Verlag, 1987.

Temple, K. *Opportunities for Sustainable Livelihoods in the Southwest Coast Lobster Fishery*. 2011. http://www.curra.ca/documents/Sustainable_Lobster_Fishery_Report_December_21_2010_Final_for_Web.pdf

Threlfall, W. "Seabirds." In *Biogeography and Ecology of the Island of Newfoundland*. Edited by G.R. South, 467-508. The Hague: Dr W. Junk Publishers, 1983.

Turner, N., C. Parrish, and S. Solberg. "Food Security in Coastal Communities in the Context of Restructuring: Coasts Under Stress. In *Resetting the Kitchen Table: Food Security, Culture, Health and Resilience in Coastal Communities*. Edited by C.C. Parrish, N.J. Turner, and S.M. Solberg, 1-12. New York: Nova Science Publishers, 2007.

Valentin A. "Structure des Populations de Sébaste de l'Atlantique du Nord-ouest dans un Contexte de Gestion des Stocks et D'évolution." Ph.D. thesis, Université du Québec à Rimouski, 2006.

Warkentin, I. and S. Newton. *Birds of Newfoundland Field Guide*. Portugal Cove-St. Phillips: Boulder Publications, 2009.

Wroblewski, J.S., L.K. Kryger, D.A. Methven, and R.L. Haedrich. "The Fish Fauna of Gilbert Bay, Labrador: A Marine Protected Area in the Canadian Subarctic Coastal Zone." *Journal of the Marine Biology Association of the U.K.* 87 (2007): 575-587.

Wroblewski, J., B. Neis, and K. Gosse. "Inshore Stocks of Atlantic Cod are Important for Rebuilding the East Coast Fishery." *Coastal Management* 33 (2005): 411-432.

GLOSSARY

Anadromous: category for fishes that are born in freshwater, migrate to the ocean to feed and grow, and then return to freshwater to spawn. An example is the Atlantic salmon.

Baleen: fibrous plates attached to the upper jaw of certain whale species and used for filtering prey from seawater.

Barachois: a shallow lagoon of brackish water separated from a river delta by a sandbar or narrow strip of land.

Biofouling organisms: aquatic organisms that naturally attach to underwater hard substrate, including boat bottoms and man-made structures.

Brackish water: freshwater diluted with seawater.

Bycatch: non-targeted species that are unintentionally caught by fish harvesters.

Catadromous: category for fishes which are born in the ocean, migrate to freshwater to feed and grow, and then return to the ocean to spawn. An example is the American eel.

COSEWIC: the Committee on the Status of Endangered Wildlife in Canada is the national body authorized by Canada's Species at Risk Act (SARA) to provide professional scientific advice to the Federal Government on the conservation status of a species.

Crab pot: a funnel-shaped trap framed with iron rods and covered with polypropylene webbing constructed so that crabs entering the trap to feed on bait cannot escape.

Demersal: a "sea bottom-dwelling" way of life.

DFO: Department of Fisheries and Oceans Canada.

Dressed fish: the catch with the head and entrails removed.

Ecology: the scientific study of the relationships between living organisms and their environment.

Eel trap: a series of funnel-shaped "hoop nets" of decreasing size that lead to confinement of eels entering the first and largest hoop net.

Endangered species: under Canada's Species at Risk Act (SARA) a species is considered "endangered" if it is facing extirpation in Canada or extinction everywhere.

Estuary: a coastal embayment where seawater is significantly diluted with freshwater draining from the land.

Extinction: the loss of a species from the planet forever.

Extirpation: the loss of a species from a terrestrial or aquatic geographic region.

Finfish: commercially important fish species with prominent fins and a tail.

Fisherman's dilemma: the circumstances when a fisherperson may forego harvesting to conserve a fishery resource only to see the resource being harvested by other fisherpersons. Such circumstances are an impediment to fisheries conservation.

Fishery: the harvest of a living resource (invertebrate, fish, or mammal) from a marine, estuarine, or freshwater environment.

Fishery management: the application of the principles of control to a fishery.

Fisheries stock assessment: the science of estimating the abundance of a fishery resource and the biological consequences of a harvest level.

Flatfish: pancake-shaped demersal fishes (flounders).

Food security: locally available, affordable, nutritious food which meets the cultural preferences of people.

Gillnetting: deployment of monofilament netting in the water column so fish swimming though the net are caught by their gill covers.

Groundfish: commercially important fishes that dwell and feed near the bottom of the ocean.

Handlining: lowering a line with a weight and baited hook to catch fish feeding near the sea bottom.

Invasive species: an organism that appears outside of its natural biogeographic range and alters local ecosystem function.

Intertidal zone: the shoreline between mean low tide and mean high tide.

Jigging: lowering a line, ending with lure-embedded hooks, which is then "jigged" up and down to attract fish to the lure.

Katabatic wind: an air mass falling from cold highlands down a land slope toward sea level.

Kayak: a small, covered boat propelled using a double-bladed paddle.

Littoral zone: the shore area between the highest high-tide line and the lowest low-tide line.

Lobster trap: the traditional lobster trap has a wooden frame with wooden slats and netting constructed so that lobsters entering the trap to feed on bait cannot escape. The modern lobster trap has a metal frame covered with plastic-coated wire mesh that endures the ocean environment but is more costly.

Longliner: a commercial fishing boat that uses long lines and hooks to catch fish.

Longlining: deployment of a "long line" with a series of baited books along the seabed or in the water column where fish are feeding.

Marine biology: the scientific laboratory study of the body structure and function, physiology, phylogeny, and genetics of marine organisms.

Marine ecology: the scientific field study of the relationships between the distribution and abundance of a marine organism and its physical and biological environment.

Mid-water trawling: towing funnel-shaped nets through the water column to catch pelagic fish. Similar to otter trawling except that the net does not touch the sea bottom.

Otter trawling: dragging funnel-shaped nets along the ocean floor to catch groundfish. Named for the rectangular "doors" or "otterboards" that keep the mouth of the net open as it is towed.

Pelagic: a "water column-dwelling" way of life.

Population: a group of individuals of one species that live in a particular geographic area and freely interbreed.

Purse seining: deployment of a net curtain around a school of fish where the bottom of the net is drawn together to enclose the fish.

Round fish: the catch as brought from the sea with head and entrails intact.

SARA: the Species at Risk Act is Canadian federal legislation enacted in 2002 to protect wild species in Canada from becoming extirpated from Canada's lands, freshwaters, or marine waters.

Seine: a wall of netting used to corral fish.

Shellfish: category for commercially important aquatic invertebrates that have an external shell or exoskeleton. Includes bivalve molluscs with shells made of calcium carbonate, and decapod crustaceans with an exoskeleton made of chiton.

Special concern: under Canada's Species at Risk Act, a species is considered of "special concern" if its numbers are in decline and will decline further unless steps are taken to protect the species and conserve its habitat.

Stock: a subgroup of an exploited animal population.

Subtidal zone: the sea bottom below the mean low-tide line.

Tides: periodic changes in water level along a coastline caused by the rotation of the earth and the gravitational pull of the sun and the moon.

Threatened: under Canada's Species at Risk Act (SARA) a species is considered "threatened" when the species is likely to become extirpated in Canada if nothing is done to reverse its decline in numbers.

Weir fishing: placement of poles into the sea bottom in a heart-shaped configuration so fish entering the trap encounter a near-continuous barrier to leaving the trap.

INDEX
OF COMMON AND SCIENTIFIC NAMES

PHOTOGRAPHY CREDITS

All photographs are by the author unless otherwise indicated.

Thank you to Dr. Robert Briggs, Jennifer Dawe, Dr. Evan Edinger, Jessica Flight, Alain Fréchet, Dr. Patrick Gagnon, Dr. David Innes, Arnault Le Bris, Wayne Ledwell, Ryan Martin, Ryan Melanson, Dr. David Methven, Ron O'Connell, Mark Pokorski, Dr. Craig Purchase, and Dr. Darroch Whitaker for their kind permission to use their photographs in this book.

ABOUT THE AUTHOR

Dr. Joe Wroblewski is a Professor in the Department of Ocean Sciences at Memorial University of Newfoundland in St. John's. He teaches a field course on estuarine fish ecology at the Bonne Bay Marine Station in Norris Point. He also teaches undergraduate and graduate courses on the St. John's campus, including a graduate course on fisheries resource management with the viewpoint that fishers and their knowledge should be part of the management process.

Dr. Joe Wroblewski (CENTRE, FRONT ROW), Dr. Craig Purchase (FAR LEFT, FRONT ROW), Arnault Le Bris (FAR LEFT, BACK ROW) and students in the field course taught at the Bonne Bay Marine Station during the summer of 2011. Killdevil Hill is seen in the background. (PHOTOGRAPH BY CRAIG PURCHASE)

ABOUT THE ILLUSTRATOR

Leah Wroblewski has an Engineering Degree in Ocean and Naval Architecture from Memorial University. She currently lives and works in Houston, Texas

Leah Wroblewski drawing illustrations for the book.